SOMALIA between
JIHAD and RESTORATION

SOMALIA between
JIHAD and RESTORATION

Shaul Shay

Transaction Publishers
New Brunswick (U.S.A.) and London (U.K.)

Library of Congress Catalog Number: 2007045401
ISBN: 978-1-4128-0709-8
Printed in the United States of America

Library of Congress Cataloging-in-Publication Data

Shay, Shaul.
    Somalia between jihad and restoration / Shaul Shay.
        p. cm.
    Includes bibliographical references and index.
    ISBN 978-1-4128-0709-8
    1. Somalia—Politics and government—1991- 2. Islam and politics—Somalia. 3. Islam and state—Somalia. 4. Islamic fundamentalism—Somalia. 5. Jihad. I. Title.

DT407.4.S54 2008
967.7305'3—dc22   2007045401

Contents

Introduction

The dramatic events in Somalia (June-December 2006) concerning the "rise and fall" of the Islamic Courts Union, a radical Islamic movement, attracted global attention to the Horn of Africa. Somalia is located in a region of strategic importance, on the vital sea route linking the Arabian Sea (the Indian Ocean) and the Red Sea. All of the oil tankers from the Persian Gulf region pass through the Bab Al-Mandab Straits, which are under the control of Eritrea and Yemen, on their way to Europe. The importance of the Horn of Africa and the Arabian Peninsula did not escape the attention of the colonial powers, which took over the region and actively controlled it until the 1960s.

Somalia is a Muslim state located at the periphery of the point of Islamic development and intensification (in the Arabian Peninsula, Egypt and the vicinity of the "Fertile Crescent"). Somalia has developed into national entity from within the reality of colonial government on the one hand, and the influence of the core Arab countries, on the other hand. The geopolitical location of Somalia attracted not only the colonial powers followed by the superpowers during the "Cold War," but also radical Islamic entities that grasped the innate potential of this region vis-à-vis the fortification and dissemination of radical Islam.

The involvement of Iran following the Khomeini Revolution and that of radical Islamic entities from Saudi Arabia left its stamp on the nations of that area and turned them into a focal point for confrontation with the West (mainly the United States). Osama bin-Laden, Al-Qaida, and members of radical Islamic organizations discovered allies and refuge in Somalia. The presence of radical Islamic entities in the area, alongside local problems and conflicts on a national, ethnic and tribal basis, turned Somalia into a focal point for nations both near and far.

In the wake of the terror attacks on September 11, 2001, the United States declared war against terror and set Al-Qaida and the Taliban regime in Afghanistan as the initial targets of the campaign. A short time after the "Coalition against Terror," led by the United States, launched its offensive in Afghanistan, the question arose as to which country would be the next target in the counter-terror campaign. Politicians, security experts, and academics named three countries that might be next in line in the war against terror: Sudan, Somalia, and Yemen.

This assumption was not coincidental. It was based on the historical record of Somalia, which was involved in one form or another in the provision of shelter and refuge to Islamic terror organizations. In Somalia, which has been defined since 1991 as a "failing state" that lacks an effective central government, the various rival factions fighting for power declared after the 9/11 attacks that they support the war against terror. They also cast accusations against one another regarding support for and involvement in Islamic terror organizations.

The United States and the coalition deployed air and sea forces in order to prevent the infiltration of Al-Qaida activists and other radical Islamic terror organizations into countries in the region. In Somalia, the United States backed an alliance of local warlords that ruled the area of Mogadishu and some other parts of south Somalia for a decade. On June 5, 2006, the Islamic Courts Union (ICU), a radical Somali Islamic movement, declared victory in its struggle against the Alliance for the Restoration of Peace and Counter Terrorism (ARPCT), a coalition of U.S.-backed warlords.

The ARPCT's defeat represents a major set back for the U.S. war against terror in the Horn of Africa. The triumph of the ICU shocked the regional states, especially Ethiopia, which feared a radical Islamic government on its doorstep. President Bush expressed concern that Somalia could become a haven for Islamic terror, like Afghanistan was in the late 1990s.[1] The United States has accused the Islamic Courts of harboring Al-Qaida leaders responsible for the terror attacks against U.S. embassies in Kenya and Tanzania in 1998 and against Israeli targets in Kenya in 2002.

Osama bin Laden in an Internet audio message, on July 1, 2006, warned the world against interfering with the ICU, which had taken control of Somalia, and urged Somalis to support the ICU in building an Islamic state in Somalia[2]: "We pledge that we will fight your soldiers on the land of Somalia and we will fight you on your own land if you dispatch troops to Somalia. You have no other means for salvation unless you commit to Islam, put your hands in the hands of the Islamic Courts to build an Islamic state in Somalia."

The defeat of the U.S.-backed Alliance for the Restoration of Peace and Counter Terrorism (ARPCT) by the ICU created a new reality in Somalia and in the Horn of Africa. Shortly after its victory, the ICU appointed Sheikh Hassan Dahir Aweys as the head of the Islamic movement. Sheikh Aweys is a radical Islamic cleric who is listed by the United Nations and the United States as a suspected terrorist with suspected ties to Al-Qaida. The ICU have denied any links to terrorism or Al-Qaida and say they are interested only in restoring law and order to Somalia.

The United States, as a response to the ICU victory, ruled out contact with Somalia's new leader, Sheikh Aweys of the ICU. State Department spokesman Sean McLormac said: "Of course we are not going to work with somebody like that, and of course we would be troubled if this [choice] is an indicator to the direction that this group would go in. Let's wait, let's see what the collective leaders of this group does."[3]

The reign of the Islamic Courts Union was short. In December 2006 they were defeated by a coalition of the Transitional Federal Government (Somalia's weak, internationally recognized government) and invading Ethiopian forces. In spite of the ICU's defeat, the internal conflict in Somalia between the ICU and the Transitional Federal Government, propped up by Ethiopian troops, is still far from over. The internal conflict could still "spill over" and turn into a regional one.

Somalia has reached a crossroads with three main alternatives:

- Remain a "failed state."
- Formation of a moderate and pragmatic state, with support of the United Nations, the United States, and the African Union.
- Turn into an endless theater of Jihad.

My book, *The Red Sea Terror Triangle*, studied three countries, Sudan, Yemen, and Somalia, which I dubbed "the terror triangle of the Red Sea," and particularly the links that each maintains with Islamic terror and the reciprocal ties between them. The triumph and the fall of the ICU in Somalia in 2006 demands a deeper insight into Somalia. This study, analyzing the background and events that led to the current situation in Somalia, provides some ideas how to prevent the foundation of a new radical Islamic state that would turn into a haven for Islamic terror in the Horn of Africa.

Notes

1. Salah Nasrawi, Bin Laden endorses Al Zarqawi's successor A.P Cairo, July 2, 2006.
2. Leave Somalia alone, alleged Bin Laden tape says, CBS News, July 1, 2006.
3. Somalia: U.S bans contact with Dahir Aweys, Reuters, June 26, 2006.

1

Somalia—Background and Historical Review

The nature and character of a people are mostly according to their natural habitat, historical events, and cultural experiences in the course of several centuries. The Somali people have had, since their origin as prehistoric people of this land, a very hostile natural habitat with scarcities of water and abundance of sandy and infertile land and repeated droughts.[1]

They have faced several political turmoils—external invasions, wars, feuds, coups, and counter-coups. All these circumstances and events have left their mark on the character of the Somali people, who have been basically nomadic pastoral people for thousands of years.

Somalia is situated in the African Horn—an important strategic location overlooking the passageway between the Red Sea and the Indian Ocean. As such, Somalia was a target for Western colonialism from the sixteenth century until the last century, and alternated between Portuguese, Italian, French, and British control.

The independent Republic of Somalia was founded in 1960 on the basis of the consolidation of two colonies—one British and the other Italian—into one state. Since its establishment, Somalia has suffered from political instability and inter-tribal conflict. The Somali state attempted to establish "greater Somalia" and consolidate a central government and a Somali national identity in a society clearly characterized by schisms on a tribal basis.

Somali Society

Most of the Somali population is Sunni Muslim, but despite the religious homogeny, Somali society is characterized by tribal divisions and infinite rivalries against a background of personal and sectorial power struggles. About 80 percent of the Somali population is nomadic and there are four main tribes:[2] Dir, Isaaq, Darood, and Hawiye. These four tribes are divided into sub-tribes, extended families and clans, which either

1

cooperate or compete with each other. The strongest basis for loyalty is family and extended family, while on the tribal and national scope, the level of solidarity and loyalty becomes steadily weaker.

The confrontations between the various social components have been a frequent phenomenon throughout Somali history, however, at the same time there were various institutions that were charged with resolving these conflict, such as councils of the tribal leaders and elders, and various Islamic institutions.[3]

Most of Somalia's population is split between nomadic tribes and non-nomadic tribes with permanent residences. The fertile and cultivated lands served as Somalia's wheat granary and provided a solution for the years of drought during which the roaming residents relied on the produce of the farmers, either via commerce or by invading the area and forcibly confiscating the food.[4]

Tradition, as transmitted orally from father to son, has the force of law among the nomads. That nomad order prescribes what to do in every conceivable situation and directs the nomad's attitude towards life. The nomad's value system is all embracing and clearly defined. It draws its content from tradition and from the mainstream of Islamic beliefs.[5]

There is strong belief in Allah, upon whose mercy and compassion one finds prosperity and luck or whose wrath destroys whole populations. It is Allah who is worshipped, his prophets professed, the saints revered, the ancestors appeased and respected. Only then can a society lead a decent life protected from natural catastrophes.[6]

The corollary of these values is manifested in the fatalist philosophy that the nomad holds true. Any conceivable situation, social or ecological takes from on the will of God. To the nomad nothing in the world of nature functions, but in accordance with God's will. The other corollary is to profess Islam, the religion ordained by the Almighty through his Prophet Mohammed, and to abide by its tenets.[7]

Since the Somali family is an extended unit, ancestors are revered and accorded holy or saintly status. Members of a clan aspire to appease their ancestors through offerings and ritual ceremonies, in the hope that they will take care of their offspring and will avert any evil that may fall on them.[8] Religious men, wadaad, play a vital role among the nomads. They treat the sick and initiate the rituals of offerings, ceremonies, feasts, of marriage and death. Traditionally, teaching in classrooms was first done by the wadaad.[9]

Another component of Somali society is the urban class, mainly consisting of merchants and clerks that were closer to the secular culture and had moved a relatively long way from the religious and tribal systems.[10] Thus, most of the internal conflicts in Somalia during the modern era have erupted due to the uprising of one of the tribal groups against an attempt to impose a collective Somali identity, and its desire to protect its self-definition and freedom as a group.

The Islamic faith is one of the identities that cut across clan lines. In the pre-colonial times, rural Somali communities recognized two distinct authorities, clan elders and religious leaders. Their responsibilities overlapped to the extent that Islam was essentially assimilated into clan culture. This symbiotic relationship has persisted throughout the colonial and post-colonial era.[11] (See Chapter 3, Islamic Movements in Somalia.)

The Period of Ziad Barre's Administration[12]

As stated above, the Republic of Somalia was established in 1960. In the first nine years of its existence, the Somali state was a parliamentary democracy that allowed unrestricted political activity, and the political and social system incorporated traditional tribal norms and values together with Western lifestyles and values.[13] One of the expressions of the conservative aspects was the marginal role of women in the political system, so that only in May 1963 was the right to vote granted to all Somali women.

In March 1969, a coup d'êtat headed by General Ziad Barre took place. The elected President Amdi Rashid Ali Shermarke was deposed and Somali democracy ceased to exist. Muhammad Ziad Barre was orphaned at the age of ten and until adulthood he struggled to support himself as a goatherd in Somaliland, which at that time was an Italian colony. He joined the Italian colonial police and quickly rose in the ranks. In 1960, when Somalia was granted independence, Barre was appointed deputy commander of the Somali army, which was being founded at the time, and five years later he was appointed commander of the Somali army. In March 1969, Barre initiated a military coup and seized control.

Barre did not only introduce governmental changes, but also aspired to instigate a Marxist revolution that would introduce fundamental changes in Somalia's political, social and economic system. The Revolutionary Council with Barre at its head served as Somalia's government, changed the political and organizational structure of the government, and formulated a new ideology that incorporated Islam and Communism. In 1971, Barre declared his intention to convert the revolutionary, military regime into a civilian government, thus leading to the establishment of the governmental party—the SRSP—Somali Revolutionary Socialist Party; the members of this party's central committee were also the members of the Revolutionary Council.[14]

In this framework, Barre became a close ally of the Soviet Union in East Africa. The Soviets supplied Barre with weapons, military equipment, and advisers. With their help, Barre proceeded to build up a strong army with which he attempted to resolve conflicts with his neighbors and his adversaries from within.

Modern political Islamic movements did not emerge in Somalia until the late 1960s, when Somali students (particularly those studying at Al Azhar in Egypt) and employment seekers were exposed to the teaching and public support for political Islam in Egypt, Saudi Arabia and other Arab countries where Al Aqwan al Muslimin (the Muslim Brotherhood) was gaining widespread support. Upon return from abroad, many of these individuals formed parallel Somali movements to Al Aqwan, seeking to peacefully transform the Somali state to be based on Islamic law (shari'a).

Their beliefs led to public resistance to Ziad Barre's plans for "scientific socialism," and ultimately to government repression. For instance, when followers of the movement publicly rejected the "Family Law" of 1975 for its recognition and promotion of the legal and economic equality of women, demonstrations were eventually put down by the execution of ten prominent clerics. Following the repression and fracturing of Al Aqwan, a period of relative inactivity followed when Islamist organizations were not prominent in Somali politics. However, instead of disappearing altogether, the remnants of Al Aqwan went to underground and began organizing for their political return at a later date.[15]

In 1977-1978 a brutal war raged between Somalia and Ethiopia due to Somalia's demand to control the Somali population in the Ogaden Desert. The Somali forces were defeated, and more than a million Somali refugees fled from Ogaden to Somalia, placing an onerous burden on its already collapsing economy. Somalia's defeat in the Ogaden War against Ethiopia, the problem of the refugees, and the severe economic crisis that struck the country from the mid-1970s, forced Barre to appeal to the international community in order to solicit humanitarian aid.[16]

The economic and social crisis also led the establishment of opposition pockets to Barre's regime from among his own tribe and party, in addition to the adversaries from rival political and tribal circles. Facing the threat against his regime, Barre began a campaign to suppress his adversaries—many were arrested, tortured, and even executed. Tribes that were hostile to the regime were severely punished.

Barre's economic and political distress from within, and his disappointment with the Soviet stance during the Ogaden War, triggered a significant shift in his policies; he abandoned his alliance with the Soviets and appealed to the United States and the West for aid.[17] The United States hastened to assist Barre, thus ousting the Soviet Union from this important strategic stronghold at the shores of the Red Sea. The United States granted Barre generous aid (directly and via international institutions like the World Bank) in order to enable his regime to survive.[18] In exchange, Somalia allowed the United States to utilize docking services at the strategic port of Berbera, which had previously served the Soviet navy.

Parallel to the stream of economic and military aid pouring in from the West, Barre was requested to implement a more liberal policy, preserve human rights in his country, and act to establish a democratic political system. Due to these pressures, in December 1979 Barre declared elections for the parliament in which the "People's Parliament" was elected, but in effect all of the elected parliament members were affiliated with the SRSP, the governing party.

Following the elections, Barre also introduced changes in the composition of the executive branch. In this framework he rescinded the roles of the three vice presidents and consequently reinstated the Revolutionary Council (in October 1980). As a result of these changes, in practical terms three congruent bureaucratic mechanisms functioned in one governmental system:[19]

1.   The Party's politburo, which held executive authority through the Central Council (which was an executive entity);
2.   The Council of Ministers or the Government;
3.   The Senior Revolutionary Council (SRC).

The multiplicity of mechanisms and the competition between them enabled Barre to fortify his own status and left him with the decision-making process through the strategy of "divide and conquer." However, the failing bureaucracy and the political power struggles prevented the restoration of the Somali economy despite the economic aid received from the West. Against this background, in February 1982, Barre set out for the United States. On the eve of this visit, in order to minimize the criticism against his regime, he made the gesture of liberating two political prisoners who had been incarcerated since 1969. But at the end of his visit, when he saw that the political criticism in his country was rising, he initiated a new wave of suppression of opposition members in addition to those entities whom he perceived as a threat to his status. On

June 7, 1982 Barre commanded the arrest of seventeen leading politicians and public figures, including the chief of staff, the former vice president, a former foreign minister as well as some politburo members. The arrests triggered an atmosphere of terror and crisis, and as a result opposition elements consolidated into a united front, mainly on a tribal basis, with the aim of toppling the government.

In July 1982, Somalia faced not only internal problems but also an external threat in the form of an invasion by Somali exiles, with the aid of Ethiopian army units and combat planes, into the state's northwestern regions and its center, thus threatening to cut the country in two. Barre declared a state of emergency and requested Western aid in repelling the invaders. The U.S. administration agreed, rushed weapon shipments and doubled its economic aid; after several weeks of fighting, the invasion was deflected and Barre was again free to deal with his adversaries at home.

In December 1984, due to his desire to intensify his government's legitimacy, Barre introduced several amendments to the constitution, including extension of the president's term of office from six to seven years, as well as an amendment according to which the president will be elected in a referendum, and not by the National Council (the executive body). It is to be noted that in referendums that Barre held during his term of office he always won 99% of the votes, and therefore the amendment of the constitution in this matter was geared at fortifying his control and granting his regime a broad, popular basis of support.[20]

A short time after his ascendancy to power, in 1969, Barre had declared that he would act against the tribal and sectorial characteristics of Somali politics and society. Barre claimed that the tribal mentality constituted a threat against Somalia's unity, and in the name of the struggle against this danger he banned all political and party activity. But in practical terms, in the 21 years of his regime, Barre also based his political power of tribal and sectorial loyalty. Most of the influential and powerful positions were allocated by Barre among the three main clans of the Daarood tribe:

1.   The clan to which he himself belonged—Mareehaan;
2.   The clan of his son-in-law—Dulbahante;
3.   The clan of his mother—Ogaden.

The remaining tribes and clans were permitted to claim the "leftover" crumbs from the Somali government's "cake."

The ban on political and party activities made the tribal association the only legal possibility for group organization, and therefore a clear link was created between the tribal and political interests. The establishment of the SRSP government party did not constitute a proper and real response for the Somali society's political needs, and therefore the protest activity was channeled into illegal directions related to political subversion and terror. Regardless of the fact that Ziad Barre's regime relied solely on force and lacked broad political support, it succeeded in surviving 21 years, but ultimately the domestic opposition forces finally overcame him and put an end to his regime at the end of 1990.

The Rival Factions in Somalia (1991)

As stated above, Somali society was characterized by a large range of powerbrokers arrayed on a tribal, clan and extended family basis. Some of these power centers established political movements and militias aimed at protecting the group's interests in the Somali political system.

It is possible to count five main movements, all on a tribal and regional basis, that were prominent in the power struggles in Somalia during the early 1990s:

1. The USC (the United Somali Congress)—of the Hawiye tribe in central Somalia, the dominant movement in the state;
2. The SNM (Somalia National Movement)—of the Isaaq tribe in the Somaliland area;
3. The SPM (the Somali Patriotic Movement)—in the Ogaden area;
4. The SSLF (the Somali Salvation and Liberation Front)—of the Mayerteen tribe;
5. The SDM—(the Somali Democratic Movement)—of the Rahanwein tribe in north Somalia.

The movements were generally divided up into two main groups:

1. North Somali movements, headed by the SNM, which represented tribes and populations from the former British colony;
2. Central Somali movements, headed by the USC, which represented tribes and populations from the former Italian colony.

Although the regional and tribal division provides a relatively convenient way to distinguish between powerbrokers, the political reality was actually far more complex, and splits and rifts within the ranks of the political movements, in addition to a shifting of loyalties, were prevalent in Somali society.

After the collapse of the Ziad Barre government in 1991, a number of different movements developed in Somalia whose ideology and objectives cover a wide spectrum of political philosophy. These include Al Islah,

Al Tabliq, Al Takfir, and Al Itihad. Even a brief overview of the interests and activities of these various movements warns against any simple conflation of all politically organized Islamist groups as "fundamentalist" or "terrorist." For instance, Al Islah, whose name translates as "reconciliation" or "meditation," seeks to infuse Somali politics with a liberal reading of Islamic values through entirely non-violent means. Membership in the movement is generally drawn from the educated elite of the Hawiye clan, including former politicians and civil servants, academics, health and engineering professionals, and businessman traders. Their activities are focused in Mogadishu, including basic literacy training in Koranic schools, vocational training and higher education at Mogadishu University. Some humanitarian organizations, such as Mercy International, are integrally connected to Al Islah. Of the modern political Islamic organizations, Al Islah appears the most moderate and, due to its adherence to internationally recognized principles of human rights and gender equality as a member of the Peace and Human Rights Network, finds itself in confrontation with more militant movements such as Al Itihad.[21]

The End of Ziad Barre's Government and the Civil War

At the end of 1990 and the beginning of 1991, there was widespread insurrection initiated by the tribes and powerbrokers in Somalia against the government of General Barre, who, as stated above, governed Somalia for twenty-one years. Due to the insurrection, Barre was forced to flee Somalia. (He was given political sanctuary in Nigeria, where he died in 1995.) Most of his associates and supporters, who fulfilled central roles in the administrative and governmental mechanisms, also fled Mogadishu, and the capital was left in governmental chaos.

Due to the collapse of Barre's government, political struggles erupted over control in Mogadishu in particular and over the entire country, in general. The two main contenders for control came from the ranks of the United Somali Congress (USC)—the dominant political movement in Somalia at that time. The two were:[22]

1. *Ali Mahdi Muhammad*, one of the USC leaders and a member of the Hawiye tribe and the Abgal extended family, which resides mainly in the Mogadishu area. Muhammad had been a teacher and a government clerk prior to his election to the House of Representatives (the Republic's National Congress) in March 1969. Following Ziad Barre's coup in October 1996, Muhammad was arrested along with many other politicians. He was released from prison several years later and launched a career in business. In the 1980s he served as the manager

of the UN offices in Mogadishu. At the same time, Muhammad used his financial resources in order to assist guerilla fighters affiliated with the USC, in their struggle against Ziad Barre.

In May 1990, Muhammad was among those who signed a petition demanding that Ziad Barre introduce democratic reforms. Barre responded with a rash of arrests; Muhammad fled to Rome where he continued to act against Barre's government from the USC offices there. In the framework of the internal struggle in the ranks of the USC Ali Mahdi Muhammad relied on the support of circles within the USC, members of his own tribe and a loose coalition with other tribes.

2. *General Muhammad Farah Aidid*—He was also one of the senior leaders of the USC, and he too was a member of the Hawiye tribe, but he belonged to the Habar Gadir extended family, which resides in central Somalia. Although his father was a simple camel raiser, Aidid studied in Italian schools and subsequently in the Soviet Union. Aidid spoke several Western languages and was considered an intelligent, though somewhat erratic, individual.

During the administration of President Ziad Barre, Aidid fulfilled senior roles; he served as a senior officer in the army with the rank of general, a cabinet member, an ambassador to India, and director of Somalia's intelligence service. Barre later suspected that Aidid was subverting him and incarcerated him for a period of six years.

In the framework of the internal struggle in the ranks of the USC between Aidid and Ali Mahdi Muhammad, Aidid was supported by his tribe and a relatively broad coalition of tribes, as well as political and military powerbrokers, called the Somali National Alliance (SNA).

Following the collapse of Barre's regime, the USC declared the establishment of a temporary government, but its actually rule was limited. The USC elected Ali Mahdi Muhammad as its temporary president. According to the 1979 constitution, the president serves as the head of state and he is authorized to appoint a government; accordingly, Ali Mahdi Muhammad appointed Omar Arta Galib, of the Isaaq tribe, as temporary prime minister. The latter established a government with twenty-seven ministers and eight deputy ministers. This step accentuated the importance that Muhammad attributed to the establishment of a coalition on a tribal basis and to the broadening of the legitimacy basis for his government.

In June 1991 elections were held for the leadership of the USC, and Aidid was elected chairman of the movement, but despite the defeat within his movement, Ali Mahdi Muhammad refused to relinquish the presidency, which he had taken at the end of 1990. Due to Muhammad's actions, Aidid strengthened his links with his allies from the SNA and initiated forceful steps to depose Ali Mahdi Muhammad and his associates.[23] Ali Mahdi Muhammad declared that it was his true intention to hold general elections the moment that the security circumstances enabled it, but the internal power struggles in the USC and the resistance of opposition elements to Muhammad's government prevented any possibility of holding elections, and the country rapidly deteriorated into a civil war.

Thus, in the beginning of 1992 a civil war erupted in Somalia, which quickly spread from Mogadishu to the other parts of the land. In the fighting in Mogadishu, Aidid had the upper hand, and his forces overtook most parts of the city, but they were unable to uproot Ali Mahdi's forces in several quarters, leaving the capital divided. After their relative success in the capital, Aidid and his men set out to dominate the central and southern part of the country.

The ruthless battle between the rival tribes and factions, the collapse of all governmental systems, including the supply of basic products, in addition to the severe drought that prevailed in the area (which reportedly caused the deaths of some 300,000 people in 1992)—all of these factors contributed to major disaster for Somali residents. Due to the growing anguish, the UN decided to offer aid to Somalia and in December 1992 operation "Restore Hope" was launched in an attempt to restore order in the state and enable the distribution of food to its inhabitants. The UN offices in Mogadishu were opened shortly after the victory of Aidid's forces over Ali Mahdi Muhammad, and in this situation it was clear to the UN representatives that they were too late to achieve any kind of compromise between the warring parties. Therefore, the UN activity focused on humanitarian aid in order to ease the starvation and suffering of the inhabitants.[24] The UN secretary-general defined the situation in Somalia as anarchy, and viewed the achievement of a ceasefire and the confiscation of weapons from the rival sides as a pivotal step towards resolving Somalia's problems.

Therefore, the United Nations decided (with U.S. support) to dispatch an international force under UN auspices with the following roles: providing humanitarian relief for Somali's starving population, disarming the fighting sides, and forming a stable central government based on the Western model.[25] The UN's steps came up against dogged resistance on the part of traditional powerbrokers and entities with political interests in Somalia, and the UN's humanitarian mission rapidly deteriorated into a violent confrontation with local militias, particularly with the forces of General Aidid, which inflicted heavy casualties on the UN forces.

The rival parties in Somalia understood that the humanitarian aid arriving via the United Nations constituted the key to control of the state and its population, and therefore did everything in their power to achieve control over the distribution of humanitarian relief.[26] Ali Mahdi Muham-mad, who continued to claim that the role of state president was his even after his defeat at the hands of Aidid, argued that he should be the only person with the authority to supervise the allocation of humanitarian aid and set standards for eligibility and prioritization for its distribu-tion. When the United Nations refused to accept this demand, his forces bombed Mogadishu port and attacked distribution sites of humanitarian aid. Ali Mahdi Muhammad claimed that the attacks were carried out by desperate and uncontrolled elements among his forces, but it was evident that he was the person who decided to deprive the general population of humanitarian aid if this was not conducted under his control. General Aidid argued that the distribution of the relief should be handled by his own people, who controlled most of the country's territory. He accused the United Nations and the Arab countries of taking sides in the conflict, and said they were accomplices to Ali Mahdi Muhammad's actions.

In view of the increasing difficulties surrounding the distribution of the humanitarian aid in Somalia in November 1992, the United States decided to dispatch a large military force whose role would be to enable the UN delegation to assist the suffering Somali citizens. The U.S. deci-sion came up against the strong opposition of various powerbrokers in Somalia, who were afraid of losing their power if they relinquished their control over the supply of food and international humanitarian aid.[27]

On November 2, 1992 Aidid threatened that any deployment of foreign forces in Somalia would end in bloodshed, and the USC spokesperson stated that the reference was to the American armed forces that were impairing Somali sovereignty. Due to the refusal of the United States and the United Nations to take his side in the confrontation, Aidid launched a series of steps aimed at reinforcing his status in anticipation of a possible confrontation with the Americans. In November 1992, Aidid convened a conference of leaders of various sectors in Somali society, in order to gain their support for the SNA and their loyalty to its leadership. At the same time, (on November 10, 1992) Aidid's forces took over 15 central intersections from gangs and local powerbrokers, thus achieving control over the country's main roadblocks and axes.[28] At the end of November Aidid visited Kismayo—a city in the southern part of the country with an important port, airport and a central junction—and he signed an agree-ment with several important powerbrokers, including:

- Ahmad Omar Jays, chairman of the SPM, whose people controlled the area (Aidid appointed him deputy chairman of the SNA);

- Muhammad Nur Iliau, leader of the SDM in the north;
- Leaders of the "Army for the Liberation of Somalia"—a relatively large underground movement whose main bases are in nearby Kenya.

In a meeting with these leaders Aidid described the dangers threatening their control and demanded cooperation in order to protect joint interests. At the same time, Ali Mahdi Muhammad acted to build up a counter-coalition, and held meetings with powerbrokers from Eritrea and Ethiopia in order to recruit aid in his struggle against Aidid.

However, despite the threats, on December 1, 1992, the two warring sides welcomed the arrival of the American forces. Nevertheless, each of the sides demanded that the United Nations and the United States recognize him as Somalia's legitimate leadership, and that the U.S. forces take action against the adversary if he disrupts the distribution of humanitarian aid.

Notes

1.   Muhammad Farah Aidid and Satya Pal Ruhela, *The Dawn of Civilization to Modern Times*, Civic Webs Virtual Library, 1994.
2.   James Cameron, *The African Revolution*, Thames and Hudson, London, 1981, pp. 176-180.
3.   Ibid.
4.   Ibid.
5.   Mohammed Farah Aidid and Satya Pal Ruhela, *The Dawn of Civilization to Modern Times*, Civic Webs Virtual Library, 1994.
6.   Ibid.
7.   Ibid.
8.   Ibid.
9.   Ibid.
10.   *CIA Fact Book*, Somalia, 2000.
11.   Andre La Sage, "Prospects for Al Itihad and Islamist Radicalism in Somalia," in *Review of African Political Economy*. Volume 27, No. 89, September 2001.
12.   This part based on: Shaul Shay, *The Red Sea Terror Triangle*, Transaction Publishers, New Brunswick, NJ, 2005.
13.   *CIA Fact Book*, Somalia, 2000.
14.   Robert F. Goreman, "The Anatomy of Somali Civil War and Famine," *Washington Report on Middle East Affairs*, March 1993, pp. 9-18.
15.   Andre La Sage, "Prospects for Al Itihad and Islamist Radicalism in Somalia," in *Review of African Political Economy*. Volume 27, No. 89, September 2001.
16.   Ibid.
17.   *CIA Fact Book*, Somalia, 2000.
18.   ABCNews.com, "Somalia's Hopes," October 26, 2001.
19.   *CIA Fact Book*, Somalia, 2000.
20.   Ibid.
21.   Andre La Sage, "Prospects for Al Itihad and Islamist Radicalism in Somalia," in *Review of African Political Economy*. Volume 27, No. 89, September 2001.
22.   "The civil war in Somalia," in *CIA Fact Book*, Somalia, 2000.

23.   Ibid.
24.   NomadNet.com, "Mission in Somalia," December 5, 1993.
25.   Ibid.
26.   Robert F. Gorman, "The anatomy of the Somali civil war and famine," *Washington Report on Middle East Affairs*, March 1993, pp. 9-18.
27.   NomadNet.com, "Mission in Somalia," December 5, 1993.
28.   Ibid.

2

The Development of Radical Islam—
From Local Jihad to Global Jihad[1]

The September 11 attacks were the fruition of meticulous and ongoing planning based on the infrastructure of the global jihad (holy war) that developed in the final decade of the twentieth century on the basis of the global Islamic Dawa (proselytizing) infrastructure.

It would be impossible to understand the September 11 attacks, the background leading to the attacks, the motivation that inspired the attackers, and the repercussions felt throughout the world in general and particularly in the Muslim world, without understanding the development processes of the jihad from local jihad movements with goals defined on the national, state and regional level, to the global jihad movement with its globally defined goals.

Only by comprehending the roots of the global jihad phenomenon, its formation and Islamic religious foundation, as well as the popular and logistic support received from the Islamic community, is it possible to grasp the dimensions of the worldwide terror conspiracy that horrifically culminated in the September 11 attacks.

The joint vision shared by all of the Jihad organizations is based on the concept of the "Umma" (the community of believers of Islam). The instruments for realizing this vision are Jihad and Dawa. Both of these terms are taken from the world of classic Islamic concepts and reflect a yearning for the glorious days of Islam. From the Islamic point of view, the world is divided into two parts: The first part—Dar al Islam, which includes territories controlled by Islam, and the second—Dar al Harb, which is controlled by the infidels (non-believers). These two means—Dawa and Jihad—are mutually supportive and complement each other. While Dawa is based on non-violent means aimed at rectifying Islamic society through the education systems, preaching, and social aid, Jihad aspires to achieve its aims through extreme violence.

These two means developed at different paces during the twentieth century. Due to the fact that Dawa is moderate, tolerant, and less threatening, it spread worldwide. Any place where there are Muslim communities in which Islamic institutions, mosques, and centers exist, Dawa activity, aimed at expanding the influence and territorial boundaries of Islam, thrived. This is true to such an extent that it is noteworthy that on the eve of the Islamic revolution in Iran in 1979, the Dawa infrastructure had already spread to many countries worldwide. In contrast, during the twentieth century the jihad movement was active mainly on the local or regional levels, with the aim of exiling a foreign leader from their land or in order to remove what they deemed as infidel governments and replace them with Islamic regimes.

The following review will endeavor to clarify how a local, radical religious struggle was transformed into a "Holy War" machine, the global jihad, which currently poses the greatest threat against the Free World.

The Local Jihad—Initial Stages

A central cornerstone of the development of radical Islam in the modern era was laid with the foundation of the "Muslim Brotherhood" movement in 1929 by Hassan Albana in Egypt. The movement's goals were to expel the British from Egypt, amend the secular constitution introduced under the British influence, and establish an Islamic state to be run according to shari'a (Islamic law). The means to achieve these goals was the use of Jihad. The latter constituted one of the three central foundations of the Muslim Brotherhood's concepts: knowledge, education, and jihad. Albana succeeded in convincing his followers that death in Allah's name is desirable and he who sacrifices his life in the name of Islam will enjoy eternal life in Paradise. During the 1930s and 1940s the Muslim Brotherhood launched subversive and terrorist activity against the Egyptian regime and the British presence in Egypt as well as cultural and entertainment sites identified with Western culture.

From the 1930s onward, Albana's teachings began to take root in the Muslim world and offshoots of the Muslim Brotherhood (or parallel organizations) began to crop up among Muslim communities all over the world. The organizations quickly established Dawa infrastructures, which met their communities' needs in terms of education, welfare, relief, and especially in the areas of faith and spirituality. Due to the fact that the nature of these movements' activities was essentially religious and social, most of the countries did not stop them as long as they did not veer to political issues or violence.

Following Hassan Albana's death in 1949, the movement's leadership split into two factions—moderate and extremist. His disciples were of one mind regarding the goals and vision related to the establishment of a religious Islamic state, but could not agree about how to bring it about:

1. *The "moderate" faction believed in the Dawa approach.*[2] Hassan al Hadibi, who headed this faction, chose to compromise with political reality, be it democratic or tyrannical, and advocated that Jihad should be adopted according to the spiritual and non-violent meaning of the word. He believed that the population should be won over in amiable ways rather than by unleashing violent force. Therefore, this faction believed that information and education (Dawa) are the main tools to be applied in the transformation of society.

2. *The extremist faction believed in the Jihad approach.*[3] It based itself on the radical philosophy of Sayyid Qutb, which called for an uncompromising struggle against the corrupt and ignorant government (jahilli) through Jihad. Qutb characterized the maladies of Muslim society and analyzed its components. He came to the conclusion that only activism, Jihad, and revolution whose message is carried by "true believers" have the ability to being about the establishment of a religious Islamic state. He emphasized that there is a sharp contrast between two images, two ideologies, two societies, two forms of government and a conflicting truth. Islam and ignorance (jahilliya), faith and heresy, truth and lies, good and evil, God's government or that of man, God and Satan, etc. One side cannot exist if it does not eradicate the other, and there is no room for compromise or mediation between the two. The change, according to Qutb, can only be achieved through revolution, terminating the leaders of the infidels and placing faithful leaders in their stead.

The followers of Qutb's aggressive, jihad-oriented theories—Shukri Ahmad Mutstafa, founder of Jamaat Al-Hijra and Al-Takfir, and Abd al-Salaam Faraj, one of the founders of the Jihad in Egypt, developed Qutb's radical line and adopted Jihad as a means to topple "the corrupt governments" and establish religious Islamic states.

These people believed that it was their duty to build an alternative society upon the rubble of the jahilli society by educating and informing the masses on the one hand, while waging a violent and unbending battle against whoever stands in their path, on the other.

In 1979 Salaam Faraj established the al-Jihad Organization in Egypt. His organization was responsible for the assassination of President Sadat on October 6, 1981. Faraj hoped that chaos would prevail in Egypt in the aftermath of the assassination, thus enabling his organization to seize the reins. *One of Faraj's disciples is Ayman al Zawaheiri, Osama Bin Laden's deputy and cohort.*

To summarize, the local approach characterized the Jihad movement until the end of the 1970s. Although the characteristics of the Jihad and its goals had become more radical, they still operated in internal state and regional arenas. The Jihad movements maintained collaborative ties to a certain extent. In contrast, the Dawa spread out a network of means and agents throughout the world. One of the prominent philosophers who advocated the Jihad was Abdallah Azzam.[4] He conducted fundraising campaigns in the Western world in order to raise money in support of the Jihad, including in Muslim communities in the United States.

Azzam regarded the Jihad as the main tool to achieve Islamic victory and the establishment of Islamic rule on earth. For a period of time he even joined the Mujahidin that fought in Afghanistan. He became the symbol and leader of the jihad movements and of the radical Islamic circles worldwide, and his impact on the world Jihad movement transcended the time and place of his lifetime. Azzam's concept of jihad constitutes the theoretical basis for the modern jihad movements. It affected the development of several phenomena and processes in radical Islam as follows:

1. The establishment of an Islamic "Internationale" on the basis of recruitment of volunteers from all over the Muslim world on behalf of the jihad in Afghanistan.
2. The creation of an international network of Islamic terror cells supported by radical Islamic organizations worldwide.
3. The victory of the Mujahidin in Afghanistan created an aura and ethos of bravery around the Muslim fighters and serves as an inspiration for Muslims all over the world.
4. A broad cadre of Islamic fighters motivated by a sense of mission and combat experience came into existence and turned into the spearhead in struggles between radical Islam and its foes, conspiring to continue the Jihad in various global arenas mainly connected to the West.

Bin Laden and Implementation of Global Jihad

Osama Bin Laden's radical worldview was influenced by the writings of the radical Egyptian Islamists and by Wahhabi Islamic concepts from his land of birth, Saudi Arabia, and it took form during his years in Afghanistan. Bin Laden was particularly influenced by the doctrine of the Palestinian Sheikh Abdallah Azzam, champion and mentor of the global jihad concept, with whom he cooperated in the running of an organization in Peshawar that dealt in the recruitment of Islamic volunteers for the jihad in Afghanistan, their training and the provision of arms, followed by their relocation to fight in Afghanistan. However, controversy subsequently arose between the two. Bin Laden parted ways with Azzam and began to recruit, train, finance and operate volunteers independently in the jihad frameworks.

The Islamic organizations that dealt in Dawa dedicated resources to humanitarian relief, but at the same time they also dealt in Islamic indoctrination in the communities where they were active. In contrast, the Jihad movement, whose activities had become increasingly radical, continued to act locally or regionally in Muslim countries against Muslim rulers or foreign occupiers.

The situation changed in the aftermath of the Islamic revolution and the war in Afghanistan in 1979. From this point onward the concept of global jihad began to crystallize. It was developed by Abdallah Azzam, who was active at the time in Afghanistan, but more importantly, it was implemented by Bin Laden and the Afghan "alumni," who founded the global Jihad in 1998 and declared the United States, Christianity, and Judaism as main targets of the global Jihad. The rapid development and expansion of the Jihad movement was based on the infrastructure of the Dawa networks that had been spread out all over the world since the 1930s.

Dawa and Its Role in Promoting Global Jihad[5]

The global Jihad, including its lethal branches, would not have succeeded in reaching its current dimensions, expanding its bases, recruiting supporters and terror activists, and conducting terror activity worldwide (particularly the September 11 attacks) if not for the prior global network of the Dawa system, which included logistics, financial channels and its community of benevolence. The infrastructure of charities as well as the system of religious and communal services that they had established over several decades served as an anchor and foundation for the activity of the global Jihad's cells and branches.

Members of Islamic terror organizations in general and Al Qaida in particular mainly originate from populations characterized by radical Islamic consciousness. This Islamic consciousness is not the fruit of a momentary epiphany but rather the result of ongoing indoctrination carried out by the organizations and their messengers, whether through Muslim states that believe in disseminating the Islamic message worldwide, or through official and semi-official religious establishments in Muslim countries. Communities, groups or individuals in Muslim countries or

Muslim communities worldwide (where the Dawa infrastructure was established during the twentieth century), were exposed to Dawa activity for years. These entities constitute the main human resource that feeds the Islamic terror organizations.

These audiences are more attentive to the calls to volunteer for Jihad in order to save the Islamic nation, even if the war is being waged far away from their countries of origin. The Mujahidins' success in Afghanistan and the incorporation of the Afghan "alumni" in world Islamic terror organizations encouraged the continuation of activity along the same course.

It is important to understand that the Afghan "alumni" are actually an "Internationale" of Islamic extremists from all over the world who went through the radical Islamic melting pot in Afghanistan. Many of the Afghan "alumni" found their way back to local terror organizations, to other Islamic areas of conflict, and some of them joined the ranks of the global Jihad.

It is noteworthy that the Dawa activity at many focal points in the Muslim world was extremist by nature. Alongside the social and humanitarian activity of Dawa organizations, the Muslim believers were expected not to be content with merely strengthening their faith, but also to take action in the defense of Islam. From there the leap to adopting jihad concepts was not great. The mobilization for Islamic terror organizations and the global Jihad among these audiences bears a procedural similarity to the model of the Afghan "alumni."

1. Stage 1: Dawa activity, education, and welfare services that bring the people closer to Islam.
2. Stage 2: Responding to the call for jihad to save Islam in areas of conflict addressed to both members of the Jihad movements and audiences that have been exposed to Dawa activity. Supportive Islamic countries and charities along with Islamic institutions dispatched the latter to combat areas and training camps. These entities financed their travels, provided the necessary fake papers and referred the recruits to training camps.
3. Stage 3: Increased exposure and a closer link between the recruits at the Mujahidin training camps and Jihad radical indoctrination.
4. Stage 4: Strengthening the link between the recruited fighters and terror organizations at various conflict areas in the world, both due to joint formative experiences alongside veteran terrorist activists during combat and also as a result of the creation of interpersonal relationships.
5. Stage 5: Recruitment to terror organizations under the umbrella of global Jihad and the perpetration of terror attacks in that framework.

The Connection between Global Dawa and Global Jihad[6]

The Dawa infrastructure all over the world was constructed by three central entities:

1. Muslim states that directly built and nurtured the Dawa.
2. Semi-official Islamic institutions and charities established and operated Dawa infrastructures in their countries of origin and worldwide.
3. The Jihad organizations and movements that also developed Dawa infrastructures as a support foundation for their activities.

The Soviet invasion of Afghanistan generated mobilization of the Muslim and Western world on behalf of the Afghan Mujahidin. This mobilization on behalf of the Jihad in Afghanistan forged the link (which was granted widespread legitimacy) between the Dawa mechanisms that originally offered humanitarian aid to the Afghans and the Jihad entities that recruited fighters for the campaign. This integration that actively worked and led to the trouncing of the Soviets in the Afghan arena, contributed to the crystallization of the global Jihad concept in the hands of Abdallah Azzam and Osama Bin Laden.

In the aftermath of the war in Afghanistan and following the formulation of the concept of continued Jihad in other arenas worldwide, Bin Laden and his associates had at their disposal tested and effective infrastructures which had earlier served the war in Afghanistan and upon its completion were free to support new Jihad arenas such as the Balkans, Chechnya, Kashmir and more. The cooperation, the joint work at the Dawa centers, the direct contact between the charities and the Mujahidin fighters, and the interpersonal relationships that had been forged as the result of their joint activities all constituted the basis for the continuation of this pattern of activity when the terror organizations began to act against Western targets and others, particularly against the United States.

This worldwide system enables optimal flexibility for diverting funds, combat means and fighters from one arena of activity to the next all over the world while maintaining operational discipline and high levels of secrecy, without any need for reorganization.

The Reciprocal Relationship between the Dawa and Jihad Factors on the Local Level[7]

When placing the emphasis on the state entity, the Dawa factors mentioned earlier in this chapter develop the Dawa infrastructures both inside the state and in Muslim communities abroad. These infrastructures serve Dawa activities abroad. An examination of the reciprocal relationship between the three factors on the level of the individual Islamic center abroad plainly clarifies the role played by the Dawa centers and infrastructures in the rapid dispersion of the global Jihad. Here follows a characteristic example that illustrates the relationship model between global Dawa and global Jihad.

1. Stage A: An Islamic state takes a decision to build an Islamic center abroad, and allocates funds for this purpose.
2. Stage B: The center is built and dedicated by government representatives.
3. Stage C: Responsibility for running the center is transferred to Islamic charities and institutions.
4. Stage D: The state continues to support the center's activities and maintains control through representatives at embassies abroad. At this stage the institutions/charities begin to recruit personnel (teachers, preachers and lecturers) to run the center.
5. Stage E: The center attracts Islamic audiences and conducts Islamic indoctrination activities based on the permanent staff. It occasionally summons special staff to teach seminars and organize Islamic conferences at the center. In cases such as these, the presence/arrival of a charismatic radical Imam at an Islamic center turns him into a magnet for extremist Islamic target audiences.
6. Stage F: The global Jihad identifies the potential that lies in the center and acts to recruit into its ranks activists from among the center's visitors.
7. Stage G: As time passes, the center turns into a gathering place for global Jihad and a base for recruitment and logistics. Around and inside it, members of the global Jihad are actively dealing in identification, mobilization, and the training of new recruits. They depart for terror attacks from this location, where they conduct Jihad indoctrination. From this point onward, the Dawa center becomes a focal point for global Jihad activity alongside the state and semi-official Dawa entities and means involved in the center's activities.

Dawa, Jihad and Global Islamic Terror[8]

The radical Islamic organizations view terror as the most effective tool to achieve their goals in the modern era. Thus, it is no coincidence that since the 1980s following the Islamic revolution in Iran, and even more markedly during the 1990s (following the Mujahidins' triumph in Afghanistan), Islamic terror has become a leading factor and a source of emulation for terror organizations worldwide.

International terror organizations in general and Islamic terror organizations in particular must develop worldwide infrastructures and secret action patterns in order to ensure their survival and low-key activity. An international terror organization like Al Qaida acts on the basis of four basic principles:

1. Secrecy and compartmentalization
2. Decentralization
3. Logistic and financial infrastructure
4. Collaboration with local terror organizations.

The terror organization has a secret command center within the organization's logistical, financial and operative setups. The logistical and operational infrastructures are spread out all over the world in autonomous, regional and local terror networks that are linked to the organization's command through regional "operators."

The organization has recruitment points based on agents who are planted in mosques and Islamic cultural centers as well as in Muslim communities worldwide. The recruitment process of a volunteer is accompanied by in-depth investigations regarding the recruit, as well as training and indoctrination, culminating in the demand for the recruit's oath of allegiance.

The terrorists' training is conducted at the organization's training facilities. The volunteers come to the facility, undergo training connected to their missions and are sent back to their lands of origin or to their destination countries.

The financial and logistic system is required to provide financial resources and means, and to send them to the terror networks in order to sustain their activities.

Mega terror attacks, like those perpetrated on September 11, are the result of the existence of a worldwide terror infrastructure based on a logistic and financial system backed by abundant resources as well as planning and implementation capabilities.

These are the product of the accumulation of capabilities and many years of experience. To summarize, an international Islamic terror organization like Al Qaida can obtain results like those achieved on September 11 on the basis of extensive infrastructures which can only be provided directly or indirectly by a state entity.

The Advantages of the Global Terror Organization

The implementation of the global Jihad concept necessitates worldwide infrastructure and alignment. The following advantages can be attributed to the international terror organization:

1. *The spreading of the infrastructures generates survivability and superiority.* The distance and deployment of the organization create a situation whereby the headquarters and sub-headquarters are spread out in safe places (Bin Laden and his headquarters continue to be active to this very day). The training areas are situated in other places and the logistic infrastructures are also decentralized. As a result, the organization has maximum survivability even if the infrastructure is damaged at one location.

2. *A global terror organization can prevent effective surveillance by a single country.* This would necessitate international cooperation, something that is almost impossible to implement on a global scope. The global terror organization has the ability to recruit and/or move terror activists all over the world so that surveillance activities related to their movements and activities would necessitate global control and coordination that simply do not exist. For example, it is possible to restrict the entry of citizens of certain countries to the United States, but the terrorists can always enter by using documentation of countries whose citizens are allowed entry.

3. *The global terror organization has maximum flexibility when choosing targets.* The organization can act against targets of a certain country on its soil or all over the world (embassies, corporations, etc.). The organization has the ability to attack by recruiting terrorists in the target countries or by collaborating with local terror organizations.

4. *The global terror organization has the initiative.* Due to the fact that the international terror organization can choose any place it desires as an attack arena, this prevents the possibility of effective defense because it is impossible to provide a global response to this type of challenge.

5. *The global terror organization is self-financing.* The international terror organization has the ability to raise financial resources and to transfer them all over the world by using the international banking system to feed and operate terror infrastructures.

6. *The global terror organization has pre-positioned agents and assets.* It operates by building sleeper infrastructures that are incorporated within the population of the target country and are activated when needed. The chance of discovery is non-existent prior to the stage when they begin acting in subversive patterns.

7. *The global terror organization has access to international news media.* Modern media amplify the advantages of the global terror organization and enable it to operate according to a global action plan. This includes gathering intelligence in target countries, transferring information to headquarters for planning purposes, transferring terror campaigns to the destination within a short amount of time, and managing decentralized headquarters work, which makes it harder to thwart.

8. *The global terror organization has an institutional mind.* It is able to investigate, learn, draw and implement lessons from one terror attack to the next. There is no doubt that the September 11 attacks were based on lessons drawn from other attacks perpetrated by Al Qaida all over the world.

Only by understanding the advantages at the disposal of a global terror organization is it possible to comprehend and explain how Bin Laden planned and executed the September 11 attacks through Al Qaida from his hiding place in the wilds of Afghanistan. By activating a worldwide system of activities, Al Qaida brought the American superpower to its knees.

Dawa and the Global Economic Jihad[9]

The violent (terrorist) Jihad is accompanied and backed by the economic Jihad, which on the one hand serves to finance and aid the infrastructures and the terror perpetrators, and on the other hand constitutes a parallel arena of contention against the enemies of Islam with the focus on the West.

Over the years, Al Qaida has built an extensive economic infrastructure that serves as a sort of "shadow economy." It acts alongside and within the official economic system in countries around the world. Most of the organization's budget is designated for the funding of local terror organizations in order to expand the alignment of the global Jihad; part of it is used as payment for host countries such as Sudan and Afghanistan, and the rest is spent on the terror attacks.

The economic infrastructure that serves as Al Qaida's foundation includes a complex and extensive network of entities, the majority of which are "legitimate." These include corporations, charities, Islamic banks, religious and educational institutions, and contributing private organizations. Thus, part of the movement's revenue comes from sources and means connected to the Dawa, both from sources controlled by the Islamic state and via those controlled by Islamic associations and institutions. The transfer of funds to the organization is achieved through sophisticated camouflage and laundering operations as well as through legitimate businesses.

This method of using businesses as a cover for transferring funding to the movement was made possible by the basic capital infrastructure that Bin Laden possessed as well as his access to business. Over the years he established a global network of commercial companies through which he succeeded in laundering funds, creating revenues, providing work to the organization's members and supporters, and funding its activities. The cornerstones of free society—including freedom of speech and religion, freedom of occupation, freedom of movement, and a free economy—make it easy for terror organizations to act within this system. They exploit it for their own purposes, and ultimately act against it in order to undermine the state-oriented system upon which it rests. The desire to preserve the free and democratic character of the West's economic and political system places many restrictions on law enforcement agencies when contending with terror that aims to undermine the foundations of democracy.

The economic Jihad claims a high toll from the Western world and poses a grave challenge to its continued freedom-based existence:

- Immediate damage stemming from attacks (the direct damage of the September 11 attacks).
- Indirect damage inflicted by attacks (damage to aviation, tourism, insurance, etc.).
- The threat of terror necessitates the investment of huge sums of money for protection against it (changing security procedures in aviation, establishing the DHS, etc.).

Another heavy blow inflicted by the global Jihad in the West stems from the need to carry out steps to thwart this activity. These steps affect the economic system and endanger the foundations of the democratic system.

Summary

The Jihad waged in Afghanistan against the Soviets generated processes of historical importance that altered the appearance of modern radical Islam:

1. The Dawa and Islamic organizations rushed to help the Islamic movements in Afghanistan, and with the aid and support of the Muslim (and Western) world established systems that provided humanitarian aid to the Afghan population.
2. Islamic fighters from all over the Muslim world arrived in Afghanistan in order to participate in the Jihad against the Soviet Union.
3. The provision and training of fighters, supplying them with weapons and sending them to the battlefield with the help of the infrastructures of Islamic organizations that were active in the arena.
4. The combination of the Dawa centers and infrastructures upon which the Jihad infrastructures were constructed created a highly efficient system that proved to be successful in the Afghan arena and has served as a model in other arenas worldwide.
5. The Jihad in Afghanistan created three central phenomena:

    First phenomenon—Globalization of the Jihad and Jihad movements, while prior to the Jihad in Afghanistan these entities generally acted locally in Jihad movements (sometimes on the basis of local or regional mutual aid) in order to topple the regime in their country. The Afghan Jihad brought about a direct encounter between the members of the Jihad movements from all over the world and generated "a brotherhood of comrades-in-arms," and joint formative experiences which at the end of the Jihad in Afghanistan created a sort of worldwide "Jihad Internationale."

Second phenomenon—A systematic model incorporating the Dawa and Jihad infrastructures on a global scale and their activation as a coordinated and integrated system to promote the Jihad's goals. Abdallah Azzam (Bin Laden's spiritual mentor) and Bin Laden himself both played key roles in molding the concepts and systems of the global Jihad whose basic components are described above.

Third phenomenon—The construction of a "learning system" that accumulates experience, learns lessons, and incorporates them within the planning processes of the attacks and realizes them in the implementation.

The contribution of the Islamic institutions and the charities to the development of Al Qaida as a global terror organization was essential and stemmed from the fact that the Dawa infrastructure had been spread all over the globe prior to the concept of global Jihad. When this idea came to full maturity and implementation by Bin Laden, it grew on the foundation and infrastructure of the global Dawa system, which was anchored in a worldwide alignment of Islamic centers, mosques, preachers, funding, and logistic sources. On the eve of September 11, the global Islamic Dawa infrastructure included thousands of Islamic institutions and sites spread out among Islamic communities all over the world, and even if only a handful of them dealt in radical Islamic indoctrination this would suffice to enable the rapid expansion of the global Jihad.

The Dawa activity provided the platform that the global Jihad founded by Bin Laden needed, and among other things it provided the following:

1. *Fundamentalist indoctrination*—A central theme in the activity of the Islamic institutions and the state institutions. Through institutional and advanced dissemination means the latter enhanced Islamic consciousness among Islamic communities as well as the motivation of these populations to take part in a war defending Islam. These entities also molded public opinion in favor of the terror activity against the West in general and the United States in particular.
2. *The logistic infrastructure*—The Dawa entities, including the Islamic institutions and the charities, built and operated a logistic infrastructure that provided shelter, a refuge and an address vis-à-vis spiritual and material help for the Jihad activists. At the same time, this infrastructure recruited young Islamic men and dispatched them to various combat zones. It purchased combat means and equipment for the forces (uni-

forms, medical equipment, vehicles, etc.) The Dawa entities also helped with the maintenance of the training camps in various combat areas, with emphasis on Afghanistan.

3.   *Financing*—Islamic institutions and charities provided direct and indirect funding for the terror organizations through deception, concealment and money laundering while carefully covering up any link between the financer and the terror organization.

It is noteworthy that the Muslim states that are acquainted with the reciprocal ties between the Dawa and the Jihad apply tight supervision over the Dawa means and entities due to the fear that it will provide the infrastructure which the Jihad needs for its development. The West, which only saw the humanistic side of the Dawa and was unaware of the powerful ties between global Dawa and global Jihad, did not restrict the Dawa activity, thereby enabling the consolidation of global Jihad upon the infrastructure of global Dawa.

Al Qaida succeeded in tapping the potential inherent to the Dawa infrastructures worldwide, became integrated within them and harnessed them to promote the terror campaign it was planning, based on its familiarity with and exploitation of vulnerabilities inherent to the democratic American society, with the aim of causing grave damage to the most sensitive and painful sites in the United States and the Free World as a whole.

The Global Jihad and the Horn of Africa

The African continent with more than 300 million Muslim inhabitants is recognized by Al Qaida and the Global Jihad as an important theater. The Horn of Africa and the Red Sea are regarded by Al Qaida as areas of strategic importance.

Abdul Bara Hassan Salman, deputy emir of Islamic Jihad Movement, an Al Qaida associate group, expressed the Islamist view regarding the region:[10]

Politically, the African Horn refers to all the countries of East Africa. It includes Somalia, Djibouti, Eritrea, Ethiopia, and Kenya. The area is of particular strategic importance as it links the East with the West through the Red Sea, that is, between the agrarian and industrial societies. The region is also oil producer and has great mineral deposits in the Red Sea. The Horn's strategic security significance increased since the establishment of a Jewish nation in Palestine. These catalysts, along with some others, made the region a highly sought-after place particularly by the colonialists and imperialists, both past at present.

Abu Azzam al Ansari, in an article in a jihadi website (sada al Jihad-Eco of Jihad) provides an analysis of Africa and the global Jihad.[11] Ansari said that: "The interest of the Mujahidin of Al Qaida in Africa is an old one but has progressed slowly."

Al Qaida has always been aware of the importance of this huge continent and since its emergence attempted at "feeling its pulse." Al Qaida has carried out many operations there and had a presence there. This all proves the awareness by Al Qaida of the importance of this region from many dimensions, as seen also by observers.

We can find the following operations that reflect the focus of the Mujahidin on Africa:

- Many operations against Western targets such as in the U.S. embassies in Kenya and Tanzania.
- The big campaign in Somalia where they managed to expel the American occupier.
- Al Qaida has been active in the Sudan for a period of time, where it was involved in military operations against the infidel John Garang.
- After September 2001, Al Qaida and its supporters carried out a number of attacks, such as in Mombassa, Kenya; in Jerba, Tunisia; in Casablanca, Morocco; and in Sharm al-Sheikh and Sinai.

Abu Azzam al Ansari claims that Al Qaida and the Mujahidin perceive the significance of the African continent for the military campaign against the Crusaders.[12]

Among the most significant advantages of Africa over other regions he highlighted the following:[13]

- The Jihad doctrines are spread in many African countries—Egypt, Algeria, Sudan, Mauritania, Morocco, Libya, Somalia, Eritrea, and Chad. These countries and others produced many Mujahidin who irrigated the lands of Islam with their blood and sacrificed themselves for the sake of Allah. This Jihadi expansion has old roots in many of the African countries.
- The political and military conditions in most of the African continent, the broad weakness of its governments, and the internal fighting and corruption of these regimes, ease the ability of the Mujahidin to move, plan, and organize themselves, far from being seen. They enjoy in Africa easier operational abilities than in other countries, which have effective security, intelligence, and military capacities.
- This general weakness brought about numerous situations of tribal conflicts in many African countries, and hotfired civil wars that produced groups and individuals willing to heroically sacrifice themselves. If these people could be channeled into the line of the Jihad they will have enormous effect in the defense of Islam and the Muslims.

- The wars and conflicts in Africa provide a golden opportunity for the Mujahidin to easily move between different African countries, without any surveillance, and in most cases needing only finances.
- The above-mentioned conditions provide huge amount of weapons and military equipment easy to obtain and in most cases much cheaper than in other regions. Weapons are found all over Africa in larger numbers than in any other continent. In many African countries there is no house without a variety of weapons for either offensive or defensive objects.
- One of the prominent advantages of Africa is the general condition of poverty and the social needs in most countries. It will enable the Mujahidin to provide some finance and welfare, thus, posting there some of their influential operatives.
- Most of the people of this continent are Muslims. The most famous Islamic trend, which the Mujahidin can approach, is the various Sufi groups. The Sufis have no doubt a huge presence in Africa, more than in any other continent. Many Mujahidin in other countries have learned that working with the Sufis is easier than working with any other trend, such as the Shi'is or the Communists. The Christian presence in this region is weak, they are not able to attack the Muslims, and if they did so it would be easy to defeat them.
- There are in Africa nests of continuing conflicts between the true Muslims and their rivals, such as in Somalia, Algeria, or the Christians of southern Sudan, There is potential of the renewal of the conflict in Egypt, especially if the government goes on with its oppression as a reply to the operations. It might lead to an explosion, whose signs are already seen.

Abdul Bara Hassan Salman expressed his perception regarding the future steps of the radical Islamic movements in the Horn of Africa:[14]

- The catalyst for the five-fold Islamist strategy is (a) the effective effort on the part of the Islamic jihad and da'wa tides in the African Horn; (b) the education of the Muslim population and their awareness of the extent of the conspiracy and plotting of the Christians both regionally and internationally; (c) the possibility of establishing a Somali government capable of maintaining a political balance; (d) the alertness of some of the Arabic countries to the danger of the Jewish presence in the region—this will help to review their position with respect to providing support to the people of the region; (e) the efforts of the Jewish government and to confine its external influence.

Somalia has become an ideal theater for the emergence of jihadist organization like Al Itihad al Islamiya (AIAI) (see chapter 3). Osama bin Laden and some of the Al Itihad leaders have apparently known each other from the Jihad in Afghanistan.

Al Itihad has worked with Al Qaida since 1993 to carry out attacks against the United States in Somalia and neighboring countries, including also Israeli targets:

- Al Qaida operatives helped orchestrate the 1993 "Black Hawk Down" incident that ended with the loss of life of 18 American soldiers.
- The "Black Hawk Down" incident led to the decision of President Bill Clinton to withdraw U.S. forces from Somalia, and encouraged Al Qaida to claim that United States was a "paper tiger."
- Al Itihad provided support to Al Qaida in the 1998 bombing of the U.S. embassies in Kenya and Tanzania.
- In 2002, Al Itihad has supported Al Qaida operatives who attacked the Israeli-owned Paradise Hotel in Kenya and made a failed missile attack against an Israeli civilian airliner.

A strategic objective of Al Itihad was the establishment of a pan-Somali Caliphate in the Horn of Africa that would bring Somali ethnic populations in neighboring Ethiopia, Djibouti, and Kenya into a territorially enlarged Somalia. In the mid-1990s with Al Qaida and Sudanese support, Al Itihad launched a terrorist campaign against Ethiopia. Bin Laden transported several hundred Arab Mujahidin veterans of the anti-Soviet Afghan struggle to assist Al Itihad in its military ambitions inside both Somalia and Ethiopia. In response to Al Itihad aggression, Ethiopian forces entered Somalia and defeated Al Itihad forces on the battlefield.[15]

This decisive defeat prompted Al Itihad to re-invent itself and, by 1999, key elements of Al Itihad had merged with Islamic Courts Union (ICU) in southern Mogadishu. One of the leaders of Al Itihad, Sheikh Hassan Dahir Aweys, who has been linked to Al Qaida, became the leader of the ICU. The victory of the Islamic Courts Union in Somalia and the nomination of Sheikh Aweys as the leader of the ICU are significant achievements of the Global Jihad in Somalia and the Horn of Africa. Somalia under a radical Islamic regime could soon become a springboard of exporting Jihadi ideology to neighboring countries.

Al Qaida's Message to the Islamic Courts Union in Somalia

Osama bin Laden addressed a recorded message on the July 1, 2006 to the "nation of Islam in general, and our people and brothers the Mujahidin in Iraq and Somalia in particular."[16] Bin Laden called Abdullahi Yusuf, who heads the Somali transitional federal government (TFG) in Baidoa, "an agent of foreign apostates," and he condemned Yusuf's recent call for support from neighboring Ethiopia.[17] Bin Laden warned "every

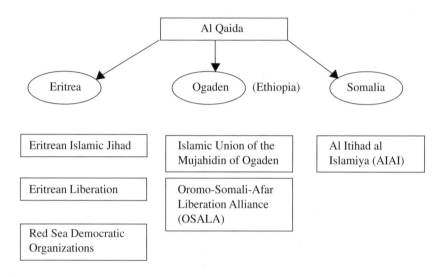

Figure 1
Al Qaida and the Horn of Africa
(1991-1996)

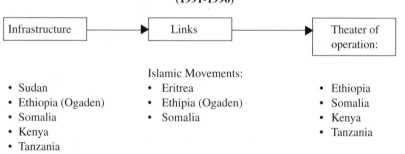

Figure 2
Al Qaida and the Horn of Africa
(1991-1996)

Muslim in Somalia" to reject such efforts calling Yusuf in particular "an obedient American agent."[18] Bin Laden called on Islamic forces to attack the Yusuf government "quickly and make sure he doesn't flee."[19]

Regarding intervention by "international forces" he instructed, "prepare what is needed especially the mines for the tanks and the (rocket-propelled grenades) for the armored vehicles." ... "We pledge that we will fight your soldiers on the land of Somalia and will fight you on your own land if you dispatch troops to Somalia."[20] He recalled the 1994 withdrawal of U.S. forces from Somalia after 18 troops were killed by a local militia. "This time," he said, "victory will be far easier."

Bin Laden also addressed President Bush, saying: "We will continue to fight you and your allies every where, in Iraq, Afghanistan, Somalia and Sudan to run down your resources and kill your men until you return defeated to your nation."[21]

The leader of Somalia Islamic Supreme Council, Sheikh Hassan Dahir Aweys, distanced his group from Osama Bin Laden after Bin Laden called on Somali Islamists.[22] In an interview with Shabelle Radio, Sheikh Aweys said that Osama Bin Laden's remarks on Somalia had nothing to do with their Islamic uprising in Somalia.[23] "It's not more than a friendly call because Osama shares the pain with the Islamic Republic of Somalia," he said.

Sheikh Aweys indicated Islamic Courts in Somalia are the wish of the Somalis and not outsider's desire. He also condemned Ethiopian government for what he termed to be plain aggression and a huge incursion against Islam.[24] "We call on Ethiopians to stay away from evil violations, Ethiopia will be responsible for the grave consequences," Aweys warned.

The prime minister of Somalia's transitional federal government (TFG), Ali Muhammad Gedi, reacted angrily to Bin Laden's statement on Somalia. He said the Somali people were practicing Islam before the birth of Osama Bin Laden and his ancestors so Osama should leave Somali affairs to the Somalis.[25] At a press conference held in Baidoa, where the transitional government of Somalia is based, Ali Muhammad Gedi was reacting to the audio message on the Internet purported to be from the leader of Al Qaida, Osama Bin Laden.[26]

The prime minister of Somalia said that after long suspicions about his involvement in Somalia, Bin Laden made clear in his recent message about Somalia that he has representatives in Somalia. He called on the representatives of Osama Bin Laden to depart the Somali territory or else they will be kicked out.[27] Prime Minister Gedi added: "Bin Laden claims that he is the international leader of Islam, which is untrue. He is a radical who spreads a theory of violence."

The intervention of Bin Laden in the internal conflict in Somalia between the TFG and the ICU reflects the strategic importance of the theater of Somalia and the Horn of Africa for Al Qaida and the Global Jihad.

Al Qaida and the Fall of the Islamic Courts Union

The defeat of the ICU by the Ethiopian and the TFG forces in 2006 was a significant setback for Al Qaida and the global Jihad. The response of Al Qaida came shortly after the final collapse of the ICU forces in Kismayu.

On January 5, 2007 an audiotape of Ayman al Zawaheiri (the deputy of Bin Laden) was posted on a website used by Jihadi groups.[28] In the tape, Zawaheiri responded to the defeat of the ICU in Somalia and called on the ICU to launch an Iraq-style campaign against the TFG and the Ethiopian forces in Somalia. "I appeal to the lions of Islam in Yemen, the state of faith and wisdom. I appeal to my brothers, the lions of Islam in the Arab Peninsula, the cradle of conquests. And I also appeal to my brothers, the lions of Islam in Egypt, Sudan, the Arab Maghreb, and everywhere in the Muslim world to rise up to aid their Muslim brethren in Somalia," he said.

Zawaheiri said this could be done "through offering sacrifices, money, opinion, and expertise so as to defeat the slaves of America that it sends to death on its behalf." He also accused the United Nations of plotting against Somalia. "The Security Council is plotting to approve this invasion by issuing its resolution to dispatch international forces to Somalia and by its failure to issue a resolution that calls for the withdrawal of the Ethiopian forces from Somalia," he said.

Zawaheiri urged the fighters to employ the tactics that have been used by insurgents fighting U.S.-led forces in Afghanistan and Iraq. "As the world's most powerful power in the world has been defeated in Afghanistan and Iraq by the believer groups, who will go to heaven, its slaves will be defeated, God willing, on the land of the mujahid Muslim Somalia," he said. "Use ambushes, mines, raids and martyrdom-seeking raids [suicide bombings] to devour them as the lions devour their prey."

Notes

1.   This chapter is based on: Shaul Shay, *The Islamic Terror and the Balkans*, Transaction Publishers, New Brunswick, 2006.
2.   Yoram Schweitzer and Shaul Shay, *The Globalization of Terror*, Transaction Publishers, New Brunswick, U.S.A, 2003, p. 13.
3.   Ibid.
4.   Rohan Gunaratna, *Inside Al Qaida, Global Network of Terror*, Columbia University Press, New York, 2002, pp. 3-43.
5.   Ibid.
6.   Ibid.
7.   Ibid.
8.   Ibid.
9.   Ibid.
10.   Rohan Gunaratna, *Inside Al Qaida, Global Network of Terror*, Columbia University Press, New York, 2002, pp. 151-152.
11.   Revuen Paz and Moshe Terdman, *Africa: The Gold Mine of Al Qaida and Global*

Jihad, The Project for the Research of Islamist Movements (PRISM) Occasional Papers Volume 4 (2006) Number 2 (June 2006).

12. Ibid.
13. Ibid.
14. Rohan Gunaratna, *Inside Al Qaida, Global Network of Terror*, Columbia University Press, New York, 2002, pp. 152-153.
15. Georgy Alonso Pirio and Herach Gregorian, "Viewpoint: Jihadist threat in Africa," *Middle East Times*, June 11, 2006.
16. Karen De Young, "Bin Laden Tape," Washingtonpost.com, July 2, 2006.
17. Ibid.
18. Ibid.
19. Ibid.
20. Lee Keath, Bin Laden planning Somalia, Iraq message, A.P. Cairo, July 1, 2006. See also: Salah Nasrawi, Bin Laden Endorses al Zarqawis success, A.P. Cairo, July 2, 2006.
21. Ibid.
22. Spiritual Leader Denies Bin Laden Links, Shabelle Media Network, Mogadishu, allafrica.com, July 3, 2006.
23. Ibid.
24. Ibid.
25. Somali PM Slams Osama Bin Laden, Shabelle Media Network (Mogadishu), allafrica.com, July 2, 2006.
26. Ibid.
27. Ibid.
28. "Al Qaeda call for Somalia Jihad," BBC News, January 5, 2007.

3

The Islamic Movements in Somalia

The roots of the Islamic faith in Horn of Africa and Somalia are over 1000 years old. Most Somalis follow a Shafi'i version of the faith that has come to be characterized by veneration of saints, including the ancestors of many Somali clans, and has traditionally been dominated by apolitical Sufi orders.[1] Islamic faith in Somalia is one of the basic identities including class, race, and location of origin, which cut across clan lines.

In pre-colonial times, rural Somali communities recognized two distinct authorities, clan elders and religious leaders whose responsibilities in the conduct of individual and community affairs overlapped to the extent that Islam was essentially assimilated into clan culture. This symbiotic relationship has persisted throughout the colonial and post-colonial era.[2]

Somali Islamicism can be traced to a common source, the Wahdat al-Shabaab al-Islami and the Jama'at al-Ahli al-Islami (also known as the al-Ahli group).[3] These Muslim Brotherhood-inspired groups developed in the 1960s and strove to be key players in shaping the state and the setting of its mixed ideological agenda.[4] The rise to power of Muhammad Ziad Barre in 1969, however, deprived the Islamists of their status. Al-Ahli was forced to disband and al-Wahdat and other Islamist groups went underground or fled to the oil-rich states of the Gulf to join the Somali diaspora.

By the 1980s, the Somali Islamist movement had grown considerably. Nevertheless, it was the ouster of the Barre dictatorship that gave a major boost to Islamic associations and organizations.[5] Their common denominator was the desire for a unique form of Islamic regime in Somalia. The differences between Somalia's Islamist movements were mainly doctrinal: Traditionalists, Reformists, Modernists, Salafis, Jihadists and others. The distinctions between the different groups were not only doctrinal but as well the difference of leadership, dominant clan affiliation and sectorial interests.

37

We may identify three main categories of Islamic movements in Somalia:

- Political Islamism.
- Missionary Islamism.
- Jihadi Islamism.

Political Islamism

Harakat Al-Islah

Harakat Al-Islah was formed in 1978 as a loose network of affiliated clandestine groups.[6] During the period 1980-1990, the al-Islah was obliged to remain clandestine because of the repressive nature of Barre's regime.

After the collapse of the Barre regime in 1991 the organization started to operate openly mainly for promotion of social and humanitarian activities. Al-Islah members played prominent roles in the state's educational system, in the foundation of the Formal Private Education Network in Somalia (FPENS), and in the foundation of the Mogadishu University.[7] The leaders of the organization are elected by a parliament (Majlis al-Shura) for five years and are limited to two terms.[8]

Al-Islah's leaders are: Dr Ali Sheikh (President of the Mogadishu University) the chairman of Al-Islah, Abdu Rahman Baadiyo is vice chairman, and Dr. Ibrahim Dusuqi is the secretary general. All of the current leaders were the founders of the organization.

Al-Islah has always been suspected by Somali and foreign security services of involvement in radicalism and association with Al-Itihad. There is much evidence, however, of a power struggle between and within al-Islah and al-Itihad's competing ideological differences and strong divergences on strategies, tactics and religious interpretations.

Al-Islah's leaders, for example condemn violence and takfir (declaring as an infidel) as un-Islamic and counterproductive. They have long called for building a shared future that transcends the extremism and bigotry embodied in al-Itihad's and Takfir wal-Hijra's Salafi-Jihadist ideology.[9]

Majma Ulimadda Islamika ee Somaliya[10]

After the fall of the Barre regime in 1991, a group of Somali religious leaders (Ulama) came together to discuss how to fill the vacuum. The result was the formation of a militia force named Horseed.[11] The primary goals of the militia were to provide security for areas of Mogadishu that were affiliated with the Majma and its newly established Sharia courts.

Majma presents, as its name denotes, an assembly of Islamic scholars who follow the Shafi'i madhhab and whose main goal is the establishment of a Sharia-based government.

Within months, the leader of southern Somalia's most powerful militia faction, General Aidid, apparently decided that the jihadi fighters of al-Itihad posed a greater threat to his authority than a modest group of Islamic scholars and sought an alliance with Majma.[12] His overtures split the organization: those who rejected Aidid's offer of partnership retained the name Majma; those responsive broke away to establish Ahlu Sunna wal-Jama'a.[13]

The declared purpose of Majma is "to protect the proper understanding and practice of Islam," ideally through establishment of a Somali government that will govern in accordance with the Shafi'i madhhab (legal school) of Sharia.[14] In the early 1990s, Majma' became involved in a variety of peace initiatives, including the mediation effort of U.S. special envoy Robert Oakley in 1992. Since then, it has concentrated more on basic social functions, such as religious education, engagement The founding chairman, Sheikh Muhammad Ma'alim Hassan, died in 2001, and Sheikh Ahmed Abdi Dhi'isow was elected to replace him. He heads an executive committee of eleven members, many of the clerics who served in government mosques under the previous regime.[15] The group's total membership is estimated at between 200 and 300 religious leaders from most clans and regions of Somalia.[16]

Ahlu Sunna wal Jama'a

Ahlu Sunna wal Jama'a (ASWJ) is another modern Islamist group created in 1991 as an offshoot from Majma to counter the influence of the most radical Islamist trends.[17] Some of the leaders believed the intensive measures were required to defend "traditional" Somali Islamic practices from foreign, and especially Islamist encroachment.[18]

The movement brings together politically motivated sheikhs whose primary goal is to unify the Sufi community under the unified leadership capable of consolidating the powers of the three primary Sufi Tariqas—the Qadiriyya, Shakihyya and Ahmadiyya—into one front whose sole mission is the rejuvenation of the "traditionalist" interpretation of Islam and the delegitimization of the beliefs and political views of al-Itihad and other radical Islamic movements.[19]

In spite of the weakness of the ASWJ compare to other Islamic groups the organization continued to provide unified leadership for Sufi turuqi mainly across southern Somalia.[20]

At the early stages of the civil war the (ASWJ) was an ally of General Farah Aidid, but later in 1992-1993 Aidid switched allegiances, associating himself with Al Itihad in his confrontation with U.S. forces.[21]

In spite of the weakness of the ASWJ compare to other Islamic groups the organization continued to provide unified leadership for Sufi turuqi, mainly across southern Somalia.[22]

From 2002 onward, the ASWJ began to play an active role in different peace initiatives promoting a moderate Islamic school as a platform for restoring peace and order in Somalia.

Missionary Islamism

Missionary Islamists largely eschew political activism—even if their brand of activism has some political objective and implications. The movement is represented by Salafiyya Jadiida (the new Salafis) and the most structured movement in Somalia, Jama'at al-Tabligh.

Salafiyya Jadiida[23]

The Salafiyya Jadiida is best exemplified by Sheikh Ali Wajis, an example of a prominent Salafi ideologue who has gone from supporting and briefly leading Al Itihad to opposing its violent dogmatic theology. Wajis' qualified repudiation of the irrational jihadi ideology of Salafi-Jihadists and his re-examination of its theoretical position in light of a rational reassessment of Islamic rules of warfare and the prevailing realities on the ground exemplify the fractures rocking the jihadi and Islamist movements. It is also an encouraging sign of the debate occurring within the new Salafis and Salafi-Jihadist circles about the need for contextualized understanding of the issues of jihad and political violence.

Jama'at al-Tabligh[24]

The Tabligh movement—launched in 1926 by the Jama'at al-Da'wa wal-Tabligh (Group for Preaching and Propagation), as an apolitical, quietist movement—constitutes the largest group of religious proselytizers in Somalia. Tablighi missionaries' aggressive and dedicated peaceful and apolitical preaching tactics are part of the reason for the growth of Tablighi sympathizers and supporters. This notable success in recruitment and significant increase in membership left the movement wide open to infiltration and manipulation by radical groups.

Out of the 500 to 700 foreign sheikhs present in Somalia, many are from the Arab world, but they also come from Afghanistan, Pakistan,

Chechnya and other countries. Given the size and heterogeneity of the movement, its infiltration by jihadi elements should come as no surprise. What is troubling, however, is the denial of the movement's leadership of any such infiltration despite mounting evidence of the group's involvement in murdering foreign aid workers in Somaliland. The movement, as the International Crisis Group reported, "Lacks any system of screening its members for prior involvement in jihadism and so is poorly equipped to respond to allegations that some may be involved in fomenting extremism and violence."[25]

Al-Ansar al-Sunna[26]

Al-Ansar al-Sunna was the product of internal divisions within the early Al-Itihad Islamic movement. The April 1991 Battle of Araare, the first military action fought by Al-Itihad al-Islami, had strengthened two emerging trends within the movement. First, it aided the jihadis in their determination to militarize the movement. Secondly, it gave the impression that Al-Itihad placed the interests of the Darood clan (the defenders of Kismaayo) above those of the Hawiye (the forces of General Aidid).

Disillusioned by these developments, a group of mainly Hawiye clerics broke away to from their own association. The result was Al-Ansar al-Sunna, a Mogadishu-based association of Wahhabi religious leaders led by Sheikh Hassan Alasow, who had preached Al-Itihad's message in the pre-war period at the city's Lafwyene Mosque. According to one account, many members were traders with links to Saudi Arabia and used aid from Saudi institutions to encourage conformity with Wahhabi-style religious conduct and dress.

Al-Ansar's lifespan was brief. Within months its leaders abandoned the project in favor of a brand of Salafism that they referred to as "Al Jama'a" and began to denounce Al-Itihad. A number of Al-Ansar's members belonged to the Abgaal sub-clan of the Hawiye; by 1993 several had drifted into the orbit of Musa Sudi Yalahow, an emerging Abgaal faction leader in Mogadishu's Madina district, where they established the city's first Islamic court.

One of the group's founders, Sheikh Ali Wajis, has remained active. An early leader of Al-Itihad, he played a key role in both the formation of Al-Ansar and its dissolution. Viewed today as a leading figure of the Salafiyya Jadiida movement, he emerged post 9/11, as a prominent Salafi critic of Al-Itihad and is considered by some observers to embody the ideological tension between the new Salafis and jihadi Salafis.

Jihadi Islamism[27]

The jihadi tendency is the third type of Islamic activism. Unlike the political and missionary currents of Islamism, the jihadi activists are committed to violence and armed resistance against what they perceive as the continuing onslaught of the enemies of Islam. This form of Islamic activism has very few sympathizers, although it is actively involved in trying to recruit or infiltrate missionary organizations like Salafiyya Jadiida and the Tabilgh movement. The Jihadi movement has had its fortunes ebb and flow during the last decade.

Al Takfir Wal Hijra[28]

The original al Takfir wal-Hijra was founded in Egypt following the radical Islamic doctrine of Sayyid Qutb. Very little in known about the Somali Al-Takfir Wal-Hijra, except that its presence first became apparent after the collapse of the Barre regime, when small Takfiri communes appeared in Mogadishu, Bosaso, and a number of other towns. They were secretive and shunned unnecessary contact with other Somalis, but had no known links to Al-Itihad or other Jihadi groups and no known record of violence. Some observes have described the Somali Al Takfir Wal Hijra as the most militant Islamist group in Somalia.

In mid-2005, reports in Kenyan media claimed that U.S. and Kenyan intelligence had identified a terrorist coalition of Al-Takfir, Al-Qaida, and the Al-Qaida-affiliated Iraqi organizations led by Abu Musa'ab al-Zarqawi operating between Somalia and Kenya.[29] The reports cited sources close to the leadership of Somalia's Transitional Federal Government (TFG), which has consistently overstated the terrorist threat in order to attract foreign assistance.

The confusion surrounding the Somali Takfiri movements is understandable. The obscurity of the group's membership, aims and beliefs lend themselves to speculation and rumor. Furthermore, like Shukri Mustafa's original group, it is quite possible that members of the group do not refer to themselves as "Takfiris" or identify themselves as such. The term "Takfir" relates more to a system of Islamist belief and conduct (Takfir is the practice of denouncing infidels or the impious) than it does to membership in a given group, so it is quite plausible that some members of other organizations share Takfiri beliefs. The little that is known about Somali "Takfiris," together with the extremist ideology and violent character of Takfiri groups elsewhere, however, suggests that the movement merits further research and close monitoring.

Al-Itihad Al-Islamiya (Unity of Islam)

This group first emerged in the late 1980s in Mogadishu, and most of its members were young academics who studied in Middle Eastern schools. They believed that the only way to liberate Somalia from the corruption, oppression, and tribalism that characterized Ziad Barre's regime was to adopt political Islam. In this, Al-Itihad was similar to many Islamic movements in the Middle East and the Muslim world.

After the collapse of Ziad Barre's regime in 1991 and the ensuing power struggle between clan-based militia factions, Islamists sought to construct a cross-clan and national movement based on the appeal of Islamist ideology as an alternative to a failed nationalism and divisive clanism.[30] In broad terms, the political trajectory of Al Itihad since the collapse of the Barre regime can be broken down into three phases: building economic power, military confrontation, and ideological regrouping.[31]

In the early days of the civil war, the strategic objective of Al Itihad was to build power by taking control of key economic installations across Somalia. Al Itihad's initial success came in Kismayo in January 1991, when the movement took control of the seaport, a lucrative transit point for taxing international aid and import/export goods. However, in March 1991, General Farah Aidid advanced on Kismayo with his United Somali Congress militia (USC), drawn from the Hawiye clan. In exchange for the right to administer the town in the future, Al Itihad offered to fight side-by-side in defense of Kismayo with the secular Somali National Front faction (SNF), drawn from the Darood clan. The offer was not accepted and, amidst continuing divisions within the Al Itihad and SNF ranks, Aidid was able to capture the town. After the fall of Kismayo, all Darood clans were targeted by harsh reprisals from the Hawiye militia—including summary executions, systematic rape and looting—due to their genealogical association with the former president.

Following these events, much of the remaining trust between cross-clan allies was undermined, and Al Itihad broke increasingly along clan lines. Fleeing from Kismayo, Darood remnants of Al Itihad re-grouped in Bosaso and Garowe towns in northeast Somalia (now known as Puntland). In 1992, Al Itihad again attended to take control of key commercial points in Bosaso. This led to a military confrontation with the Somali Salvation Democratic Front (SSDF), drawn from the Darood clan, in which Al Itihad was again defeated and forcefully displaced.

The movement relocated to the towns of Luuq and Dolo in Gedo region. There, it was able to court support from Darood Marehan residents. The clans formed the backbone of the SNF faction, leading to an intra-clan confrontation between Al Itihad and the SNF in southwestern Somalia. Originally, Al Itihad participated with the SNF in the defense of Marehan territory from SNA-Haber Gidir incursions. Once victorious, Al Itihad found itself in control of the district administrations in Luuq and Dolo towns, and temporarily extended their influence to Bulo Hawo and El Wak.

Again, however, the group was seen as a threat to the authority of secular powers—this time by both the SNF faction and the Ethiopian government. The latter, fearful of the importation of radical Islam into its restive southern region, supported the SNF to overthrow Al Itihad. The movement was known to have links with both the Ogadeni National Liberation Front (ONLF), and accused of supporting the overthrow of the Ethiopian government following bomb attacks in Addis Abba hotels during 1996. In that year and again in 1997, the Ethiopian military crossed into Somalia numerous times, defeating Al Itihad and driving them further south along the west bank of the Juba River. These activities were the reason why the Al-Itihad movement was included in the US State Department's list of terror organizations.

From the year 1996 onwards, Al-Itihad adopted a new strategy:

- The movement decided to withdraw from direct military activity and gave up of holding territories on a permanent basis, as this turns them into an easy target for Ethiopia and other enemies.
- The movement decided to assimilate and act within various Somali communities, a fact that made it difficult for its adversaries to thwart its activities. Based on the understanding that Somali tribalism found it hard to accept an integrative Islamic perception, the movement decided to act on a tribal basis and leave the goal of a united Somalia under the wings of an Islamic regime for the subsequent stages. The movement achieved varying levels of influence in different tribes, but no tribe agreed to subjugate its leadership to the movement's policies.
- The movement became decentralized, much like the social structure of Somalia, causing the movement to take on a different character in the various areas of Somalia. In some areas the organization cooperates with Western relief organizations and refrains from maintaining ties with radical Islamic organizations, while in other locations the movement acts independently, and in still other areas it is involved in violent activity against Somali adversaries and Westerners.
- Al-Itihad has decided to attain its long-term goals—the establishment of the Islamic regime in Somalia—through "dawa" activities (education, indoctrination), and it pursues the development of long-term political and social infrastructures by investing in education, in the development of a local judicial system based on Islamic law, in

communications and information. The organization operates relief and charitable organizations and deals in the development of the movement's economic infrastructure and in the recruitment and infiltration of its members into influential focal points in Somali society.

Al Itihad Al Islamiya's Financial Sources

Funded by wealthy Saudis, Al Itihad had extensive connections with the Somali expatriate community in Kenya in Nairobi and the predominantly Muslim costal regions. AIAI was extensively connected to Al Barakaat, a Somali business conglomerate and money transfer organization described by former U.S. Treasury Secretary Paul O'Neill as one of the "financiers of terrorism."[32] Al Barakaat allegedly provided Al-Qaida with money laundering services.[33]

On September 24, 2001, Al Itihad Al Islamiya's finances were sanctioned by U.S. President George W. Bush under Executive Order 13224. Its then-head, Hassan Dahir Aweys, was also sanctioned under EO 13324 in November of that year.[34]

In addition to Somalia's largest traders, remittance banks (also known as the "hawildad system") became a significant source of revenue and patronage for Al Itihad. In the mid-1990s, when militia-factions fragmented and turned against one another, direct remittance support for the factional struggle decreased. Instead, the Somali diaspora increasingly channeled money directly to war-affected kin. Trust networks established on common commitments to political Islamist agenda gained Somali businessmen easy access to capital through connections to Islamist counterparts in Dubai and Saudi Arabia.

Faith-based credit schemes left Islamist businessmen well positioned to take over Somalia's $500 million per year remittance business. In order to conduct their business across the country, the remittance agencies slowly built a sophisticated telecommunications network to serve their needs. This has created an independent and primarily legitimate financial sector in its own right. Yet, the remittance companies—as a source of profit sharing and a channel for foreign support—remain an essential financial asset for Al Itihad. In addition, these companies are considered to be sources of employment for devout, young followers of the movement.

The financial strength gleaned from these connections has been spent in two ways. First, Al Itihad has cultivated public support by delivering welfare services to the urban poor in major centers across the country. For instance, during the 1997-98 El Niño floods in Somalia, Islamic organizations were an essential and well organized part of the relief response. This strategy is not different to that of Al Islah, except for Al Itihad's concentration on the most disenfranchised communities susceptible to indoctrination to more militant agendas. Second, to build a patronage network within each clan. By increasing the influence of likeminded individuals within each clan to assume the reigns of traditional authority, this is evidenced during the recent constitutional crisis in Puntland. As President Abdulahi Yusuf's tenure elapsed, Al Itihad used its influence within the Bosaso business community and financial payoffs within the Majerteen councils of elders to disrupt reconciliation with Yusuf and propose alternative presidential candidates.

Al Itihad Al Islamiya after the 9/11 Attacks

Following the September 11 attacks, suspicions were raised regarding cooperation between Al Itihad and Al Qaida. According to the United States, Al Itihad enabled Al Qaida to use its bases and other infrastructures prior to Al Qaida's terror attacks in 1998 against the U.S. Embassy in Nairobi (Kenya) and in Dar al Salaam (Tanzania). The Al Qaida liaison vis-à-vis, the Al Itihad organization was Osama Bin Laden's aide, Muhammad Attaf, who was killed in the U.S. offensive in Afghanistan.[35]

The Al Itihad organization apparently continues to operate several training camps for Islamic terrorists, including the Ras Kamboni Camp located near the Kenyan border.[36] According to U.S. sources, this camp served as a base for Al Qaida terror activity in Africa (mainly in nearby Kenya). In view of the links between Al Itihad and Al Qaida, it was feared that Al Itihad might offer Al Qaida members fleeing Afghanistan a safe haven in Somalia, and that the latter would serve as the organization's main base to replace the lost one in Afghanistan. Al Itihad has a strong infrastructure in Mogadishu, and it operated a legal system based on the Sharia in the city before the temporary government was founded (TNG).

The movement supported the Arta process and the establishment of the temporary government, and in exchange demanded government portfolios, particularly the Ministry of Justice (due to its critical importance to the application of the Sharia as the state law), but this request was turned down and instead it had to be satisfied with several seats in parliament. This support served as the basis for charges that the temporary government (TNG) was merely a Trojan horse planted by Al Itihad, as Al Qaida's tool. From this point of view, the temporary government in Somalia was perceived as similar to the Taliban government in Afghanistan, which championed the Al Qaida organization.

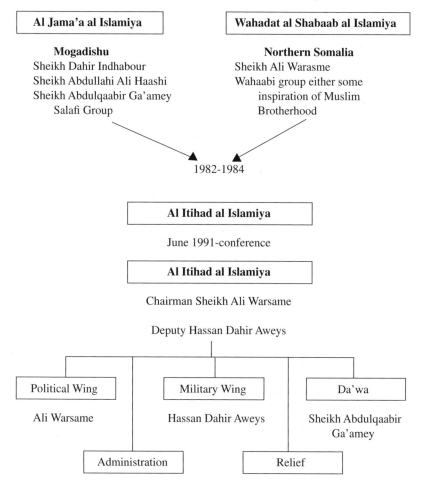

Figure 1
The Foundation of the Al Itihad al Islamiya

Al Jama'a al Islamiya

Wahadat al Shabaab al Islamiya

Mogadishu
Sheikh Dahir Indhabour
Sheikh Abdullahi Ali Haashi
Sheikh Abdulqaabir Ga'amey
Salafi Group

Northern Somalia
Sheikh Ali Warasme
Wahaabi group either some
inspiration of Muslim
Brotherhood

1982-1984

Al Itihad al Islamiya

June 1991-conference

Al Itihad al Islamiya

Chairman Sheikh Ali Warsame

Deputy Hassan Dahir Aweys

Political Wing

Ali Warsame

Military Wing

Hassan Dahir Aweys

Da'wa

Sheikh Abdulqaabir
Ga'amey

Administration

Relief

Saudi Arabia and Charitable Organizations[37]

Saudi Arabia's prominent status as a central donor to the Muslims in Somalia calls for a brief discussion of the exceptional complexity characterizing the relationship between the Saudi Arabian regime on the one hand, and radical Islam and terror, on the other. Consequently, this chapter will discuss the activity of Saudi charities and analyze Saudi Arabia's policy.

Saudi Arabia's status vis-à-vis the issue of Islamic terror is unique and particularly complex. On the one hand, Saudi Arabia is an American ally that opposes and fights Islamic terror endangering its regime, while on the other hand, Saudi Arabia supports and assists radical Islamic organizations in their activities in distant arenas.

The roots of the Saudi "Islamic dilemma" lie in the historical alliance between Muhammad Ibn Saud, founder of the Saudi dynasty, and Muhammad Ibn Abd Al Wahab. The Saudi dynasty was granted religious legitimacy and in exchange promised to include the Wahhabian dynasty in the government and award legitimacy to the religious school of thought that it represents. However, there is a basic contradiction between the lifestyle and pro-Western policy of the Saudi monarchy, and the puritanical, radical worldview of the Wahhabist school of thought.

Saudi Arabia constitutes the bastion and influential factor of the Wahhabist movements that act to export the radical Islamic concepts of the Wahhabi school to Islamic focal points throughout the Muslim world (the Balkans, Chechnya, Afghanistan, Africa, and elsewhere). It acts to disseminate radical Islam through charities and welfare organizations who serve radical Islamic organizations and entities with the authorities' knowledge. In this framework, Saudi Arabia openly aids Islamic terror organizations (based on the claim that these entities are supposedly not terror organizations, but rather legitimate liberation organizations).

Saudi Arabia was also one of only three countries in the world that recognized the Taliban regime in Afghanistan, which sponsored Bin Laden and Al Qaida and even aided this regime until September 11, 2001. Saudi Arabia enables wealthy "private" entities to aid and support radical Islamic entities. The support and "adoption" of these entities are sometimes accomplished as part of the internal power struggles within the Saudi Arabian royal family.

In the early 1980s, the Saudi regime praised the Saudi volunteers who joined the struggle in Afghanistan, including Osama Bin Laden. Even after the danger inherent to the "Afghani alumni" became apparent, the Saudi authorities allowed volunteers to set out for areas of conflict where Muslim populations were in dire straits, such as the Balkans and Chechnya.

Upon his return to Saudi Arabia after the Jihad in Afghanistan, Osama Bin Laden was given a hero's welcome by the Saudi public and the authorities as well, but his growing criticism against the stand that Saudi Arabia had taken during the Gulf War eventually prompted the Saudi authorities to deport him from the country and revoke his passport. Bin Laden's deportation from Saudi Arabia did not prevent widespread solidarity of radical circles with Bin Laden and his worldview, and many joined the ranks of Al Qaida and the terror infrastructures that he established worldwide. It is no coincidence that fifteen of the perpetrators of the September 11, 2001 terror attacks were Saudi citizens.

The Saudi royal family is threatened by opposition entities that are motivated by a combination of social, economic, ideological, and religious factors. The ostentatious and extravagant lifestyle of the Saudi royal family, the inequality in distributing resources, the country's opulence and its "non-Islamic" behavior according to the view of Islamic parties, have contributed over the years to the development of extensive cadres of opposition entities that aspire to overthrow the regime and establish a "true" Islamic state in Saudi Arabia.

Threats against the regime have also been posed by external factors such as subversion by Iran and the latter's attempt to export the Khomeini revolution to Saudi Arabia, or the activities of erstwhile Iraqi president Saddam Hussein against the Saudi regime.

The threats that the Saudi regime faces on the one hand, and its dependency on Western support and power factors close to the throne on the other, compel the regime to follow a careful and intricate policy vis-à-vis the handling of radical Islam and terror.

The Saudi regime takes all necessary measures against entities that constitute a threat to the regime's stability, including executing terrorists, but it nevertheless allows radical Saudi entities to act outside of its borders almost without disruption, thus creating a *modus vivendi* with these forces.

Thanks to its "petrodollars," from the 1970s onwards Saudi Arabia set up an extensive system of charities that deal in the dissemination of Wahhabi Islam all over the world. Between the years 1990 and 2000, Saudi Arabia spent some 70 billion dollars from government sources on humanitarian aid and dissemination of Islam worldwide. A Saudi weekly reported that thanks to these funds, some 1500 mosques, 210 Islamic centers, 202 Islamic colleges and almost 2000 schools were built all over the world.

Today, in addition to the official charities functioning in Saudi Arabia, there are some 240 private charities including about 20 that were founded by Saudi intelligence in order to support the Mujahidin all over the world. The funds raised totaled between 3 and 4 billion dollars annually. Some 10-20 percent of these funds were dispatched outside of Saudi Arabia's borders to charity branches all over the world.

The link between Saudi charities and the activities of terror organizations was manifested in two ways:

- Charities transferred hundreds of millions of dollars to terror organizations that dealt in Jihad worldwide, including Al Qaida.
- The charities served as a logistic infrastructure and cover for the terrorists' activities through the provision of documentation, work places and flight tickets.

Since the September 11 attacks, Saudi Arabia has vehemently denied any link between itself and the terror organizations. This also applies to Shiite charities that were active in the Balkans and had contacts with Islamic terror organizations.

Prince Sultan Ibn Aziz, the Saudi Minister of Defense and a significant contributor to some of the charities, claimed that the organizations deal in humanitarian relief and that in any event the Saudi authorities could not supervise the activities of private charities.

Despite these claims, investigations conducted in the United States after September 11 indicated that princes from the Saudi royal family, as well as prosperous entrepreneurs, sat on the boards of directors of many of the large Saudi charities. Moreover, a significant part of the funds donated to these charities came from government sources and were the personal donations of members of the royal family.

In May 2003, under American pressure, Saudi Arabia informed all of the Saudi charities that they must suspend their activities outside of the country until further notice pending a security examination to ensure that they are uninvolved with or linked to terror organizations. Since that time, many charities have renewed their activities, including some that were revealed to have been involved in terror activity. In some cases, the organizations changed their names and the addresses of their offices, and in other instances the organizations' directors or employees who were suspected of involvement in terror were replaced, after which the organization renewed its activities.

Islamic Charitable Organizations in Somalia

Islamic charities in Somalia do not maintain ties with Western and other philanthropic organizations, and do not adopt the behavioral norms and transparency customary in organizations of this sort. The "closed" policy of these Islamic organizations enables them to cooperate closely with radical Islamic organizations that exploit these charities to promote their goals in this country. It is also possible that some of the Islamic charities actually constitute "front organizations" for al-Itihad as well as other radical Islamic organizations.

Following the collapse of the Barre regime and the humanitarian crisis in the early 1990s, Islamic charities, both foreign and domestic, expanded dramatically. The finding of a recent study on the phenomenon estimates that there are "literally dozens" of Islamic charities in Mogadishu alone, most notably the Africa Muslims Agency (based in Kuwait); the Red Crescent Society of the United Arab Emirates (UAE); the World Association of Muslim Youth (WAMY, based in Saudi Arabia); the Al-Islah Charity, linked to Harakat al-Islah; the Muslim World League (Rabitat al-Islam al-alamiyya) and its subsidiary, the International Islamic Relief Organization (IIRO), both based in Saudi Arabia; Dawa al-Islamiyya; and the Al Wafa Charitable Society, which is listed as a "specially designated terrorist entity" by the U.S. government.[38]

Some of these, and others not listed here, have been linked to militant Islamist groups inside and outside Somalia. As described above, the Muslim World League, the IIRO and the now-defunct Mercy International Relief Agency (MIRA) were all used to channel funds to al-Itihad during the early 1990s. As part of the wider investigation into the Saudi-based Al Haramain Islamic Foundation's links to international terrorism, the United States cited the Somali offices of Al-Haramain as directly linked to terrorism, persuading Riyadh to suspend their staff in 2003. In April 2005, an employee of the Al Haramain office in Somaliland, was arrested for involvement in the assassination of several foreign aid workers.[39]

The vast majority of Islamic charities in Somalia have no such links with extremism: they are private NGOs that provide essential services to the public. In Mogadishu alone, Islamic charities either manage or support three universities, a major management training institute, two hospitals, and schools that furnish education for over 100,000 students. Many Islamic also support work in other regions of the country.

The term "Islamic charities" implies a distinction from NGOs assisted by Western donors, but in reality that is not so clear-cut. Many Somali Islamic organizations are simply committed to providing a service that is consistent with their beliefs and practices as Muslims and have little or no qualms about partnerships with non-Muslim organizations or donors.

Some Islamic charities in Somalia do indeed use social services as a platform for proselytizing, political activism, and promotion of an Arab national identity.[40] Most ordinary Somalis resent such activities as religious and cultural interference and are resistant to their messages.

But many Islamic charities seem to lack any parallel agenda. Much of the instruction in Islamic teaching institutions is in Somali or English, not Arabic, and is focused on academic or vocational skills rather than religious education. Likewise, as a close observer recently noted, "Islamic charities are doing some of the most practical and intensive work in Somalia to promote the education, advancement and empowerment of women."[41] Women constitute a significant proportion of the students in Islamic learning institutions at all levels, and classes are often mixed.

The expansion of Islamic charities in Somalia in recent years is primarily a response to need and the availability of funding. Most Islamic NGOs profess a belief that their faith offers a way out of the crisis that has engulfed their country for nearly fifteen years and perceive their missions and actions in that context. Islamic social activism is not necessarily a sign of growing radicalism, nor is it inherently anti-Western; on the contrary, the endeavors of many Islamic NGOs are a pragmatic response to a crisis for which all support is welcome.

Al Haramain Islamic Foundation[42]

The Al Haramain Islamic Foundation is a Saudi charity that operated offices in 49 countries worldwide and annually raised some 30 million dollars in donations in Middle Eastern countries as well as throughout the Muslim world[43] and Macedonia.[44]

According to American intelligence sources, the organization's offices in Somalia and Bosnia were directly involved in Al Qaida activities. The director of the Al Haramain Islamic Foundation, Sheikh Aqeel al Aqeel, was investigated by the Saudi authorities in connection to suspicions that additional worldwide offices affiliated with the organization (in Indonesia, Kenya and other countries) were connected to Islamic organizations' terror activities. This branch was in direct contact with the Internet website of Azzam Publications, one of the sites that Al Qaida used for Jihad related propaganda.

In March 2002, the Al Haramain Islamic Foundation was designated a terrorist entity by the U.S. authorities and all of its assets in the United States were frozen. Following the implementation of this step by the Americans, NATO forces raided seven of the organization's branches in Bosnia. The raid on the organization's office in Sarajevo exposed documents connecting the charity to Al Qaida and also revealed letters calling for Jihad against NATO and U.S. forces. In the framework of its investigations, the U.S. Treasury exposed links between the Al Haramain Islamic Foundation and the Egyptian terrorist organization Jamaah al Islamiyah (this organization has also been included in the U.S. list of terror organizations since November 2, 2001).

The International Islamic Relief Organization (IIRO)[45]

The IIRO was established in 1978 and its headquarters is located in Jeddah, Saudi Arabia. The IIRO is a critical component in the financial activity of the Muslim World League (MWL), which is financed by the Saudi government.[46] The director of the MWL is appointed directly by the Saudi King Fahed and he serves as chairman of the IIRO's board of trustees. The IIRO is one of the largest and most affluent Islamic charities and it has offices in over 90 countries worldwide.

Al Barakaat and Somalia[47]

In 1991 the Ziad Barre regime collapsed in Somalia and the country descended into a bloody civil war. At that time many Somalis left Somalia and some of them immigrated to the United States. The Somali immigrants in the United States sought a safe and quick way to move money earned in United States back to their families in Somalia. Somalia at that time had no central bank by which foreign exchange could be made. Thus, a different way had to be found to get money to Somalia.

The al-Barakaat network of money remitters was set up to address this need. Founded by Ahmed Nur Ali Jumale in 1985, al-Barakaat at the time of 9/11 had more than 180 offices in 40 countries, all existing primarily to transfer money to Somalia. The financial headquarters for Al Barakaat was in the United Arab Emirates, where Jumale had opened a number of accounts at the Emirates Bank International (EBI) to facilitate the transmission of money.

At the time of the 9/11 terrorist attacks, Al Barakaat was considered the largest money remittance system operating in Somalia; In addition to being used by a significant number of Somalis who had fled the anarchy in their home country, it was the primary means that the United Nations used to transmit money in support of its relief operations there.

A money remitter, described most simply, collects money from an individual at one point and pays it to another in another location, charging a fee for the service. The money itself does not actually move; rather, the originating office simply sends a message to the destination office, informing it of the amount of money and the identity of the sender and of the recipient.

Al Barakaat has been commonly called a hawala, but it is not one.[48] There are similarities between the two systems. In both, there is a need to compensate the agent who has paid out money pursuant to a money transfer. In both, the money is not sent for each individual transaction;

rather, there is a larger settling transaction conducted periodically to adjust for the differences in what each office took in and what it had to pay out.

The key difference is in how the money or value moves between the office obtaining the money from the customer and the office paying the ultimate beneficiary. In transferring value between the sending and the receiving offices, a money remitter uses the formal financial system, typically wire transfers or a correspondent banking relationship. A hawala, at least in its "pure" form, does not use a negotiable instrument or other commonly recognized method for the exchange of money.

Hawaladars instead employ a variety of means, often in combination, to settle with each other: they can settle preexisting debt, pay to or receive from the accounts of third parties within the same country, import or export goods (both legal goods, with false invoicing, or illegal commerce, such as drug trafficking) to satisfy the accounts, or physically move currency or precious metal or stones.

There are other distinguishing characteristics of a hawala. Many hawalas operate between specific areas of the world, or even specific areas within a specific country. An individual wanting to send money from Canada to one area in Pakistan, for example, might use one hawaladar; to move money to a different part of Pakistan, it may be necessary to use a different one. Hawalas typically do not maintain a large central control office for settling transactions. Instead, a loose association of hawaladars conducts business with each other, typically without any formal or legally binding agreements. Hawaladars often keep few formal records; those that do exist are usually handwritten in idiosyncratic shorthand and are typically destroyed once the transaction is completed. Osama Bin Laden and al Qaeda made significant use of hawalas to move money in the Middle East—particularly in Pakistan, the United Arab Emirates, and Afghanistan.

Through the years (1991-2001) different American intelligence agencies claimed that Al Barakaat has connections with Islamic terror organizations including Al Itihad al Islamiya (AIAI). In the late 1990s, the intelligence community also began to draw links between AIAI, Al Barakaat, and Osama Bin Laden.

The reporting centered on a few key facts. First, it alleged that Osama Bin Laden was in fact a silent partner of Al Barakaat. Second, the reporting indicated that Al Barakaat was associated with AIAI, in that al-Barakaat managed the finances of AIAI, and AIAI used al-Barakaat to send money to operatives.

Variations of that reporting stated that the head of al-Barakaat was part of the AIAI leadership, or that Osama Bin Laden, using Al Barakaat, actually assisted in procuring weapons for AIAI or sold weapons to AIAI. There were specific reports, for example, of Al Barakaat's supplying Somalia's Sharia court with 175 "technicals" and 33 machine guns between January and mid-July 2000, and AIAI with 780 machine guns, which it had procured from sources in China and Chechnya. Other reporting indicated that al-Barakaat was founded by members of the Muslim Brotherhood in order to facilitate the transfer of money to terrorist organizations, including Hamas and AIAI.

Lastly, there was fairly detailed information from a U.S. embassy in Africa in July 1999. Two sources known to the embassy claimed that Osama Bin Laden was a silent partner and frequent customer of al-Barakaat, which did not practice any kind of due diligence in making financial transactions. Both sources claimed that al-Barakaat security forces supported Osama Bin Laden by providing protection for Bin Laden operatives when they visited Mogadishu. The embassy cautioned that the allegations could not be confirmed and noted the risk that the sources may simply be spreading negative information about their rivals.

During these years, many international NGOs and agencies in Somalia used Al Barakaat services. Al-Barakaat had become Somalia's preeminent remittance company and the largest provider of telecommunications services.[49] On November 7, 2001, U.S. federal agents entered eight Al-Barakaat offices in different places in United States and the U.S. government placed al-Barakaat, its chairman Jumale, and its managing director, Abdullah Hussein Kahiye, on its list of individuals and groups linked with terrorism.

The president of the United States, with the secretary of the treasury and attorney general, announced the action in press conference, describing Jumale as a "friend" and supporter of Osama Bin Laden. Secretary of the Treasury Paul O'Neill described al-Barakaat offices as "the money movers, the quartermasters of terror a principal source of funding, intelligence and money transfers for Bin Laden." He later announced that "we estimate that $25 million was skimmed from the al-Barakaat network of companies each year, and redirected toward terrorist operations."

Al-Barakaat offices were closed in the United States, the United Arab Emirates, Djibouti, and Ethiopia. Before the action against al-Barakaat, the CIA surmised that AIAI would easily move to other financial institutions in the event that al-Barakaat was shut down. It also understood that the loss of money from al-Barakaat would only temporarily disrupt AIAI, which had other revenue sources. Early intelligence reporting after the freeze indicated that AIAI came under financial pressure was the closure of al-Barakaat, but moved quickly to develop alternative funding mechanisms. There was no analysis of whether that pressure was the natural result of the closing of the country's largest conduit of funds or was due particularly to al-Barakaat's alleged complicity in funding AIAI.

Al-Barakaat ultimately moved its offices to other locations in Dubai and Somalia and changed its name. Moreover, AIAI was able to move money through alternative means. Even as early as mid-November 2001, the CIA judged the Islamic terrorist funding networks to be composed of "robust," interlocking Islamic NGOs and financial entities in the Gulf region.

The U.S. government has given no public evidence in support of its claim, which many Somali analysts consider "questionable"[50] Instead Al Barakaat is actively promoting its own version of events. In the absence of a transparent legal process, many Somalis view the case against Al Barakaat as persecution of an ostensibly Salafi business enterprise.[51]

Notes

1.   Somalia's Islamists, Crisis Group, *Africa Report*, No. 100, December 12, 2005.
2.   Andre Le Sage, Prospects for al Itihad and Islamist Radicalism in Somalia, published in *Review of African Political Economy*, Volume 27, No. 89, September 2001.
3.   Anouar Boukhars, "Understanding Somali Islamism," *Terrorism Monitor*, Volume 4, Issue 10, May 18, 2006.
4.   Roland Marchal , "Islamic Political Dynamics in the Somali Civil War" in Allex Dewall (ed.) *Islamism and Its Enemies in the Horn of Africa*, Indiana University Press, 2004.
5.   Anouar Boukhars, "Understanding Somali Islamism," *Terrorism Monitor*, Volume 4, Issue 10, May 18, 2006.
6.   Somalia's Islamists, Crisis Group, *Africa Report*, No. 100, December 12, 2005, p. 13.
7.   Anouar Boukhars, "Understanding Somali Islamism," *Terrorism Monitor*, Volume 4, Issue 10, May 18, 2006.
8.   Ibid.
9.   Ibid.
10.   Somalia's Islamists, Crisis Group, *Africa Report*, No. 100, December 12, 2005, p. 13.
11.   Meaning "Vanguard."
12.   Somalia's Islamists, Crisis Group, *Africa Report*, No. 100, December 12, 2005, p. 11.
13.   Ibid., p. 16.
14.   Ibid., p. 16.
15.   Ibid., p. 16.
16.   Somalia's Islamists, Crisis Group, *Africa Report*, No. 100, December 12, 2005, p. 13.

17. Anouar Boukhars, Understanding Somali Islamism, Terrorism monitor, Volume 4, Issue 10, May 18, 2006.
18. Somalia's Islamists, Crisis Group, *Africa Report*, No. 100, December 12, 2005, p. 13.
19. Ibid., p. 13.
20. Ibid., p. 13.
21. Ibid., p. 13.
22. Ibid., p. 14.
23. Ibid., p. 15.
24. Ibid., p. 16.
25. Marc-Antoine Perouse de Montclos, "Des NGO sans government: movements islamiques et velleites de substitution a l'Etat dans la Somalie en guerre", Colloque organize dans le cadre du programme MOST (UNESCO), en partenariat avec l'IRD, le CEDEJ, le CEPS d'Al Ahram. March 29-31, 2000 au Caire.
26. Somalia's Islamists, Crisis Groups, *Africa Report*, No. 100, December 12, 2005.
27. Ibid.
28. Ibid.
29. Andre Le Sage, Prospects for Al Itihad and Islamist Radicalism in Somalia, in *Review of African Political Economy*, Volume 27 No. 89, September 2001.
30. Andre Le Sage, Prospects for Al Itihad and Islamist Radicalism in Somalia, in *Review of African Political Economy*, Volume 27 No. 89, September 2001.
31. Ibid.
32. *Dawn*, Pakistan, November 26, 2001.
33. Suspected Terrorist List (http://www.sec.state.ma.us/sct/sctter/teridx.htm), list maintained by the U.S. Commonwealth of Massachusetts.
34. Al Itihad al Islamiya, *Wikipedia*, the free encyclopedia.
35. Charles Cobb, Jr. "Hints of Military Action Cause Puzzlement and Worry," allAfrica.com, December 23, 2001.
36. Somalia "Next U.S. target after Taliban," *The East African*, November 2, 2001.
37. This chapter is based on: Shaul Shay, *The Islamic Terror and the Balkans*, Transaction Publishers, New Brunswick, NJ, 2006.
38. Andre Lesage, "The rise of Islamic charities in Somalia: An assessment of impact and agendas," unpublished draft paper presented to the 45th Annual International Studies Association Convention, Montreal, Canada, 17-20 March, 2004, p. 9.
39. See Crisis Group Report, Counter-Terrorism in Somalia, op. cit, pp. 5-6.
40. See Crisis Group Report, Somalia: Countering Terrorism in a Failed State, op. cit, p. 12.
41. Andre Le Sage, "The rise of Islamic charities in Somalia", op. cit, p. 19.
42. This section is based on the document Islamic Fundamentalists' Global Network—Modus Operandi Model: Bosnia, Documentation Center of the Republic of SRPSKA, Banja Luka, September 2002. The organization's Arabic name is Mu'assasat al Haramain al Kharyiy and it is also known as The Charitable Establishment of the Two Holy Mosques.
43. Based on the organization's website.
44. Declassified 1996 CIA report regarding involvement of Islamic Charities in terrorism.
45. The organization is also called The International Humanitarian Relief Organization. The organization operated in the Balkans under the name Haya'at al Ighata al Islamiyya al Alamiyya.
46. "IIRO-Welcome" http:/www.arab.net/ iiro.

47.   This part is based on: Al Barakaat Case Study, The Somali Community and al Barakaat, National Commission on Terrorist Attacks upon the U.S., chapter 5.
48.   The following discussion is aided by two reports, both produced by FINCEN: A Report to Congress in Accordance with Section 359 of the USA PATRIOT ACT, (2002) and Hawala: the Hawala Alternative Remittance System and Its Role in Money Laundering, (undated, probably 1996).
49.   Somalia's Islamists, Africa Report No100—December 12, 2005.
50.   Ibid.
51.   Ibid.

4

Islamic Involvement in Somalia[1] (1992-1993)

The involvement of Islamic relief organizations in Somalia began as early as the late 1970s, when Ziad Barre severed his ties with the Soviet Union and the Communist Bloc. Islamic charity and aid organizations, with the encouragement of Saudi Arabia and the Persian Gulf states, poured financial and humanitarian aid into Somalia, most of which was transferred to the government via a Somali liaison named Muhammad Sheikh Othman.

In the summer of 1991, following the collapse of Barre's regime, Othman transferred his camp's loyalties to General Aidid. Othman's step was apparently taken with the blessings of the Islamic entities that made use of his services, as the ideological and financial support of these entities was also transferred to Aidid's camp.

During the civil war in Somalia, Islamic factors from Saudi Arabia and the Gulf states were active in the country; they incorporated humanitarian aid with Islamic preaching aimed at bringing the Somali population closer to their religious worldview. These organizations were diverse and represented various interested parties and several religious sects from the Arabian Peninsula, that sought exclusivity in aiding Somalia. They regarded UN and US involvement as counterproductive to their interests and as an attempt by Western powers to take over Somalia under a pretext of humanitarian aid. Thus, for example, Islamic charities like the Islamic World Association and the Muslim World Relief Organization declared that "only Muslim organizations act to provide true humanitarian aid to Somalia, and the humanitarian relief from the West is meant to serve Western control of Somalia."[2]

Among those entities active in Somalia under the guise of charitable organizations was Osama Bin Laden, who acted in coordination with the

radical Islamic leader of Sudan—Hassan al-Turabi. Bin Laden viewed the
deterioration of the central government in Somalia and the intensification of radical Islamic influences as a window of opportunity to develop
and boost an Islamic terror infrastructure. The Islamic terror infrastructure that Bin Laden deployed all over the world relied on a network of
companies and financial institutions that served as camouflage for the
terror networks and ensured the flow of the required resources for their
operation. Thus, with the aid of Muhammad Sheikh Othman's financial
infrastructure, Somalia quickly became an important component in the
financial network established by Bin Laden worldwide.

Bin Laden's activities in Somalia were largely coordinated with Sudan,
whose leader—Hassan al-Turabi—regarded Somalia as an important destination for the export of the Islamic Revolution. The Sudanese involvement was supported by Iran, Sudan's patron at that time, and became a
part of an Iranian strategic plan to export the Islamic revolution to Africa
and to attain important strategic footholds in the Horn of Africa and on
the shores of the Red Sea.

It is thus accurate to state that since the beginning of the civil war in
Somalia, four radical Islamic entities acted there simultaneously and
sometimes even in coordination:

1.   Iran—Directly and indirectly through its ally Sudan;
2.   Sudan—Directly and through Somali powerbrokers which it sup-
      ported;
3.   Bin Laden and Al-Qaida—Independently, but in coordination with
      Sudan;
4.   Radical Islamic entities from Saudi Arabia and the Emirates in the
      Persian Gulf.

Somalia rapidly turned into an arena of confrontation between the
United States, which aspired to restore stability and peace to Somalia and
to strengthen its own status and influence in the strategic Horn of Africa
on the one hand, and the Islamic powerbrokers, who aspired to perpetu-
ate the anarchy in Somalia with the aim of strengthening the influence
of Islam and achieving a free hand for Islamic terror entities.

Iranian Involvement in Somalia[3]

As stated earlier, Iran regarded the Horn of Africa, Somalia included,
as an important target for the export of the Islamic Revolution and as a
key to achieving control over the coasts overlooking the vital waterway
between the Red Sea and the Indian Ocean. The creation of a chain of fun-

damentalist Islamic regimes associated with Iran would have generated a new geopolitical reality that would enable Iran to "surround" the Arabian Peninsula—from Iran in the east, on to the Horn of Africa states in the west, and finally to Yemen in the south. In addition, this would intensify the Islamic threat against Egypt and the North African countries.

Under the government of Hassan-al-Turabi and Omar al-Beshir, Sudan had already become Iran's close ally in 1990, and served as an active partner and a springboard for the realization of strategic Iranian interests in the region. Iran and Sudan regarded the United States and the West as the main enemy impeding the realization of the Islamic vision in the Horn of Africa, and therefore took joint action to block and remove this threat.

On November 28, 1992, following the U.S. declaration of its intention to dispatch forces to Somalia, an Iranian delegation headed by Ayatollah Mohammad Yazdi arrived in Khartoum for consultations. During the visit, a new security cooperation agreement was signed between Iran and Sudan, according to which Iran undertook to boost Sudan's military and security capabilities and to help with the building of the necessary infrastructures for the export of the revolution to African countries.

Iran and Sudan decided to establish a joint committee headed by the Iranian General Rahim Safawi and Ali Othman Taha, Hassan al-Turabi's aide, who had planned the action in the Somali arena against the American forces with the help of local powerbrokers, the Somali Islamic Union Party (SIUP). In addition, Iran decided to establish and fund the Somali Revolutionary Guard (SRG). Its members were to be trained in Sudanese camps by Iranian and Hizballah experts. The establishment of the SRG was placed in the hands of an Iranian intelligence officer named Ali Manshawi.

The strategy formulated by Ali Othman Taha's team postulated that the Islamic activity should focus on inciting the Somali public against the American presence and encouraging guerilla and terror activity by local powerbrokers. A frontal confrontation between the organizations supported by Sudan and the United States was to be avoided as long as the conditions were not yet ripe, and provided that there was no direct threat against Sudanese and Iranian interests.

Nonetheless, the Iranians believed that there was an urgent need to perpetrate terror acts against the United States, which would give expression to the opposition of radical Islam to the American presence in Somalia. The target for attack was Aden, which served as a base for American activity in Somalia, but was located outside of the African continent. The mission in Aden was assigned to Osama Bin Laden, who undertook the task with alacrity and efficiency (see the subsequent subchapter on this issue).

In the framework of the preparations for the activity in the Horn of Africa, Iran incorporated the "Al-Quds forces," whose role was to facilitate the export of the revolution via subversive activity in the target countries. Several hundred Afghan "alumni" were active in these activities, some of whom were sent by Iran to Sudan prior to their operations in the Horn of Africa. In addition, Iran presented Sudan with "Stinger" anti-aircraft missiles for possible use in Somalia. At the end of 1992 and in the beginning on 1993, groups of "Al-Quds" fighters were dispatched from Sudan to Somalia and Ogaden in order to organize infrastructures and prepare for their operation.

In February 1993, a conference was held in Khartoum under the patronage of Hassan al-Turabi, and with the participation of senior Iranian representatives, the SIUP representatives, and delegates sent by Aidid, with the aim of establishing a combat strategy against the United States. After the conference in Khartoum, for the following six to eight weeks, Aidid and several of his senior aides visited Iran, Yemen, and Sudan numerous times in order to coordinate the aid to be offered his forces in Somalia. The Iranians poured combat means, instructors, and consultants into Sudan and through that country to Somalia. According to various reports the latter helped the Islamic forces and Aidid's people in the fighting in Mogadishu.

The U.S. decision to withdraw its forces from Sudan following the losses that it had sustained there (particularly in the fighting on October 3-4 1993; see subsequent elaboration), was perceived by the Iranians and the Sudanese as a major victory of radical Islam over the American superpower. Iran, which had succeeded via Hizballah in causing the withdrawal of the U.S. forces from Lebanon in 1983, again forced a humiliating retreat on the United States, this time in Somalia.

On March 1, 1994, most of the U.S. forces withdrew from Somalia, and the country was plunged into total anarchy, which enabled Iran and its allies—Sudan and Bin Laden—to tighten their grip on strategic territory that, in practical terms, had ceased to function as a state.

Sudanese Involvement in Somalia[4]

The escalation and deterioration vis-à-vis the situation in Somalia occurred at the same time as (and perhaps as part of) an Iranian-Sudanese campaign aimed at exporting the Islamic Revolution to East Africa.

During the years 1990-1991, an infrastructure of training camps was established in Sudan, which was sponsored by the National Islamic Front (NIF). Islamic volunteers from Ethiopia, Eritrea, Kenya, Uganda, and Somalia arrived at these camps. Dr. Ali Alhaj, one of Hassan al-Turabi's cronies, was responsible for the operation of these training camps and for the training of the foreign terrorists.

In the fall of 1992, Hassan al-Turabi ordered the escalation of the campaign to undermine the stability of regimes in East Africa. The terrorists who had completed their training were sent back to their native countries in order to facilitate and lead subversive Islamic activities. This step by Hassan al-Turabi was initiated around the time that the United States decided to send a humanitarian task force to Somalia.

The civil war and anarchy that prevailed in Somalia presented a convenient opportunity for Iran and Sudan its ally to attain influence and a base in a strategically located Muslim country on the shores of the Red Sea. American involvement in Somalia was perceived by Iran and Sudan as a threat against their interests and the actions that they aspired to facilitate. It was also viewed as American imperialism under the guise of humanitarian aid. Thus, in the eyes of Iran and Sudan, the U.S. forces became a central target that should be expelled from Somalia through a terror and guerilla campaign that would be based on local powerbrokers hostile to the Americans and the United Nations. Sudan aided Islamic terrorists trained in its camps to reenter Somalia via various ways (the sea, Ethiopia, and Kenya) and supplied them with weaponry.

Hassan al-Turabi's three main allies in the Somali arena were:

1. Abdel al-Rahman Ahmed Ali Tur, an Islamic leader in the Somaliland area who enforced a rigid Islamic regime in the area under his control and enjoyed Sudanese and Iranian aid.
2. General Muhammad Abshir, former chief of the Mogadishu police and a central figure in the leadership of the Somali Salvation Democratic Front (SSDF); thanks to his close ties with Hassan al-Turabi, the militia was joined by many volunteers from Sudan, Egypt, Pakistan, and Afghanistan.
3. General Aidid was Hassan al-Turabi's most important ally, but the extent of Sudanese or Iranian influence on his actions was relatively limited.

Sudan granted Aidid financial and military aid with the aim of broadening and boosting its influence in Somalia, and Hassan al-Turabi even sent volunteers trained in Sudan to fight alongside Aidid against the forces of Ali Mahdi Muhammad. But as stated above, Aidid succeeded in maintaining a large degree of political independence, and his dependence on his friends in Khartoum and Teheran was limited.

As noted earlier, through Osama Bin Laden Hassan al-Turabi established a covert financial and logistic infrastructure in Somalia for the funneling of financial aid to Hassan al-Turabi's allies. In 1992, Hassan al-Turabi established the Somali Islamic Union Party (SIUP) in Somalia, an umbrella organization that consolidated several radical Islamic entities sharing a common denominator of tribal loyalties. The SIUP became the main and direct platform for infiltrating the Sudanese influence into the Somali arena, under Hassan al-Turabi's express guidance.

The formal leader of the SIUP was Muhammad Othman, who was based in London and dealt mainly in informational and propaganda-related activities, but the subversive activities and the fighting were run by local commanders in Somalia, who received instructions directly from Sudan and Iran. The SIUP initiated military activity in June 1992 via an offensive launched in the area of Bosaso, in northern Somalia, but the attempt failed. Following the military debacle, a delegation of experts headed by Rahim Safawi, the deputy commander of the Iranian Revolutionary Guard and Ali Othman Taha from Sudan, arrived in Matka, Somalia in August 1992 to investigate military and other needs of the SIUP together with the latter's commanders, and prepared a plan for the improvement of its operational skills. Starting from the fall 1992, weaponry was supplied and training camps were set up for the organization in Somaliland and in Ogaden inside Ethiopian territory (Bin Laden played a major role in arranging the establishment of the camps on Ethiopian soil).

Following the landing of the U.S. Marines in Somalia, a joint Sudanese-Iranian decision was made to initiate a struggle against the American presence, on the basis of Sudan's allies in the Somali arena and the terror infrastructure established in this country prior to the arrival of the American forces.

Osama Bin Laden and the Campaign in Somalia[5]

From the beginning of the 1990s, Osama Bin Laden resided in Sudan, and under the patronage of the regime of Hassan al-Turabi and Omar al-Beshir, built up an economic empire and a terror infrastructure with which he planned to launch a Jihad against the West. Bin Laden, who was a close associate of Hassan al-Turabi, became an active partner in the granting of aid to various Islamic terror organizations that gained Hassan al-Turabi's support.

Bin Laden and his organization, Al-Qaida, were partners to the formulation of the Iranian-Sudanese strategy for the dissemination of the Islamic Revolution in the Horn of Africa (Bin Laden's main partner in the Somali activity was his right-hand man Aiman al-Zawaheiri).

Admittedly, most of the tasks assigned to Bin Laden were logistic and organizational, but they enabled him to accumulate valuable experience in organizing an infrastructure to support complex operations against the United States in East Africa. They also helped Bin Laden to fit in as a significant player in the decision-making processes in the framework of the Iranian-Sudanese coalition.

The establishment of an effective front of the Islamic terror organizations in the Somali arena necessitated the foundation of a logistic and financial infrastructure to enable the provision of fighters, weaponry, and funds. As stated earlier, the task of establishing and operating this infrastructure was assigned to Bin Laden, who utilized his economic and organizational experience, as well as his worldwide connections, and within a short period succeeded in placing an efficient logistic and financial infrastructure at the disposal of Iran and Sudan. Bin Laden founded several international companies that dealt in agricultural development in Ethiopia, Somalia's neighbor. In the Ogaden Desert, near the Somali border, these "companies" established farms that served as cover for training facilities for Somali terrorists, storage for combat equipment and the supply of money for funding activities.

Toward the middle of 1993, in the framework of the preparations for the escalation of the struggle against the American forces in Somalia, Bin Laden managed a complex campaign involving the transfer of Afghan "alumni" from Pakistan and Yemen to Somalia. Some of the fighters were transported in a fleet of fishing boats and dropped off at desolate beaches in Somalia, from whence they were taken by local networks to the Mogadishu combat area; others were flown in on light aircraft, which landed during the night at landing areas situated in Somalia; the rest infiltrated Somalia via its borders with Ethiopia and Kenya.[6]

Bin Laden apparently visited Somalia several times but did not take part in the fighting. On the other hand, his right-hand man and assistant (Aiman al-Zawaheiri), and Ali al-Rashidi (an activist of the Egyptian Islamic Jihad), who was an Afghan "alumnus" and Aiman al-Zawaheiri's closest aide, reportedly were in direct command of the fighting forces in Mogadishu. Bin Laden's main involvement in connection to the Somali campaign was expressed in organizing the attack against U.S. targets in Aden (see subsequent elaboration).

The heavy losses that the United States sustained in the fighting in Somalia and its decision to withdraw its forces from Somalia by March 1, 1994 were perceived by Islamic entities and the Somalis, as well as by Bin Laden, as proof of their ability to defeat the United States. In an interview with Robert Fisk of the *Independent*, Osama Bin Laden declared:[7]

> We believe that God used our holy war in Afghanistan to destroy the Russian army and the Soviet Union ... and now we ask God to use us one more time to do the same to America to make it a shadow of itself.
>
> We also believe that our battle against America is much simpler than the war against the Soviet Union, because some of our mujahidin who fought here in Afghanistan also participated in operations against the Americans in Somalia, and they were surprised at the collapse of American morale. This convinced us that the Americans are a paper tiger.

In another interview that Bin Laden granted to the al-Jazeera television network, he stated:[8]

> Based on the reports we received from our brothers, who participated in the Jihad in Somalia, we learned that they saw the weakness, frailty and cowardice of U.S. troops. Only eighteen U.S. troops were killed. Nonetheless, they fled in the heart of darkness, frustrated after they had caused great commotion about a New World Order.

The Campaign in Somalia—Summer 1993

In the beginning of the summer of 1993, the Iranian and Sudanese preparations for the campaign in Somalia were completed, and Islamic terror cells started to act against the UN forces in the neighborhoods that were under Aidid's control. The attacks included ambushes and the planting of explosive devices.[9]

These activities peaked on June 5, 1993 in an ambush laid by the terrorists for a Pakistani UN force, in which twenty-six Pakistani soldiers perished. Following the brutal attack against the Pakistani force, the UN declared the SNA an illegal organization. Aidid was officially estranged from the contacts for the economic and political restoration of Somalia, and the commander of the UN forces declared a prize of $25,000 for anyone who could bring about the capture of Aidid.

The attack, which was attributed to Aidid, boosted his stature among the Somali public, and many tribes as well as powerbrokers joined the SNA coalition under Aidid's leadership. The counter-response of Aidid's radio station to the UN's declaration was to offer a prize of one million dollars to anyone who would bring in the commander of the UN forces in Somalia, Admiral Howey, dead or alive. Following the heavy losses suffered by the UN forces, they began to respond with heavy fire against the terrorists, and in the exchange of fire Somali citizens were often hit.

On June 11 1993, Aidid and several of his aides set out for Khartoum in order to coordinate the coming steps with Sudan. The Sudanese propaganda machine blamed the United States and the United Nations for the deterioration of the situation in Somalia, and alleged that the U.S. aim was to take over the entire Horn of Africa, with Somalia only the first target in the overall American plan. The Sudanese foreign minister warned the United States that if it attacked Sudan, the former would encounter harsh opposition and the declaration of a Jihad against America.

Following Aidid's visit to Khartoum and according to Sudanese instructions, Bin Laden poured weaponry and additional fighters into Mogadishu, with the aim of fortifying the combat ability of the Islamic entities. In June 1993, the Islamic forces in Somalia included the following entities:[10]

- Aidid's forces under the SNA umbrella (whose headquarters were located in Mogadishu and Galacio);
- The SIUP forces (whose headquarters were in Marka);
- The forces of the SRG accompanied by Iranian advisers (whose main base was in Bosaso);
- Forces and volunteers from Iraq.

The forces were equipped and prepared to operate a prolonged terror campaign and guerilla warfare against the American and the UN forces, according to the policy and instructions issued by Iran and Sudan.

During June 13-15, 1993, the United States conducted a series of land and air offensives against Aidid's positions and forces. On June 17, Aidid's house was raided—the house was surrounded and searched, but Aidid was not found.[11] In response to these actions, the SNA announced that it would fight until the last UN soldier departed from Somalia, and Aidid's people called on the residents of Mogadishu to go out and fight the Americans and give their lives for the freedom of Somalia.

Aidid's troops intensified the attacks against the UN forces in Mogadishu and throughout Somalia, and his followers incited demonstrations and riots of unarmed citizens against the presence of the UN forces in the country. The violent activity of Aidid's troops was accompanied by an intensive war of propaganda in which the UN forces were accused of neo-colonialism under the guise of humanitarian aid, and the American forces were charged with the genocide of the Somali people and the destruction of mosques and holy sites.

In August 1993 Islamic volunteers acting under the organizational name of "The Vanguard of the Islamic Salvation" arrived in Somalia.

The organization founded its own radio station, which broadcasted propaganda, including a call to the Somali nation to join a Jihad against America's diabolical forces.[12]

During August 1993, Aidid and the Islamic forces continued with their preparations in anticipation of an American offensive against Aidid. On August 11, 1993, Aidid's men activated an explosive device by remote control and caused the death of four American soldiers. The attack was perpetrated by a new organization that was established on the basis of fighters from Aidid's extended family—Habar Gadir. The organization was called the Somali Islamic Salvation Movement—SISM.[13]

In September 1993 the Sudanese instructed the SIUP to join in the fighting against the Americans. Although the SIUP was established and prepared for combat even prior to the Americans' arrival in Somalia, it was not active before September 1993, and up to that time only Aidid's forces were involved in the fighting in the arena.[14] Already on September 3 1993, the organization's spokesman announced from Iran that his organization had perpetrated a series of attacks against UN forces in Somalia. The situation in Somalia continued to deteriorate and on September 5 1993, Aidid's men attacked a Nigerian UN force and killed seven of its members. Only massive U.S. intervention enabled the rescue of the Nigerian force.[15]

On September 10, 1993, a new phase was initiated in the combat against the UN forces, with Sudanese encouragement. Islamic forces from Aidid's extended family of Habar Gidir, began attacking Somali individuals identified as UN supporters throughout Somalia. In consequence, widespread riots and fighting erupted throughout the country. The UN and U.S. forces were summoned to make order, but soon found themselves trapped in ambushes laid in advance by the Islamic forces.

The fighting spread from the periphery to the capital Mogadishu, and on September 13, 1993, heavy fighting broke out between the American troops and Aidid's forces. The Americans sent in Cobra helicopters to fight Aidid's forces and among other sites hit a hospital that also served as Aidid's headquarters and logistical warehouse. Many Somali civilians were hurt in this attack, and Aidid's supporters called for revenge. On September 15, 1993, Aidid's troops attacked the UN headquarters in Mogadishu with mortar fire, and in retaliation, the U.S. forces bombed Aidid's headquarters. Aidid's supporters, including women and children, stoned UN patrols on the streets of Mogadishu, and UN soldiers opened fire and injured Somali citizens. This incident exacerbated the situation in the city even further and Ali Mahdi Muhammad, Aidid's opponent, took advantage of the window of opportunity and accused Aidid of bringing disaster and destruction on the country.

The United States, which up to that time had carefully refrained from taking a formal stand in the internal Somali conflict, decided to come out publicly against Aidid in September and to try to break his strength. At the end of September a task force of the Rangers raided Aidid's head-quarters and captured his right-hand man, Othman Hassan Ali Atto. Aidid retaliated with ambushes aimed at knocking down US helicopters, and on September 26, 1993 his men did indeed succeed in shooting down an American "Blackhawk" helicopter over Mogadishu. An enraged crowd mutilated the bodies of the American pilots and dragged them along the streets of Mogadishu. The incident, which was documented on television, shocked the American public and forced the American forces to respond ruthlessly. The confrontation between Aidid, the Islamic forces and the U.S. task force culminated in a battle on October 3-4 1993, which con-stituted the high-water mark in the American involvement in Somalia.

The "Snatch and Grab" Mission[16]

The aim of the "Snatch and Grab" mission was to apprehend two of Aidid's senior aides—Osama Salah and Muhammad Hassan Awali. The aim was to apprehend them at the "Olympic Hotel" in an area called the "Black Sea," General Aidid's stronghold, located near the busy marketplace in Mogadishu, the Somali capital. The mission was based on intelligence information that necessitated rapid organization on the part of the Ameri-can forces in order to execute the mission while its targets were at the said location. The Ranger task force, under the command of General William P. Grison, had drilled similar missions many times and had also acquired combat experience prior to the "Snatch and Grab" campaign. But what had originally appeared to be a simple mission, based on precise intelligence, rapidly evolved into a bitter battle that generated far-reaching consequences.

The American task force blundered into a well-planned ambush laid by hundreds of Somali and Islamic fighters. During the fighting two "Black Hawk" helicopters were downed and an additional helicopter was forced to make an emergency landing at the Mogadishu Airport. The American force took over its target and apprehended Aidid's aides, but were swiftly surrounded and forced to fight for their lives. An end was finally put to the ensuing bitter combat only after a rescue mission was launched by land forces using attack helicopters.

Eighteen American soldiers were left dead and seventy-eight wounded. American pilot Michael Diorent was taken captive by the Somalis. The mission of the U.S. task force was accomplished despite the delay and the heavy toll in casualties and injuries. General Grison's men did indeed win the battle, but it was a "Pyrrhic victory" which led to U.S. defeat in the overall war.

Information gleaned from various sources indicates that forces of Islamic volunteers made up of Afghani "alumni" participated in the October 3, 1993 battle, and not only the forces of the warlord Aidid.[17] According to this version, the entire operation was under the command of al-Rashidi (an Egyptian Jihad activist and Afghani "alumnus," personal aide to Aiman al-Zawaheiri, head of the Jihad organization and Osama Bin Laden's partner).

The main assault force was made up of SIUP fighters and Afghani "alumni," who used 23-mm anti-aircraft artillery and RPG7 launchers to shoot down the helicopters. Aidid's people, who played a secondary role in the fighting, isolated the battle arena and instigated mass riots of unarmed civilians, which made the American rescue mission even more cumbersome. These claims were confirmed in the charge sheet brought against twenty-one Al-Qaida members who were accused of assaulting U.S. and UN forces in 1993 and with directing terror conspiracies together with Sudan, Iraq and Iran.[18]

The consequences of the action were disastrous for the United States. The heavy losses and traumatic film footage aired on television channels worldwide of masses mutilating the bodies of American soldiers aroused strong opposition in American public opinion and in the Congress to American involvement in Somalia. Following the military fiasco in Mogadishu, and due to the combined pressure of public opinion and the Congress, President Clinton decided to discontinue the activities of the U.S. task force in Somalia. As a lesson drawn from the activities of the American forces in Somalia, the Clinton administration established the principle of "involvement without intervention," according to which the United States will refrain from sending soldiers to fight in foreign countries in order to realize goals that do not directly serve American interests.

An inquiry committee was set up in the U.S. Senate, which heard testimony about the action in Somalia. At the end of the hearings, the committee published a paper placing the blame for the debacle on President Clinton and Defense Secretary Les Aspin. Aspin submitted his resignation two months later, and General Grison ended his career earlier than planned.[19]

The American experience in Somalia in general, and in the October 3 battle in particular, became a warning sign for the United States in all matters related to the sending of troops to resolve conflicts overseas. This was apparently the reason for the lack of UN and U.S. intervention in the civil wars in Zaire and Rwanda. The American policy was revised in connection to Bosnia and Kosovo when there was a fear that the conflict would spread outside of the Balkans. It also underwent change as a result of the attacks of September 11, 2001, which led to the U.S. declaration of war against terror, the offensive in Afghanistan, the resultant collapse of the Taliban regime (Bin Laden's sponsor), and the destruction of the Al-Qaida organization's infrastructure in this country, and later operation "Iraqi Freedom" against the Saddam Hussein regime in Iraq.

Notes

1. This chapter is based on Yosef Bodansky, *Bin Laden—The Man Who Declared War on America*," Forum, New York, 2001.
2. Ibid.
3. Ibid.
4. Ibid.
5. Ibid.
6. Peter L. Bergen, *Holy War Inc.—Inside the Secret World of Osama Bin Laden*, Weidenfield & Nicolson, London, 2001.
7. *Independent*, March 1, 1994.
8. Interview with al-Jazeera television network, June 10 1999.
9. Yosef Bodansky, *Bin Laden—The Man Who Declared War on America*, Forum, New York, 2001, pp. 62-64.
10. Ibid., pp. 65-70.
11. Mark Bowden, *Black Hawk Down, A Story of Modern War*, Atlantic Monthly Press, New York, 1999, p. 89.
12. Yosef Bodansky, *Bin Laden—The Man Who Declared War on America*, Forum, New York, 2001, p. 69.
13. Ibid., pp. 69-70.
14. Ibid., pp. 69-70.
15. Keith B. Richburg, UN Officials Misjudged Size of Aidid Militia Armaments, *The Washington Post*, October 8, 1993.
16. This sub-chapter is based on the book, Mark Bowden, *Black Hawk Down, A Story of Modern War*, Atlantic Monthly Press, New York, 1999.
17. The source for this information is the book: Yosef Bodansky, *The Man Who Declared War on America*, Forum, New York, 2001.
18. Martha Crenshaw, "Why America? The Globalization of the Civil War," *State and Society*, Volume 2, Issue 2, August 2002.
19. Patrick J. Sloyan, "Somalia Mission: Clinton Called the Shots in Failed Policy Targeting Aidid," *Newsday*, Inc. December 5, 1993.

5

Somalia after the Withdrawal of UN Troops (1993-2005)

Following the withdrawal of the UN forces from Somalia in 1994, the civil war continued and the UN efforts to achieve a ceasefire and reconstruct the country's political system were put temporarily on hold.

General Muhammad Farah Aidid died on August 1, 1996, at the age of 60 and there are various versions regarding the circumstances surrounding his death; according to "South Mogadishu Radio" he died of a heart attack; other sources claim that he was injured on July 24, 1996 in fighting against a rival faction, and subsequently died due to infection.

Aidid had 14 children, most of whom grew up in the United States and live there to date. Muhamad Farah Aidid's heir is his son, Hussein Aidid, who was raised and studied in the United States, served in the Marines and even arrived in Somalia with the Marines forces in 1992. After completing his military service Hussein Aidid lived in the United States several more years and returned to Somalia in 1995. After his father's death he became the leader of the factions that had supported his father and continued in the rigid policy of struggle to gain control of Somalia.

Starting from 1995 various political entities renewed their attempts to intermediate in the matter in an effort to stop the war in Somalia. Among those intermediaries are:

- Neighboring countries—Kenya, Ethiopia, Djibouti;
- International organizations—Islamic organizations, the African Union, and more;
- European and Islamic countries;
- Various UN committees.

Over the years, several conferences were held, leading to the establishment of two central political and tribal blocs:

1.   Transitional National Government—TNG, which controls most neighborhoods in Mogadishu and several districts in the state;
2.   Somali Reconciliation and Restoration Council—SRRC—an umbrella organization of some militias structured on a tribal basis and headed by Hussein Aidid, whose only common interest is to oust the Transitional National Government (see subsequent elaboration on this matter).

The Transitional National Government (TNG)

The declaration regarding the establishment of the TNG in August 2000 came after two months of discussions conducted in the framework of the Somali National Peace Conference held in the city of Arta in neighboring Djibouti. Previous attempts to achieve national agreement had failed and had put in question the ability to achieve national reconciliation in this country. The conference in Arta instilled cautious hope regarding the chances to implement its resolutions.

The transitional government was the result of a sensitive agreement regarding the manner of distributing power in the country; each tribe was assigned representation in the parliament, which contains 245 seats, in addition to several key roles in the national transition government. Ali Caliph Galiar was appointed prime minister, and Abed al-Kassem Salad Hassan was appointed president.

Hassan is the son of the leader of the extended Habar Gidir family, one of the most important families in Somalia. He served as a minister in Barre's cabinet and when Barre's government was ousted in 1991, he fled to Egypt. Several years later Hassan returned to Somalia and began to boost his political power with the ultimate goal of restoring Somali national unity and putting an end to the civil war. The establishment of a temporary government headed by Hassan received an enthusiastic welcome in large sections of Somalia. The residents of Mogadishu were the government's most prominent supporters because its foundation assured the return of public order and the provision of services and work places.

The leadership of the transition government dealt extensively in the restoration of Somalia's diplomatic status, and accomplished several significant achievements when it reinstated Somalia's representation at the UN, the Arab League, and the Organization for African Unity. These accomplishments notwithstanding, few countries in the world recognized the transitional government in Somalia, while the United States and most Arab states decided to adopt a policy of "wait and see" prior to recognizing the government. The transitional government appealed to various countries worldwide to introduce a "Marshall Plan" for the restoration of Somalia, but the response was minor (the funds allocated as aid for Somalia are estimated at only twenty million dollars, most of which came from Saudi Arabia). Other countries and organizations stipulated that the provision of funds would be contingent upon proof that the interim government was indeed in control of the country.

The unwillingness of the Arab world and the West to come to the aid of the transitional government caused considerable frustration among its members and increasing difficulties due to the lack of economic resources to enforce its authority over the country. In September 2001, the transitional government was immersed in a serious governmental crisis. The transitional government did not succeed in establishing an efficient administrative system even in Mogadishu, and half of the city was under the control of opposition factors. Moreover, the government did not succeed in reopening Mogadishu's airport or seaport, and the enforcement systems vis-à-vis law and order functioned on a very limited basis.

The transitional government gradually lost the support and legitimacy that it had enjoyed in the beginning and opposition entities—including the rulers of the northern districts (Somaliland and Pontland), the SRRC organization and some of the heads of the stronger militias—posed an acute challenge vis-à-vis its very existence and control. Hyper-inflation resulting from financial manipulations and accusations regarding corruption and the theft of donation funds also contributed to the weakening of the transitional government.

Aside from the internal problems in Somalia, the transitional government also needed to contend with an external adversary—Ethiopia—which had originally supported the establishment of a temporary government, but quickly revised its policy and regarded it as a threat due to its close relationships with Arab and Muslim states. Ethiopia suffered from the activities of a radical Islamic movement within its own boundaries and, due to the long border that it shared with Somalia, was sensitive to any internal shift in Somalia that might turn that country into a base for radical Islamic activity. Ethiopia claimed hegemony in the region of the Horn of Africa and regarded itself as party to a drawn-out competition vis-à-vis Egypt and Arab states in relationship to its status and influence in the region.

The transitional government in Somalia made no effort to improve its ties with Ethiopia and alleviate its fears. On the contrary, it invested serious efforts in reinforcing its ties with the Arab world, thus increasing the tension with its neighbor. In consequence, several months after its establishment, the Somali transitional government was forced to contend with opposition groups that enjoyed Ethiopian support. The tension between the sides developed into the form of "a war of emissaries" with the opposition forces supported by Ethiopia acting against the Somali government which had the support of the Arab countries. In the meantime, autonomous regions of Somaliland and Puntland cropped up in Somalia that declared their independence and enjoyed the aid of the SRRC and countries such as Ethiopia and Kenya.

Despite the perpetuation of the political and tribal conflicts, during the years the fighting died down (although it never stopped completely), and a status quo of parallel governments by rival factions prevailed in different areas.

Opposition factors in Somalia opposed to the TNG pointed out the links and ties between the government and the Al-Itihad and Al-Qaida organizations, and call on the US to topple the government and expel the Islamic terrorists from Somalia. [1] The president of the transitional government of Somalia (TNG), Abed al-Kassem Salad Hassan, denied any presence of Islamic terror entities in his country as well as any ties with them, and charged the opposition of casting false accusations against his government.[2]

The Somali Reconciliation and Restoration Council (SRRC)

The SRRC was an umbrella organization that incorporates the entities opposed to the national transitional government in Somalia. The organization was established in 2001 with the aid and support of Ethiopia, which regards the TNG as a threat to Ethiopian interests. The SRRC was headed by Hussein Aidid (son of Muhammad Farah Aidid), one of the leaders of the USC and the extended Habar Gidir clan. Additional powerbrokers in the SRRC were: the RRA, the factions led by Othman Hassan Ali Ato (who was the ally and right-hand man of the senior Aidid), leaders of the autonomous northern region, and others.

The SRRC has conducted a political propaganda blitz in an attempt to persuade the United Nations and individual countries to recognize the SRRC as a legitimate governmental factor in Somalia, and at the same time waged a violent campaign against the TNG forces. In its attempt to win Western support, the SRRC emphasizes its aspiration to establish a Western-style democratic state in Somalia and insists that radical Islam is the main common enemy of the West and Somalia.

In 2002 Abed al Kassem Salad Hassan was replaced by Hassan Abbhir Farah that got three years mandate to found a permanent national government. The TNG held Somalia's seat in the United Nations and was recognized as the official government of Somalia by the African Union, but only few nations outside of the region recognized its legitimacy.

The Disintegration Trends in Somalia(1994-2001)

In late 1993 and early 1994, several conferences between faction leaders were held in Ethiopia and in different regions of Somalia. Various factors—including conflicting strategies from within UNISOM and strife between Somali factions—prevented the reaching of any substantial agreements. In February 1994, the United Nations voted to gradually reduce its troop strength. This process continued until March 1995, when the last of the UN, and the U.S. troops left Somalia.

With the withdrawal of international forces, conflict between regional and clan-based factions continued. Furthermore, unarmed UNOSOM personnel and relief workers who remained in Somalia become increasingly vulnerable to banditry. Some aid organizations simply declared the situation unworkable and pulled out of Somalia altogether. Others have taken to hiring bodyguards and paying "protection" to local leaders for the right to continue humanitarian operations in the area.

As a consequence of these events, two regions of Somalia, Somaliland and Puntland, reclaimed their sovereignty and achieved de facto independence from Somalia.

Somaliland

Somaliland is that region in the Horn of Africa, separated from the Arab world by the Gulf of Aden, that sits astride Djibouti to the west, Ethiopia to the south, and Italian Somalia to the east. Somaliland has an estimated 3.5 million inhabitants. Somaliland's main sources of income are semi-nomadic livestock cultivation and remittances sent from relatives abroad. Its historical links with the Middle East goes back to the age of the pharaohs. Somaliland was a British protectorate from 1884 until June 26, 1960 when it gained independence. Somaliland, however, ceased to exist as a sovereign state after the union with Italian Somalia in the south and the foundation of the Somali republic.

The union, however, was troubled from the beginning, especially after Muhammad Ziad Barre, seized power in a military coup d'état in 1969, suspending the constitution, abolishing the national assembly, banning political parties, and taking the country he renamed the "Somali Democratic Republic" into the orbit of "scientific socialism."[3]

Somaliland had reclaimed its sovereignty and abandoned the union on May 18, 1991, after the collapse of the Barre regime. Somaliland has followed a very different trajectory from the rest of Somalia, which turned into a "failed state." Over the last 15 years, Somaliland has adopted a process of internally driven political, economic, and social reconstruction. Somaliland developed its unique political and social system combining tradition with western democracy.

After some fitful starts, by 1996 a national accord had emerged around a civilian government led by Muhammad Ibrahim Egal. It included a bicameral parliament, which balanced an elected legislation-initiating House of Representatives and a conflict-resolving House of Elders (Guurti) which was vested with traditional moral authority. A formal constitution was drafted and approved by 97 percent of voters in May 2001. Under it, municipal elections were to be conducted in December 2001, followed by a presidential poll in March 2002. Both polls, however, were delayed due to difficulties with passing an election law and establishing an election commission.[4]

The president of Somaliland, Muhammad Ibrahim Egal, died in May 2002. He was replaced by his vice president, Dahir Rayale Kahin, in a peaceful transfer of power. Under Rayale, the delayed municipal elections were held in December 2002, with the president's Union of Democrats (UDUB) Party winning 41 percent of the votes and two opposition groups, Kulmiye ("Solidarity") and the Party of Justice and Welfare (UCID), making strong showings with 19 and 11 percent respectively. The results of the March 2003 presidential election were much closer. The incumbent President Rayale defeated his closest challenger, the standard-bearer of Kulmiye, by 80 votes out of nearly 500,000 ballots cast. The opposition peacefully conceded the race after it failed to win a court challenge. The September 2005 parliamentary election to fill the 82 seats in the House of Representatives resulted in UDUB winning 33 seats; Kulmiye, 28 seats; and UCID, 21 seats.[5]

The breakaway province of Somaliland is not recognized by a single country, but is considered to be the only effectively governed area of Somalia.

The Puntland Regional Government

Northeastern Somalia, under the leadership of Colonel Abdullahi Yusuf, formed its own government called the Puntland regional government. Abdullahi was deposed in 2001 by a council of tribal leaders, a decree Abdullahi refused to recognize. Military supporters of his then declared a separate state within the statelet of Puntland. In 2002, Yusuf, backed by Ethiopia was attempting to regain power, and had won major battles against his rival for the Puntland presidency, Jama Ali Jama.

The question of Somali unity is still pending and has been complicated by Yusuf's election. The self-declared Republic of Somaliland rejects Puntland's claims to the regions of eastern Sanaag and Sool, which lie within the colonial boundaries inherited by Somaliland. Within two weeks of Yusuf's election, unusually bloody clashes between Somaliland and Puntland forces in the Sool region had left over 100 people dead. Violence has since subsided. Both sides are employing various channels of communication to defuse the tension, but Somaliland's claims to independent statehood have yet to be addressed by the international community and will continue to be a source of friction throughout the transitional period.

The Rahanwein Resistance Army (RRA)

On September 17, 1995, militias of General Muhammad Farah Aidid invaded Baidoa, most of whose inhabitants were members of the Rahanwein tribe, and established a tyrannical regime based on terror. On August 1, 1996, upon the demise of Muhammad Farah Aidid, his son, Hussein, took the reins of power. He perpetuated his father's policy, and inflicted punitive actions and massacres in order to sustain his control in that region. Despite the efforts to establish a reconciliatory government in Somalia, Hussein Aidid remained in the opposition and continued to control certain areas including the Riverine region and Baidoa in its center.

The Rahanwein Resistance Army (RRA) was founded in October 1995, in order to combat the invasion and liberate the region of Aidid's men. For some four years the RRA underground waged its battle until finally, on June 7, 1999, it succeeded in defeating Aidid's men and liberating Baidoa. In the following months, the RRA succeeded in liberating most of the Riverine region, and on December 9, declared the establishment of an autonomous government in the area. On May 18, 2000, convoys carrying food and UN humanitarian aid (via the World Food Program) succeeded in reaching Baidoa and provided assistance to the population, which was in severe distress. During the year 2000, once security and stability had been restored in the region, economic rehabilitation began with the assistance of the UN and humanitarian aid organizations such as Care International.

The RRA is headed by Colonel Hassan Muhammad Nur Shargodod, who advocates the idea of establishing autonomous governments in various regions of Somalia, which will eventually be incorporated into an integrated federal administration. Shargodod oppose attempts to establish a central government that will control all of Somalia, and refrained from attending talks held in Djibouti with the aim of introducing a peace agreement in Somalia, claiming that this was a conspiracy designed to promote foreign interests.

In April 2002, the Rahanwein Resistance Army (RRA) in Baidoa announced the formation of an autonomous "Southwest State of Somalia," making it a third separatist region in Somalia (in addition of Puntland and Somaliland). As of the end of 2002, hundreds had been killed and thousands displaced by fighting between the forces loyal to RRA chairman, Hassan Muhammad Nur Shargodod, and two of his deputies, Sheikh Adan Madobe and Muhammad Ibrahim Habsade.

RRA leaders expressed their support for the American decision to dispatch forces to Somalia in order to arrest or eliminate Al-Qaida members active in this state.[6] One of the more senior RRA members claimed that Somalia is a paradise for terrorists, due to the lack of an effective central government, and noted that Afghanistan and Somalia are very similar. Thus, he stated, only the United States can help to banish the terrorists from this country.[7]

According to the former Governor of Baidoa, Aduwan Muhammad, his organization aspires to liberate all of Somalia, and he had talks with US entities regarding the possibility of aiding the RRA in the event of a US decision to act in Somalia.

The Transitional Federal Government (TFG)[8]

In 2004 the defunct TNG came to an end and was replaced by the Transitional Federal Government (TFG). The declaration, in Kenya, of the TFG in October 2004 was heralded as a breakthrough in Somalia's crisis of governance. Colonel Abdullahi Yusuf Ahmed was elected by the Transitional Federal Parliament as interim president.

Yusuf had advocated a federal structure for Somalia; this position and his close ties with neighboring Ethiopia place him firmly in one camp in Somalia's long-running conflict. In order to cement his victory, Yusuf called for a compliant prime minister. The composition of the first TFG cabinet confirmed his pursuit of a narrow political agenda, provoking a parliamentary revolt in the form of a no-confidence vote (ostensibly for other reasons) and dissolution of the government.

The December 15, 2004 deadline for the return of the TFG to Somalia, set by the member states of the regional Intergovernmental Authority on Development (IGAD), expired with it still in Nairobi, citing insecurity in its homeland. Divisions between regional powers and the wider international community have impeded the emergence of a common orientation toward the interim Somali leadership.

The TFG had to reconstitute itself and return to Somalia; the decision whether to go to Mogadishu or establish an interim seat of government was charged with political significance and had repercussions on the security situation in parts of the country as well. Restoration of a secure environment was a top priority. It was for this reason that the TFG chose Baidoa as the interim location of the new government.

The TFG was born impoverished and quickly needed to secure revenue. Few governments were willing or able to provide direct budgetary support, so the TFG had to tap domestic sources such as ports and airports. Although most faction leaders have agreed in principle that these should be turned over to the control of the interim government, their commitment remained questionable, and no agreement had been reached as to how or when revenues will be shared and managed.

Over the longer term, the elaboration of a federal structure and the development of a permanent constitution were delicate issue fraught with risk. Despite agreement on a Transitional Federal Charter, many (if not most) Somalis will need to be persuaded of federalism's merits. As yet, there has been little substantive discussion on the form it might take. The demarcation of new administrative boundaries, control of revenue, and the future of existing institutions, such as regional "governors" and parliaments, are just some of the issue that were contested.

The victory of the TFG over the ICU (December 2006), thanks to the Ethiopian intervention gave the TFG the opportunity, for the first time, to implement their rule over Mogadishu and the southern and central parts of Somalia. It's too early to judge its success.

The Relationship between Somalia and Ethiopia (2000-2003)

Somalia shares a long and problematic border with Ethiopia in the Ogaden Desert. Territorial and ethnic controversies, which have yet to be resolved, led to the eruption of the "Ogaden War" in the 1970s, which claimed many victims in both countries and created pressing refugee problems in Somalia.

The loss of a central government in Somalia, which occurred in the early 1990s, had a crucial impact on the relationship between Somalia and Ethiopia, which became particularly complex and problematic. Ethiopia fears the spreading of radical Islam from Somalia into its own territory, and therefore takes resolute action against these entities inside and outside of Ethiopia. In the framework of the internal Somali conflict,

Ethiopia supports the powerbrokers who are willing to serve Ethiopian interests. This support is reflected in the provision of economic and military support, and when necessary also in the form of direct military intervention in Somali events.

In the long-term view, Ethiopia is interested in the establishment of a stable government in Somalia that will maintain good neighborly relations and prevent the penetration of subversive Islamic influences into its territory. Therefore, it supports the various intermediary processes aimed at restoring government and stability to Somalia. However, as long as the reality in Somalia does not change, Ethiopia concurrently acts against internal Somali powerbrokers in order to ensure its interests in this arena, thereby contributing to the continued internal power struggles and instability.

When Salad Hassan was nominated to be president of the TNG in 2000, Ethiopia was among the supporters of the new regime. It later turned out that Ethiopia had never accepted the legitimacy of the TNG and accused it of being led by Muslim radicals.

The relationship between the two countries has experienced ups and downs during recent years. On June 9, 2001, the provisional government in Somalia accused Ethiopia of invading its territory. Diplomatic dialogue was launched between the two countries in order to defuse the tension, but it ended without any positive results, and the temporary government in Somalia continued to accuse Ethiopia of meddling in its internal affairs.

In November 2001 the relations between the two governments deteriorated further. On November 15, 2001, Ethiopia shut down the offices of the largest commercial Somali company—Al-Barakaat. This step was initiated after the United States had frozen this company's assets due to the suspicion that it was linked with Al-Qaida. The company's management and the Somali government adamantly denied any connection with Al-Qaida, and were even willing to expose the company's documents and accounts to an external auditor in order to prove the justice of their claims, but to no avail.

Moreover, the Somali government claimed that during November 2001 Ethiopian forces invaded Galkayo in northeast Somalia. This area, which declared itself autonomous, does not accept the authority of the temporary government. The Somali government claimed that the invasion of the Ethiopian forces was in response to a request made by Abdullahi Yusuf Ahmed, with the aim of reinforcing his forces in the internal Somali conflict. The Ethiopian government refuted the Somali claims regarding any request to dispatch its forces and denied their presence in Somalia.[9]

On May 20, 2002, the Somali government lodged a complaint with the Security Council, in which it accused Ethiopia of invading its territory and supplying combat means to various powerbrokers in the country. In response, the Ethiopian ambassador to the United Nations accused the Somali government of trying to impede the discussions to achieve a peaceful agreement between the rival factions in Somalia, and denied any military involvement of his country in the internal Somali conflict. He reiterated that his country has a vested interest in a stable Somalia.

Al Qaida Terror Attacks in the Horn of Africa and Somalia (1998-2002)

The terror infrastructures established during the nineties by Iran, Sudan and Bin Laden continued to exist in the country without disruption, under the patronage of local allies, but the focuses of activity and the issue of Islamic terror gradually shifted to new destinations. American and Saudi pressure finally induced neighboring Sudan to expel Bin Laden from its territory (1996), to "lower its profile," and to some extent reduce its support of terror; nevertheless, East Africa remained an important focal point for Islamic terror, and several prominent attacks were executed there:

- The assassination attempt against Egyptian President Hussni Mubarak in Addis Ababa, Ethiopia (1995);
- Attacks against the US embassies in Kenya and Tanzania (1998);
- The attack at the Paradise Hotel in Mombasa, Kenya (2002).

Nonetheless, quite surprisingly the terrorists did not avail themselves of the Islamic terror infrastructure in Somalia, but acted on the basis of terror networks prepared in advance in the target countries. According to U.S. intelligence sources, some Al Qaida members that took part in this terror attack escaped to Somalia and found shelter there. After the September 11 attacks and the war that the United States declared against terror, Somalia's name resurfaced as a possible target for an American offensive against Islamic terror points. Towards the end of the campaign against the Taliban and Al-Qaida in Afghanistan, the Americans suspected that Bin Laden and his people might try to flee to Somalia and reconstruct the organization's infrastructure from there.[10] Thus, in October 2001, the United States and its allies began air and sea patrols opposite the Somali shores in order to locate Al-Qaida activity in this arena.

The United States noted two entities in Somalia that it believed were involved in Bin Laden's terror activity: One was the Al-Itihad al-Islamiya, which the United States included in its list of terror organizations; and another—an economic concern called "al-Barkaat," that deals in a wide range of economic activities such as: Banking, international commercial companies, cellular companies and more. The United States suspected that this organization has commercial ties with Bin Laden's businesses and serves for the transfer and "laundering" of funds for him.[11]

The Attacks in Kenya and Tanzania (August 7, 1998)[12]

Al-Qaida itself perpetrated only a small number of the many attacks carried out by terror organizations affiliated with Sunni Islamic terror. Al-Qaida, which for many years supported a long chain of terror organizations and Islamic terror cells, entered the direct activity related to attacks only after the official declaration regarding the foundation of the umbrella organization called "the Islamic Front for Jihad Against the Crusaders and Jews" (February 1998). From this point on, Al-Qaida adopted a leading role in the perpetration of terror attacks, while previously the organization had been satisfied with the provision of training and operational and logistic aid for terror activities, which were conducted independently by Islamic terror organizations and terror cells worldwide.

The African continent was chosen for Al-Qaida's first attacks because it was considered a relatively convenient spot for terror activity due to the limited ability of the local security forces to keep a close eye on the preparations and Al-Qaida activists who had arrived on the continent at the end of 1993. In addition, the easy passage to and from Africa to countries on other continents, in combination with the lax level of security at U.S. embassies in Africa, turned these embassies into attractive targets for Al-Qaida attacks.

The first operations perpetrated by Al-Qaida members were the suicide attacks at the U.S. embassies in Kenya and Tanzania in August 1998. While these attacks were planned over a five-year period prior to their actual execution, the timing was chosen by the Al-Qaida command in Afghanistan and was meant to demonstrate the "Islamic Front's" intention to realize its declarations and lead the Jihad undertaken by Bin Laden at the time of its establishment and the announcement of the "fatwa" (the religious ruling) of February 1998. Al-Qaida struck again in Kenya in November 2002, when it carried out attacks against Israeli targets in Mombasa (see subsequent elaboration).

On August 7, 1998 at 10:00 a.m. a car bomb carrying about three-quarters of a ton of explosives was detonated next to the United States embassy in Nairobi. The car was driven by two suicide terrorists (one of whom, al-Awli, survived because he had gotten out of the vehicle to pursue the embassy's guard who was fleeing). As a result of the explosion, 213 people were killed, the majority of whom were Kenyans, as well as a dozen American citizens who were embassy employees. Over 4,000 people were injured. Simultaneously, an additional suicide attack was perpetrated by the same organization near the US Embassy in Dar al-Salaam in Tanzania. Eleven people were killed and scores were injured. These attacks signaled the organization's intention to perpetrate indiscriminate mass slaughter in attacks against American targets throughout the world, and reflected its characteristic modus operandi, as it was to be expressed subsequently in September 2001 in the United States.

The apprehension of a number of key activists in the terror network responsible for the planning and execution of the attacks led to a series of arrests and the preparation of a detailed charge sheet, which clearly indicated the direct responsibility of the organization headed by Bin Laden for the terror campaign in East Africa. The investigation's findings offered a unique preliminary opportunity to closely observe the organization, thus providing in-depth knowledge of its modus operandi.

The Attack in Kenya

The terror cell that perpetrated the attack in Nairobi was composed of a small nucleus of 6-8 activists under the command of Fazul Abdallah Muhammad, an Al-Qaida member born in the Comoros Islands.[13] Their original plan had been to drive a car bomb into the embassy's underground parking, detonate it with the help of suicide drivers and bring the building down upon its inhabitants.[14]

The terror team included three people who drove to their destination in two vehicles. The first car was driven by the mission commander and served as an escort vehicle for the car bomb. The second carried the two suicide bombers, the driver who committed suicide and his escort Rashed Daoud al-Awali, who survived the attack and after being apprehended was extradited by Kenya to the United States, where he is currently standing trial.

The car bomb driver, an Egyptian by origin, tried to enter the embassy's underground parking facility, but was unable to do so because of the Kenyan guard's refusal to open the embassy's gates. His attempt to circumvent the barrier was prevented by a car driving up from the underground parking area that blocked his way. Awali (the surviving suicide terrorist) threatened the guard and demanded that he open the gate, but when the latter refused, he lobbed a stun grenade at the guard and proceeded to run after him, moving away from the vehicle. The driver detonated the bomb in a compound containing three buildings, about ten meters away from the embassy wall. The explosion resulted in a large number of casualties and the collapse of several buildings near the embassy. The embassy building itself, the attack's main target, did not collapse although it was damaged.

Preliminary preparations for the attack already began in 1993.[15] Senior Al-Qaida personnel including Bin Laden and his assistant, the military commander Abu-Hafez, participated in the planning. Preparations for the attack were divided into several stages: As noted, the first stage was in 1993 when Bin Laden conceived the idea and sent his representatives to Kenya. One of them was Muhammad Ali, a former sergeant in the U.S. military who subsequently served as a state's-witness in the trials of the attack perpetrators in Kenya and Tanzania held in New York, who confessed that he had met with Bin Laden and given him photographs of the embassy in Nairobi. Bin Laden sent several emissaries to Kenya with the aim of learning the lay of the land. Some even married local women and took work enabling them to gather qualitative information about the potential targets, mainly the U.S. and Israeli embassies.

The second stage of preparations in anticipation of the attack was launched in May-June, 1998 (about two months before the attack). The decision was made following Bin Laden's public declaration in an interview with ABC in which he threatened to perpetrate mega attacks against U.S. targets in retribution for the United States' anti-Islamic policy. The practical preparations for the attack were administered from the network headquarters in the target country, the "Top-Hill" Hotel in Nairobi. The network members also rented a house in Nairobi where they hid the weapons; explosives, stun grenades and handguns smuggled into Nairobi from the Middle East via the Comoros Islands. A short time prior to the attack, three cell members gathered intelligence about the U.S. Embassy in Nairobi, and when all the preparations were in place, the date for the attack was set.

Several days prior to the attack date most of the network members left Nairobi, with the exception of Harun Fazul, the team's commander, who escorted the car bomb with the suicide terrorists to the target in order to personally supervise the operation. After the explosion, Harun returned to the safe house in order to cover their tracks and then disappeared.

The Attack in Tanzania

On August 7, 1998 a car bomb exploded near the U.S. Embassy in Tanzania. Eleven people were killed in the explosion and about 85 were wounded, all local residents. The Tanzanian cell contained six members and additional individuals, who assisted in the preparations for the attack in various stages of the planning. The members of the team underwent training in Afghanistan in the course of 1994, and it was composed of a variety of nationalities including Kenyans, Tanzanians and Egyptians.[16]

With the help of local collaborators, the team members rented a private safe house two months before the attack. The house was outside of the city and it was used for storage of the car bomb (a van) and the purchased weapons. The van had been bought two months earlier and was rigged as a car bomb a short time before the attack.

The cell members collected preliminary information about the routine procedure for cars delivering water to the embassies, and took advantage of the information to infiltrate a car bomb into the embassy. The suicide bomber arrived separately in Dar-al-Salaam and was kept at a safe house. On the day of the attack, the suicide driver of the car bomb drove to the embassy building and followed the water truck that arrived at its entrance. When the water truck was about to enter the premises, the car bomb drew up close and the suicide driver detonated the car that was loaded with a quarter ton of explosives.[17]

The Terror Campaign in Kenya against Israeli Targets (November 28, 2002)[18]

On November 28, 2002 a terror campaign was perpetrated against Israeli targets in Kenya:

- A car bomb driven by terrorists exploded at the Paradise Hotel in Mombasa.
- Two Strella (SA-7) shoulder missiles were fired at an Arkia airplane immediately after takeoff but they missed their target.

Responsibility was claimed by an unknown organization called the "Palestine Army."

The organization released an announcement via the Hizballah TV station "Al-Manar" in which it stated that the attack had been perpetrated to commemorate the 55th anniversary of the UN partition resolution (November 29). The announcement added that the organization's headquarters had decided that the entire world must hear of the suffering of the Palestinian refugees, and therefore it was decided to send a cell to Kenya with the aim of attacking Israeli targets.

The message ended with a statement that the attacks had gone according to plan. The leader of the Islamic Organization "Al-Muhajrun" in London, Omar al-Bakhri, stated that during the week preceding the attack the organization had issued a warning in chat sites on the Internet that an attack was about to be launched against Israeli targets in Kenya. In an interview with the Al-Jazeera TV network, Bakhri said "our sources are based on open forums on the Internet." According to Bakhri the message was as follows; "Brothers, you will receive good news during the last twenty days of the month of Ramadan," and it was also stated that the target would be in East Africa.

On December 2, 2002 responsibility was claimed via publication in several Internet sites affiliated with Al-Qaida - al-Jihad. It would appear that it was Al-Qaida that was claiming responsibility although the style differed in its characteristics from earlier claims of responsibility issued by that organization.[19] The announcement, which was particularly long and was worded in the organization's characteristic style, also stated that the attacks in Mombasa were aimed at "eradicating all of the dreams of the Jewish-Crusader alliance, meant to preserve their strategic interests in the region." The mission was meant to deal an additional blow to the Israeli Mossad, like the blows that struck the synagogue in Djerba in the past.

The announcement went on to say that both attacks, the attack at the Paradise Hotel and the attempt to shoot down the Arkia plane, "were meant to clarify to Muslims all over the world that the mujahidin stand by their brethren in Palestine and continue in their path." The announcement also refers to the Jewish-American connection, saying that the attack was retaliation for "the conquest of our holy sites" and Israeli acts in Palestine. "For killing our children, we will kill yours, for our elderly we will kill your elderly, and for our homes your turrets."

With the aim of justifying the attack, in which many Kenyan citizens were killed, Al-Qaida appealed to the citizens of Kenya and all of Africa as follows: "Ultimately these two actions are meant to declare that the nation, including its Arab and non-Arab sons, the black and white ones, stood as one and faced this enemy and this assault that was declared against the Muslims. We call upon our dark-skinned brothers on this continent, the peoples that have suffered most from colonialism, which stole their lands, robbed their countries, turned them into slaves and deprived them of their basic human rights, that they follow in the footsteps of the heroes of the two missions in Mombasa and turn the land into hell under the conquering feet of the Jews and Crusaders."

The Attack at the Paradise Hotel

On the morning of November 28, 2002 some 200 Israeli tourists landed at the Mombasa Airport, Kenya. They disembarked from an Arkia charter flight, and passed through the various inspections and border control. They boarded two buses and five minibuses, which took them to the "Paradise Mombasa" Hotel some 35 kilometers north of the city, where they were to spend the Hanukkah vacation.

It appears that already during the journey to the hotel, a green Mitsubishi Pajero jeep was following the convoy. After disembarking from the buses, the Israeli tourists registered at the hotel and most of them went to their rooms. At about 7:30 a Land Rover jeep burst through the hotel's security gate. According to eyewitnesses, hotel employees, and the Kenyan Police, there were three passengers in the jeep. One of them jumped out of the jeep at a run, entered the reception area and detonated the explosive charge that he was carrying on his body. At the same time, the two other passengers detonated the booby-trapped jeep, which was carrying 200 kilograms of explosives and gas balloons.[20] A Kalishnikov was found in the jeep's wreckage.

Thirteen people were killed in the attack, three Israelis and ten Kenyans, including dancers from a dance troupe that received the Israeli tourists at the entrance to the hotel. According to the various reports, 60-80 people were injured in the attack, including some 20 Israelis.

The Firing of Missiles at the Arkia Plane

Several minutes after the attack at the Paradise Hotel (a short time after 7:30) two shoulder-fired missiles were launched at Arkia Flight 582, which was taking off from Mombasa on its way to Israel. The missiles missed the aircraft and did not cause it any damage. There were 261 passengers on board in addition to 10 crewmembers.

About a minute and a half after takeoff, at a height of 3,000 feet, the passengers felt a thump against the aircraft's hull. Immediately afterwards, the flash of two missiles was identified near the aircraft. The crewmembers rushed to report to the security team on land, and the latter launched searches in the area in an attempt to locate the missile launchers.

Two missile launchers and two additional SA-7 (Strella) missiles were found hidden among the bushes outside of the airport's perimeter, at a distance of several hundred meters from the fence. According to U.S.

sources, the missiles found in Mombasa were from the same series and production line as the missiles fired by Al-Qaida at an American military plane in Saudi Arabia in May 2002.[21]

Searches carried out by the police investigators in the area where the missiles were fired indicated that the attack was perpetrated from a hill with an excellent vantage point of the airport and particularly the takeoff areas; this made the operation easier for the attackers. It was fortunate that they missed the plane they were aiming for during a phase that is considered the vulnerable point of a flight—takeoff.

The Strella is a relatively outmoded missile that was developed about 30 years ago. It is used by armies and guerilla organizations and it is known that various entities in Africa also have some in their possession. The Strella homes in on heat. It is usually adjusted according to the heat waves emanating from the plane's engines or its landing and takeoff lights. The missile's effective range is defined at four to six kilometers. Its flight velocity is 580 meters per second and its warhead's weight ranges between one kilogram and 1.2 kilograms. The missile is considered uncomplicated to operate and in regular circumstances its ability to hit a passenger plane during takeoff—which is considered an easy target—is relatively high.

The attempt to down the Arkia plane in Mombasa, Kenya, is not the first time that terrorists have tried to fire shoulder missiles at Israeli aircraft, and it is also not the first attempt to be made in Kenya. In 1969 a Palestinian cell was apprehended in Rome. It had shoulder-fired missiles in its possession and the intention was to shoot down an El Al plane. In the 1970s, two Germans who had been planning to shoot shoulder missiles at an El Al plane were caught in Nairobi the capital of Kenya. The Germans, who were affiliated with left-wing terror organizations in Germany, were extradited to Israel, tried and imprisoned, but were released several years later.

An investigation of the attacks in Mombasa in 2002 indicates that the mastermind behind them was Al-Qaida senior activist—Haron al-Fazul (Fazul Abdallah Muhammad) who was also behind the attack against the US Embassy in Kenya in 1998. The Kenyan authorities arrested five men suspected of involvement in the attack. The five stood trial in June 2003 and are awaiting sentencing.[22]

Additional Intentions to Perpetrate Attacks in Kenya

In the course of 2003, the U.S. and British intelligence agencies received warnings regarding Al-Qaida's intentions to perpetrate additional attacks in Kenya. Thus, in May 2003, El Al and British Airways flights to Kenya were stopped due to these warnings.[23] In June 2003 the U.S. Embassy in Kenya was closed after warnings were received that Al-Qaida was planning on attacking the embassy with an airplane that would crash into the building.[24] In the wake of this threat, Kenya sealed its airspace to flights from Somalia and banned the flight of small aircraft from local airports in Kenya (flights from the international airport in Nairobi continued undisrupted).

Despite efforts made by the Kenyan authorities to improve security arrangements in their country and enhance the supervision over individuals suspected of involvement in terror, it appears that Kenya continues to constitute a relatively convenient arena for Al-Qaida terror for several reasons:

- A large and poor Muslim community from which volunteers can easily be recruited to perpetrate attacks;
- Limited supervision and thwarting capabilities of he Kenyan authorities;
- The long and vulnerable border between Kenya and Somalia, which serves as a safe haven for Islamic terror entities.

Due to the low level of security in Kenya, in the course of 2003 the United States and Britain considered shutting down their embassies and have issued warnings to their citizens to refrain from visiting there.

Notes

1.   This chapter is based on: Shaul Shay, *The Red Sea Terror Triangle*, Transaction Publishers, New Brunswick, USA, 2005, pp. 86-87.
2.   BBCnews.com, "Somalia's Role in Terror," December 21, 2001.
3.   Peter Pjan, "Facing reality in Somalia," *World Defence Review*, May 11, 2006.
4.   Ibid.
5.   Ibid.
6.   Ibid.
7.   Jeff Koinage, "US Seeks Allies Against Terror in Somalia," CNN.com.world, January 13, 2002.
8.   "Somalia: Continuation of a War by Other Means," *Africa Report* No. 88, December 21, 2004.
9.   ArabicNews.com, November 24, 2001
10.   Charles Cobb Jr., "Hints of Military Action Cause Puzzlement and Worry," al-lAfrica.com, December 23, 2001.
11.   Jeff Koinange, "US Seeks Allies against Terror in Somalia," CNN.com.world, January 13, 2002.
12.   This chapter is based on the book by Yoram Schweitzer and Shaul Shay, *The Globalization of Terror*, Transaction Publishers, New Brunswick, U.S.A, 2002.
13.   Yosef Bodansky, Bin Laden, *The Man Who Declared War on America*, Forum, 2001, p. 263.

14.   Ibid.
15.   Ibid, p. 223.
16.   Peter L. Bergen, *Holy War Inc—Inside the Secret World of Osama Bin Laden*, Weidenfeld & Nicolson, London, 2001, p. 118.
17.   Ibid, p. 119.
18.   This chapter is based on articles in the *Ha'aretz, Yediot Aharonot* and *Ma'ariv* newspapers between the dates November 29 and December 5, 2002.
19.   *Ha'aretz*, December 3, 2002.
20.   *Yediot Aharonot*, December 2, 2002 quoting the Israeli Minister of Defense, Shaul Mofaz.
21.   *Ha'aretz*, December 3, 2002.
22.   *AP Nairobi*, July 8, 2003.
23.   Reported by CNN from Nairobi, June 22, 2003.
24.   Ibid.

6

The Islamic Courts in Somalia

Following the collapse of the Barre regime in 1991, Somalia descended into a civil war. As a result, many public services that were supplied by the government have been "privatized." In such a "chaotic" environment, NGOs and Islamic organizations replaced the government in providing necessary services.

The Da'awa institutes and the Islamic Sharia courts were the main components of the Islamic infrastructure that emerged in Somalia. Some experts claimed that it was a part of a strategy of the Islamic organizations to take power in Somalia. As early as 1993 Sharia courts had been established in some parts of Somalia. Their modus vivendi was to establish law and order in conjunction with the secular authority of local faction leaders and the traditional customary law.

Mogadishu's earliest Islamic court was formed in the Madina district in 1993. Some of the founders of the court were former Al Itihad members.[1] After 1997, however, a new round of Sharia courts emerged in south Mogadishu and later in Merka with integral connections to Al Itihad. This owed a great deal to the failure of the militia-factions to provide a stable environment for the investment of the local business community. In the absence of law enforcement forces, each court had its own militia. Compared to the various clan and factional militias, the Islamic courts militias had a reputation for discipline and good conduct.[2]

Following the failure of the Cairo and Sodere peace accords, as well as the short lived agreement between Aidid and Ali Mahdi to establish the Benadir administration in 1998, the secular militia-factions were unable to maintain the support of the business community.[3] The alternative for the business community was to support the Islamic Sharia courts, many of them affiliated with the Al Itihad.

In early 2000, a group of court leaders from Mogadishu formed the Sharia Implementation Council (SIC) in order to unify and coordinate the various courts.[4] The organization had an assembly (Majlis) with 63 members. The secretary general of the SIC was Hassan Dahir Aweys one of the leaders of AIAI.

In September 2000 when the Transitional National Government (TNG) returned to Mogadishu from Djibouti,[5] some members of the TNG argued that the courts should simply be absorbed wholesale into the new judicial system, others argued for a more selective approach based on qualifications and merit. Eventually the dispute was resolved in favor of examinations, to which many judges refused to submit. But the decision had little impact, since the TNG never became a functional administration.[6]

In 2004 a new umbrella organization (of 10 different courts), was established for Mogadishu's Sharia courts: the Supreme Council of Islamic Courts in Somalia. The elected chairman of the council was Sheikh Sharif Sheikh Ahmad. Under the leadership of Sheikh Ahmad, the Sharia court system in Mogadishu has expanded.

The Supreme Council of the Islamic Courts founded a 400-strong militia based on combatants of the different courts. Towards the end of 2004, the council's militia had been involved in clashes with other militias in the area of Mogadishu.

The formation of the Transitional Federal Government (TFG) in October 2004 and the anti Islamist approach of President Abdullahi Yusuf led to confrontation between the Islamic courts and the TFG. President Yusuf's plans to invite foreign forces to restore peace and order in Somalia pushed the Islamic courts into alliance with other Islamic organizations and Yusuf's political rivals. The TFG members blamed the Islamic courts as extremists and supporters of terror but a majority of the Mogadishu residents backed the Islamic courts in their confrontation with the TFG.

In July 2005 the council of Islamic Courts accepted the appointment of Adan Hashi Ayro as commander of the militia. During the years 2004-2005, the Islamic courts implemented the Sharia laws in the areas that they controlled. On December 31, 2004 the Supreme Council of the Islamic Courts issued a "fatwa," a religious judgment, that celebration of the New Year was an offense punishable by death.[7] Another judgment argued that any terrorist suspects found on Somali soil should be tried by Somali courts rather than extradited to foreign countries.[8] In November 2005 militias from several courts has operated to shut down cinemas in northern Mogadishu that they blamed for screening corrupt and immoral Western films.[9]

In March 2006 fierce fighting broke out within the U.S.-backed coalition of Somali warlords that controlled the Mogadishu area for a decade and the Islamic Courts Union (ICU). In the fighting between the ICU and the Alliance for the Restoration of Peace and Counterterrorism (ARPCT), hundreds of Mogadishu residents lost their lives.[10] After several months of clashes in the area of Mogadishu on June, 2006 the ICU declared victory in their struggle to control the capital of Somalia—Mogadishu.[11]

After taking Mogadishu, the focus of military operations immediately shifted to Jowhar, 90 kms north of the capital. Jowhar was a former base of the TFG. The ICU said hostile militia and "technicals" [heavy weapons mounted on trucks] were being mobilized in Jowhar. A group of warlords led by Muhammad Qanyare fled to Jowhar after their defeat in Mogadishu on June 4, 2006, trying to reorganize there. In a pre-emptive strike, the ICU attacked the town and took it without much resistance on June 14, 2006. Qanyare and his group had fled the town the night before.

Sheikh Sharif Sheikh Ahmad, one of the ICU leaders, agreed to a new system of governance for the town of Jowhar, with elders heading the administration while the militias would ensure security in the town. Sheikh Ibrahim Farah, a prominent elder and imam of the town, said: "We agreed to collaborate with the Islamic courts in the establishment of new administrations."[12]

In Jowhar, after captured by the ICU, there has been a marked change. Journalist Muhammad Ibrahim Malimow reported there was "a sense of relief" that the Courts had taken over, as people were no longer under duress to pay the exorbitant taxes that warlords used to impose. Food prices have fallen by between 15 and 20 percent since the takeover. Elders, intellectuals, religious leaders and business people are directly involved in decision-making, and there is a resurgence of debate and discussion over issues of leadership.[13]

After the Mogadishu takeover, structures set up the ICU were based on the existing organization of the Courts. The original aim was to bring together clans and sub-clans in an area to establish an Islamic court to provide a forum for justice and the handling of disputes. This was critical in trying to establish security in areas of Mogadishu where people were at the mercy of chaotic warlord rule. The Courts were comprised of the chairman of the Islamic court militia; and the chairman of the local Shura (council).[14]

The challenge in the post-victory era was to extend and broaden the organization without being weakened by inter-clan politics or being seen to impose the kind of central authority so weakened by Somalis. This expectation contrasted sharply with the keenness of Somali professional classes and the international community to identify a "type" of government as defined by centralized administrative structures and a definitive political ideology.[15]

The Islamic Supreme Consultation Council of Islamic Courts had 91 members, and acted like a parliament for all the courts and was headed by Sheikh Hassan Dahir Aweys. Since June 2006, it had expanded to include representatives of all the established courts. It had no executive powers, but according to one observer, "sorts out any problems in outlying courts, keeps all the programs in line, and makes sure everyone is reading from the same script." Known as the Shura (council), it acted as an advisory body of the ICU.[16] The ICU had also established a 15-member executive council, headed by Sheikh Sharif, which acted as an executive branch of government and implemented decisions.[17]

On July 27, 2006, the ICU claimed that they had set up a Sharia court inside a vast complex in Mogadishu that once served as the country's presidential palace- a highly symbolic move. "This is the place where Somalia will be ruled from and we appreciate the cooperation with the courts," said Abdel Rahman Janaqaw, a senior member of the Supreme Islamic Courts Council (SICC).

After the victory of the ICU over the ARPCT the next stage of the ICU is to defeat the TFG that remained the last obstacle on the ICU's way to control south and central parts of Somalia. In the wake of the ICU's victory, the TFG reiterated its long-standing call for foreign "peacekeepers" to intervene.[18] In response to the TFG call, Ethiopia has sent several hundred troops to support the TFG. The government of President Abdullahi Yusuf was based in a provincial town, Baidoa, where witnesses said Ethiopian soldiers were guarding key buildings. Addis Ababa backed Yusuf and regarded the Islamists as led by "terrorists."

Since taking Mogadishu, the ICU had accused Ethiopia of sending troops across the border into Somalia, a claim denied by the Ethiopian government. "Ethiopia had absolutely nothing to do with the latest fighting in Mogadishu and other towns between the militia of the warlords and the ICU, "said a statement from the Ethiopian Foreign Ministry.[19]

The ICU has rejected the TFG call for foreign troops and opposed the deployment of foreign troops on the grounds that it would make the country more dangerous and unstable, adding that they were already providing security in the capital. However, the African Union (AU) announced on June 19, 2006 that it would propose sending a peacekeeping mission to

Somalia and that it would be sending an assessment team to evaluate the situation on the ground. "We agreed that priority be given to dialogue, and [this] should take place with the transitional federal institutions and all the parties in Somalia, "AU Peace and Security Commissioner Said Djinnit said in the Ethiopian capital, Addis Ababa.[20]

However, the ICU's leader, Sheikh Hassan Dahir Aweys, declared that: "As long as Ethiopia is in our country, talks with the government cannot go ahead." [21]

"If the government cares about the Somalis, it should remove our enemy from the country... Ethiopia has invaded us," Aweys said.

Aweys denied that the Islamists planned to expand to Baidoa. "There has never been an intention of attacking Baidoa," he said. On the other hand Sheikh Aweys called Somalis to join the Jihad (holy war) against the Ethiopian forces on Somali soil.

In order to prevent further bloodshed, the United Nations, Sudan, Kenya, and other states made efforts to bring the TFG and ICU to the negotiation table. Representatives of the TFG and the ICU met on June 22, 2006, in Khartoum and agreed to meet again on July 15, 2006. However, the TFG failed to attend the meeting in July, accusing the ICU of violating the earlier agreement.[22]

Later, the TFG agreed to attend talks with the Islamists in Khartoum on August 1-2, responding to a UN drive to avoid war. "We will go to Khartoum without any preconditions," said Abdul Rizak Adam, TFG's chief of staff, after talks with a senior UN envoy in the government's base in Baidoa.

The talks in Khartoum ended without any significant results, but after meeting with a Kenyan delegation led by the assistant foreign affairs minister of Kenya, both the ICU and the TFG agreed to resume talks in Khartoum on August 31, 2006.[23]

Meanwhile, the ICU seized Baladwayne, a town on the Ethiopian border, on August 9, 2006. The ICU claimed that they had attacked the government-appointed regional administration in the town, forcing the local governor and provincial commissioner to flee towards Ethiopia.[24] The ICU militia were also said to be advancing on Galkaayo, 465 miles north of Mogadishu. Galkaayo is a town on the border with semi-autonomous Puntland, the home of the president of the TFG, Abdullahi Yusuf.[25]

On August 13, 2006 the ICU seized control of the town Haradere, 300 km north of Mogadishu on the Indian Ocean coastline. Haradere was a base of piracy and dozens of hijackings of ships. The pirates called themselves the "Defenders of Somali Territorial Waters" and were loyal to regional warlord Abdi Muhammad Afweyne.[26] Afweyne and the pirates fled before the Islamic courts militiamen arrived at Haradere.

The Islamic militia was welcomed by the local inhabitants, who were terrorized by the pirates. The Islamic militias' move to Haradere came shortly after a statement of Sheikh Hassan Dahir Aweys that he would forcefully stop all acts of piracy in Somalia.

The next move of the ICU was on September 24, 2006. The militia of the ICU captured the strategic port town Kismayo, 260 miles southwest of Mogadishu. Kismayo is the most important city in south Somalia after Mogadishu and the third key city in the country.[27] Two international harbors and an airport make Kismayo a strategic gate to Somalia.

The ICU forces took control of the town without a fight after local forces from the militia of the "Juba Valley Alliance" (JVA), loyal to the TFG defense minister, Barre Shire Hirale, fled the town.[28] The ICU said they took Kismayo to prevent it being used to bring foreign peacekeepers into the country, as requested by the TFG.[29] The prime minister of the TFG, Ali Muhammad Gedi, said the takeover of Kismayo was a "violation" of the ceasefire agreed between the ICU and the TFG in Khartoum.[30]

On September 25, 2006 several thousand demonstrators protested against the ICU in Kismayo. The ICU militiamen with white bands on their heads opened fire on protesters, killing a 13-year-old boy and injuring two other children.[31] The ICU imposed curfew in town and shut down the local radio station that was blamed for anti-ICU propaganda.

The TFG's interior minister, Hussein Muhammad Farah Aidid, told Al Jazeera network that "there are foreign forces … which attacked Kismayo."[32] In response to this accusation, Hassan Turki, a leader of the ICU militia, acknowledged for the first time that foreign fighters were helping the ICU militia. Turki said: "[The government has] called foreigners … and we are getting help from our Muslim brothers to train us."[33]

On October 13, 2006 a militia loyal to the TFG defense minister, Col. Barre Shire Hirale, tried to retake Kismayo. This was three weeks after losing the town to the ICU. The fighting on the town's outskirts lasted for two hours as rival forces used heavy machine guns and rocket-propelled grenades. The Islamic forces pursued Hirale's retreating fighters toward the town of Barhani, some 30 miles west of Kismayo, Islamic Courts official Abdullahi Warsame said.[34] Some locals were arrested for helping plan the attack, including Hirale's wife.

The ICU continued to advance with the symbolic takeover of Brava, a coastal town 125 miles southwest of Mogadishu and one of the small pockets in the south still outside their control. The town's leaders were sympathetic to the Islamic courts, but pledged to hand over their weapons.[35]

Earlier on October 12, 2006 Hirale's militia and the ICU clashed briefly in the town of Bu'aale, 220 miles south of Baidoa, where Hirale had been regrouping his forces.

Restoring Order and the Implementation of Sharia Law

In Mogadishu, the ICU has concentrated on dismantling the notorious roadblocks, thereby effectively demobilizing the clan-based militias and neutralizing the warlords and local faction leaders, and denying them much-needed resources for the militia. Critically, it allows the population freedom of movement, and removes the daily threat of intimidation and extortion. It also removes the threat of spontaneous conflict from the "freelance" militia, who live off what they can demand or steal. Many are addicted to qat and other drugs and attack indiscriminately.

Sheikh Abdulakdir Ali, ICU vice chairman, said that after the takeover the ICU had given priority to areas of high insecurity, particularly the main Bakara market and other business centers. Civilians, such as Halima Ali, a small trader, said people were taking full advantage of the new freedom of movement: "In the past I was robbed a number of times as I went to the market; [now] I go and come back with everything." In the areas under the ICU control the Islamic movement imposed strict Sharia law.

The ICU decreed in June 2006 that sport is a "satanic act." Thus, sport was banned during Ramadan. A group of teenagers playing soccer in Mogadishu was taken into custody in September 2006 and only released when their parents promised they would never allow their children to play soccer again. The Somalis segregated seating for male and female sports fans. The ICU has also prepared mosques at all playing fields in the country so that players will not miss prayers.

In the first week of July 2006, Islamist militiamen shot dead two soccer fans watching the World Cup in Mogadishu. They have banned cinemas showing the World Cup, Western and Indian movies, wedding parties, and what they call the "satanic music of the West." The Islamic Courts militias beat members of the Mogadishu Stars, a musical band, with electric cables after performing at a wedding ceremony, since the wedding included the mixing of men and women as well as playing music, which were regarded as un-Islamic.

The ICU has introduced corporal punishment and public flogging of youth accused of "indecent behaviors." Sheikh Abdallah Ali, a senior official of the ICU, has declared that: "He who does not perform prayers will be considered an infidel and sharia law orders that that person be killed."

The ICU enacted repressive measures against the media. It declared that "the media must not publish or disseminate information contrary to the Muslim religion, the public interest, or the interest of the nation: the media must not disseminate information likely to create conflicts between the population and the Council of Islamic Courts: the media must not serve foreign interests: the media must not publish or disseminate elements of foreign culture contrary to Islamic culture or promoting bad behavior, such as nudity on film."

The ICU has opened the mosque of the "Islamic Solidarity" the largest mosque in the Horn of Africa. The mosque had been closed for 16 years since the outbreak of the civil war in Somalia. The "Islamic Solidarity" mosque was established in 1987 by Saudi King Faisal bin Abdel Aziz Foundation and it accommodates about 10,000 worshipers.[36] Parts of the mosque have collapsed as it had not been restored since 1991 and the ICU called for collecting donations for restoring the mosque.[37] Sheikh Abdul Rahaman Ganko, deputy chairman of the ICU executive committee, also called on Somali businessman and merchants to join efforts to restore the mosque.[38]

The ICU has reopened the Mogadishu port for shipping more then a decade after competing warlords closed it in February 1995. On September 5, 2006, a ship chartered by the United Nations World Food Programme (UNWFP) docked in Mogadishu loaded with food for the drought stricken regions in Somalia.[39]

Somalia's people's reactions to the ICU's victory have been mixed, on one hand the ICU restored order and security after the lawlessness of about a decade under the rule of the warlords, on the other hand, some people were concerned by the imposition of radical interpretations of Sharia law.

The Radicalization of Somali Society

After the victory of the ICU over the ARPCT, the ICU recalled former experienced officers that served in the Somali armed forces before 1991, and reestablished at least four training camps. The ICU has recruited more than 1,000 "moryaans" (former fighters in the warlords militias), rehabilitated, and trained them.

The "moryaans" had to learn personal and religious discipline so they could be integrated into the ICU militia. The training included Islamic indoctrination and military trainings. The young militiamen were brainwashed with the principles of being devoted Muslims and learned about the jihad (the holy war) that they have to be ready to fight against the enemies of the ICU and Islam.

On October 9, 2006, Sheikh Sharif called a press conference and appeared in military uniform to announce a jihad against neighboring Ethiopia, accusing its government of interfering in Somali affairs and sending its troops across the border to support the Transitional Federal Government. He said the declaration of jihad "was not concerning the international community, but Somali citizens, and all Somali citizens are ready to defend their country with jihad if the Ethiopians don't stop their intervention."[40] Many Mogadishu residents have taken the call, and see "US-backed Ethiopia" as the main threat to the ICU.[41]

In October 2006 the ICU held seminars, including for women, where they were taught household management and first aid to support the fighters.[42] Earlier in the background of the war in Lebanon, and as a part of the radicalization of Somali society under the Islamic courts rule, more than 2,000 people held a rally in Mogadishu on August 11, 2006, calling for a Jihad (holy war) against the enemies of Islam in Middle East, United States and around the world.

"Look at what's happening in the Middle East and the whole world is silent, and when Somalia was in the anarchy still the world was silent," said Sheikh Sharif Sheikh Ahmad, a leader of the ICU. "It is compulsory to join the holy war (Jihad)," Yusuf Ali Sayyid, a leader of the ICU, told the Associated Press.

A similar protest was held in neighboring Kenya, drawing about 300 people to Nairobi's main mosque. The protesters, most of them young men, carried signs saying "Israel stop killing our brothers and sisters" and "end America's terrorism of army invasion in Iraq."

An Italian nun was shot dead by Somali gunmen on September 17, 2006. The nun was shot at the S.O.S hospital in Mogadishu by two gunmen. The nun's bodyguard and a hospital worker were also killed. The assassination took place shortly after a leading Somali cleric criticized the comments Pope Benedict XVI made in a speech that offended Muslims. The pope had cited the words of a Byzantine emperor who characterized some of the teachings of the Prophet Muhammad as "evil and inhuman."[43] The pope's remarks created angry responses in all the Muslim world, but Somalia was the first and only place that a Christian was murdered as revenge. The violent response in Somalia was a part of the radicalization of the Islam in this state after the victory of the ICU.

Financing the ICU

Before the ICU's victory over the ARPCT they were backed and financed mainly by the Somali business community and Islamic charities. The head of the Bureau of African Affairs at the U.S. State Department, in a June 29, 2006 hearing of the House's International Relations Committee, accused Saudi Arabia of supporting the ICU. He did not directly accuse the Saudi government of funding Somalia's ICU, but said that money is flowing from the kingdom and Yemen in support of the Islamic Courts.[44]

Saudi Crown Prince Sultan, deputy premier and minister of defense and aviation, denied the charges that the kingdom is offering assistance to Somalia's Islamic Courts Union (ICU). He was speaking at a press conference following the opening of an armed forces exhibition.[45]

On July 11, 2006 the ICU established control over Mogadishu's seaport after a two-day battle in which over 100 people died and about 200 were wounded. The port had been closed for 15 years following disagreements among the warlords over who should run it. While the port was still used unofficially, it was not under any central control, making its use unpredictable.[46]

Sheikh Sharif Sheikh Ahmad and other top leaders of the ICU have described the control of the port as a monumental, progressive development.[47] The port falling into the hands of the ICU was a positive development for the movement, which planned to reopen it and profit from its commercial activities. The ICU could facilitate arms imports through control of the ports (the port of El Maan and Marka are associated with the Mogadishu port), and could generate revenue through a thriving qat trade, the livestock trade, a profitable charcoal business, and the control of the fishing trade on the Somalia coastline.

To finance their expansion the ICU planed to profit from various trades that moved through the ports, one of them is the qat trade (a kind of drug) that may provide the ICU millions of dollars every year. Alongside the qat business are exports of livestock to the Gulf states. In the past, Mogadishu's ports have failed to ship thousands of animals due to the chaos in the city. For example, 3.2 million heads of cattle were exported through the port of Berbera in northern Somalia in 1997 and more than $100 million in annual cargo was imported to Somalia from Dubai Creek. The ICU planed to continue this trade out of the Mogadishu ports.[48]

Another source of income for the ICU was the charcoal trade. In the past, the Gulf states have provided a market for charcoal, which is transported by sea to Saudi Arabia. In the Gulf, the profit from charcoal bags is enormous, with trades earning more than $6 million profit for an 80-90 kilogram bag. Traders, for example, purchase a bag of charcoal for 35,000 Somali shillings ($3-$4) and sell it for $10 in Saudi Arabia.[49]

The fishing trade also helped to fund the ICU's operations. The warlords generated funds through the issuance of fishing licenses, and used the money to pay their militias. Those caught fishing without a license often fell victim to the pirate patrols skimming the coastline. After the warlords were defeated, the ICU was able to oversee the fishing trade and earn money through the issuance of fishing licenses.[50]

With the new Islamist authority in control of Mogadishu's ports, the ICU started to impose taxes on trade traffic. The money earned from this trade helped to fund the Islamists' operations, and also make it easier for them to receive arms shipments. Additionally, ICU control over the ports will stabilize trade traffic through Mogadishu and restart a lucrative economic artery.[51]

The Leadership of the Islamic Courts

Sheikh Sharif Sheikh Ahmad

Sheikh Sharif was born in Chabila, a town in central Somalia in January 1964. Sheikh Sharif taught geography, Arabic, and religious studies in Juba secondary school. He has attended university in Libya and Sudan. Sheikh Sharif is regarded as a moderate Islamic leader. In an interview when asked about claims that he is a Washhabsit and trying to impose Wahhabism in Somalia he said: "I myself I don't know Wahhabism at all. I am from a family that followed a Sufi order. I have no Idea about Wahhabiya, I only heard about the name."[52]

Sheikh Sharif lives with his wife and two children in a modest house in Mogadishu, and he doesn't own a computer or a satellite phone. In an interview to *Asharq al Awsat* he said:[53] "I live a simple life, like the majority of Somalis."

In an interview to *Asharq al Awsat,* Sheikh Sharif told the newspaper a story of an event that has changed his life:[54] "A few years ago, a local gang in Mogadishu kidnapped a young student and demanded a ransom from his family in return for releasing their son. This incident was one of countless other kidnappings and killings perpetrated by armed groups in the Somali capital who exploited the disintegration of the central government, after President Muhammad Ziad Barre was ousted from power."

This event marked turning point in the life of Sheikh Sharif. "I met with [the student's] teachers and decided to act. We issued a statement that attracted people's attention in Mogadishu. I began speaking to the residents of the neighborhood where kidnappers tended to hide their victims and implored them not to cover up for them."

Prior to the kidnapping, Sheikh Sharif had no affiliation with the Islamic courts organization, which was modestly established in 1996 and grew in 1998. He was surprised to be nominated to lead the organization that maintains a strong armed militia. "I was visiting a friend when I heard I was nominated for the post. I thought of turning it down and continuing to work as a teacher and guide pupils. But I soon agreed for fear that the organization might fail while still in its infancy."

With armed clashes erupting around Mogadishu, Sheikh Sharif indicated that he might need to reconsider the security measures he takes to safeguard his life. "By nature, I do not like have guards around me. But I was forced to seek the help of highly trained and armed bodyguards." This was because of the recent flare up of violence, which Sheikh Sharif blamed on "the devil's allies," a reference to U.S.-backed warlords. "I used to go out quite often without guards and I enjoyed it.[55]

Asked about the number of forces loyal to him, Sheikh Sharif said he could not discuss exact figures for security reasons. "This is top secret information. If I tell you, some parties might underestimate us if the numbers are small. We might exaggerate our force if we mention large figures. Since the beginning of the civil war, all Somalis are armed. We have not banned anyone from joining us."

Sheikh Sharif did not regret becoming the leader of the Islamic courts organization. "This is our fate and responsibility. Our aim is to protect the Somali people and defend their rights and dignity."

According to Western intelligence sources, the Islamic courts organization is sheltering Muslim extremists, some of whom have ties to Al Qaeda, including three suspected of carrying out the attacks on U.S. embassies in East Africa in 1998. Sheikh Sharif had denied systematically all such accusations, but answering specific questions in an interview with Awdal News his answers were quiet different:[56]

Q: There are people suspected by the U.S. government of having links with international terrorism, particularly Al Qaida. One of them is Hassan Aweys, a former head of Al Itihad, who is on the American blacklist. What will you do if the U.S. government requests you to arrest him?

A: [Sheikh Sharif] I don't think anybody will asks us to do that. We are not assigned to arrest people for them, as you know.

Q: If the U.S. government includes this in the agenda of its talks with you what you will do?

A: [Sheikh Sharif] They have no right to do that, as you know, we don't work for the Americans.

Q: Are your fighters all Somalis? Some reports say that they include some foreign elements. And if they are all Somalis do they all belong to Mogadishu or do they include Somalis hailing from Somaliland, Puntland, Ethiopia, and Kenya?

A: [Sheikh Sharif] All our fighters are Somalis. There may be people who arrived here during the battles and joined the fighting. I am not sure of that because all the fighters are volunteers. There may also include people who are residents of Mogadishu, but originally came from the other regions, but the fighters who are officially enlisted for us are all from Mogadishu. They are all natives of the city; they are known people and they are the people who established the Islamic courts.

Q: Some reports from the West say that your courts comprise people from various Islamic schools of thought such as Al Itihad Al Islami, Al Takfiir Al Hijra, Al Islah and Al Tabliq and that they are all against the moderate Sunni, Shafi'i and Sufi schools of Islam. If this is true, don't you think this could lead to a clash between them?

A: [Sheikh Sharif] There is no truth in this. The people are ordinary people who organized themselves. Each one of them has been selected on individual basis to lead a court. They could be from Sufi orders or Al Itihad or others. But as you know Al Itihad doesn't exist anymore. It has ceased to exist a long time ago.

Q: Where do you get support in terms of arms and finance?

A: [Sheikh Sharif] The support comes from the people who have established these courts.

For his part, Sheikh Sharif emphasized that Osama Bin Laden's group did not have any presence Somalia. "There are no fugitives from Al Qaeda or any other organization, as the U.S. and Ethiopian intelligence services are claiming. This is an open country and strangers will be found out very quickly. Look at the number of lies Washington is telling about Iraq and Afghanistan. It is trying to repeat the same thing in Mogadishu, but we will not let it."

Denying receiving financial aid from aboard, Sheikh Sharif said the organization's popularity stern from people's love and appreciation from its actions, given the absence of a central government." Rely on our limited resources and what ordinary citizens give us, we welcome financial contributions, however small they are, but do not oblige citizens to contribute."

He denied having any contacts with the transitional federal government (TFG) led by President Abdullahi Yusuf and Prime Minister Ali Muhammad Gedi, currently based in Baidoa, adding that he had no objection to future talks, if they serve the interests of the Somali people. Criticizing the U.S. administration's role in the recent fighting, Sheikh Sharif said Washington was not acting in the interest of Somalis, but was repeating past mistakes. President Bush's remarks on the presence of Al Qaida in Somalia were "lies," to promote the U.S.'s war on terror, he added. In spite of this criticism, Sheikh Sharif welcomed discussions with the United States to improve relations between the Islamic courts and the United States.

At the end of June 2006, the leaders of the ICU took the decision to change the leadership of the organization and Sheikh Hassan Dahir Aweys replaced Sheikh Sharif as the head of the ICU. Sheikh Sharif was named the chairman of the organization and remained an influential member of the ICU, but he lost power to the more radical elements in the organization under the leadership of Aweys.

Sheikh Hassan Dahir Aweys

Sheikh Hassan Dahir Aweys is an Islamic cleric, believed to be 61 years old, and has appeared as the most powerful figure in the ICU. Aweys is a former prisons colonel who started preaching in the 1970s.

Aweys was among the founders of the Al Itihad al Islamiya (AIAI) and was the head of the organization for several years. At the formation of Islamic courts in Mogadishu, Aweys became the head of one of the most powerful courts in Mogadishu.

In 2000, at the formation of the Joint Islamic Courts Council (JICC), Aweys became the secretary general of the organization. Aweys was accused by the United States of collaboration with Al Qaida while Bin Laden lived in Sudan (1991-1996). Aweys went into hiding following the September 11, 2001 attacks and reemerged only in 2004 to run Ifka Halanica, a powerful court in south Mogadishu.

Around June 2005, Aweys accused the TFG of selling the country to enemies such as Ethiopia, and indicated that he was preparing for war. He had called for jihad, warning that his faction would not be mere spectators in the Somali crisis.[57] Aweys identified Ethiopia as a threat to Somalia, and in the late 1990s the AIAI under his leadership was involved in small-scale attacks against Ethiopia (1996) until Ethiopia weakened the AIAI's power.[58]

According to A.P. reports, the leaders of the ICU took the decision to change the leadership of the organization and Sheikh Hassan Dahir

Aweys was appointed leader of the organization at the end of June 2006, replacing Sheikh Sharif. In his first interview to the media since being named head of the organization he has said:[59]

- Somalia is a Muslim nation and its people are also Muslim, 100 percent.
- The organization will support only a government based on Islam. Any government we agree on would be based on the holy Quran and the teachings of our prophet Muhammad.
- Somalis always wasted to act on Islam, but the former colonial powers diverted them from that. I hope now the only option open for them is to support an Islamic state.

The Islamic organization also changed its name from the Islamic Courts Union (ICU) to the Somali Supreme Islamic Courts Council (SSICC). The United States has said it will not deal with Aweys, because of "links to terrorism." In an interview with the BBC after his nomination as head of the SSICC, Aweys said:[60] "I am not terrorist. But if strictly following my religion and love for Islam makes me a terrorist, then I will accept the designation."

U.S. State Department spokesman Sean McCormack said the United States would be troubled if Aweys' promotion was an indication of the direction the Somali Supreme Islamic Courts Council was heading in.[61] The United States has said it is willing to work with other leaders allied to Aweys, but it fears that a Somalia run by Islamists could be used by international Islamic fighters (Mujahidin).[62]

Sheikh Yusuf Muhammad Sayyid[63]

Sheikh Yusuf Muhammad Sayyid is also known as Yusuf Indaha'adde. Indaha'adde belongs to the Ayr clan. He was trained in Afghanistan before the American invasion, (Operation Enduring Freedom). Indaha'adde was one of the Islamist warlords before he joined the ICU. He named himself as a sheikh and the governor of the Lower Shabelle region.

After joining the ICU, he was nominated as the deputy of the executive committee of the ICU. Indaha'adde had a key role in arming the ICU militia. He started receiving arms from Eritrea together with Aweys (now the head of the ICU), around 2005.[64]

According to the UN Monitoring Group on Somalia, the arms were transported by aircraft from Eritrea to Baledogle airport near Mogadishu and by ship to the port of Marka. (March 25, 2005 and April 10, 2005).[65] The arms shipments included anti-aircraft guns and mines. On November

2005, Indaha'adde visited Asmara (Eritrea) to discuss the continuation of the arms supply to the ICU.[66]

Adan Hashi Ayro[67]

Adan Hashi Ayro is a militia commander of the Islamic courts. He is considered an extremist Muslim and was trained in Afghanistan. He came to the fore following the recent attacks that involved the desecration of Italian cemeteries in Mogadishu and was blamed for killing five Western aid workers and BBC journalist Kate Peyton in 2005. Ayro was blamed for the 2005 assassination of Abdul Qadir Yahya Ali, the founder of the Center for Research and Dialogue, an NGO, in Mogadishu in front of his family.[68] In 2005, Ayro and his followers disinterred all the bodies from the colonial-era Italian cemetery in Mogadishu and dumped them in the trash. In their place they set up an Islamic militia training camp.[69]

An ICU-made propaganda video titled "Punishment of the Converts," obtained by *Newsweek* from an Islamic militiaman in Mogadishu, shows the Somali Islamists training in cemetery, interspersed with speeches from several of the ICU's leading military figures, including a partially masked man who appears to be Ayro, according to Somalis who know him. The dialogue is Pan-Islamic and pro-terrorists; the voice-over features Osama bin Laden and Ayman al-Zawaheiri'. "Every Muslim who is victimized in the world, we are calling him to come here," says one masked Somali fighter. "It will be a safe haven for him." The Islamic militias' internal newspaper, *Al Jihad*, puts it more bluntly: "terrorism is compulsory," reads a July 3, 2006 headline. According to the newspaper, "Terrorism, extremism and fundamentalism are part of Islam and good."[70]

Ayro is largely viewed as a newcomer on the Somali scene, being mentored by Aweys. Reports in 2005 said that Ayro and Aweys were running camps where religious extremists received military training. The training also included indoctrination into fundamentalist ideology aimed at advocating jihad in Islamic states.

When the ICU leader Sheikh Sharif was asked about Ayro's involvement in terror activities in the past he said:[71]

Q: It happened sometime in the past that Italian cemetery was dug up and the remains of dead people exhumed. There is a suspicion that Adan Hashi Ayro was behind this. We know Ayro is now a commander of the Ifke Halane Court. What does Sheikh Sharif have to say about this to the Italian people?

A: [Sheikh Sharif] A lot of things have taken place in the country. A lot of mistakes have taken place. Many Somali cemeteries have been built on others. People have been killed, some have been raped, and others have been taken hostage and sold. So this [Italian cemetery] is just one of the many mistakes that happened in the country.

There was great misery in the country. The life of the whole Somali people have been completely destroyed. Millions have left the country, millions have become handicapped and other millions are suffering inside it. Therefore, I think the answer is obvious.

Q: Some of Ayro associates have been convicted in Hargeisa for the murder of foreign aid workers. What is your stand on this issue?

A: [Sheikh Sharif] Brother, I have no idea about it. I have no information on this matter, I cannot, therefore, comment on it.

The leader of the ICU Sheikh Aweys described Ayro as "a good man" who's never been convicted of a crime.[72]

Hassan Abdullah Hersi Al Turki[73]

Al Turki was born in 1949 in the Ogaden region in Ethiopia. He had played a significant role in the Ethiopia-Somalia war over the Ogaden region in 1977. After Somalia lost the war over Ogaden, Al Turki left to Somalia to continue the war against Ethiopia. Al Turki is keen to see Ogaden secede from Ethiopia and become a separate state.

Al Turki joined the AIAI in Somalia and had links to Al Takfir wal Hijra and Al Qaida.[74] The United States put him on the list of terrorists and froze his financial assets. In 2004 Al Turki joined the ICU and became one of the commanders of the ICU's militia. In the Battle of Jowhar (July 2006), against the warlords of the ARPCT, Al Turki was one of the leading commanders of the ICU's militia who had defeated the ARPCT warlords at Jowhar.

The Confrontation between the Islamic Courts and the TFG

Under the growing pressure of the ICU on the TFG at least 20 members of Somalia's parliament resigned on July 27, 2006. They accused the TFG of corruption and of failing to bring peace: "Our government failed to implement national reconciliation, so we have decided to resign" said Othman Hassan Ali Atto who stepped down as public works minister.[75]

The treasury and government relations ministers resigned as well and other Cabinet members were expected to add their names to the list.[76] In August 2006, twelve more ministers walked away from the weak, Western-backed interim government of Somalia, raising fears of its imminent collapse, said reports from the area. Minister of minerals and water Mahamoud Salad Nur and three other assistant ministers announced their resignation less than a week after, dealing a blow to the TFG, the fragile interim government.

Eight more ministers and assistant ministers later resigned after Prime Minister Ali Muhammad Gedi called for peace talks with rival Islamists to be postponed. "We had to option but no resign because we believe if the talks are postponed again it will affect the reconciliation efforts, "Minister of Fisheries and Ocean Resources Hassan Abshir Farah told Reuters. "Gedi's government is unpopular among most members of parliament and its work plans will not be accepted by the national assembly," Water and Mineral Resources Minister Muhammad Salad Nur told reporters.

On July 26, 2006, Muhammad Ibrahim Muhammad, chairman of the parliamentary committee for constitutional affairs, was shot.[77] Abdallah Isaaq Deerow, Somalia's minister for constitutional and federal affairs, was shot by an unidentified gunmen, who than escaped.[78] Deerow was not among the 29 TFG members who resigned.

Meanwhile the Islamic Courts continued to expand their control over Mogadishu and the southern part of Somalia. On July 27, 2006, the militia said it was setting up a religious court inside a vast complex in Mogadishu that once served as the country's presidential palace, a highly symbolic move that further marginalized the official administration.[79]

"This is the place where Somalia will be ruled from and we appreciate your cooperation with the courts," said Janaqaw, a senior member of the Islamic courts."[80]

In this regard, experts believed that the Islamic Courts' formal acceptance of the legitimacy of the TFG, and the TFG's reciprocal recognition that the Islamic Courts constitute the new reality in Mogadishu and the country, were compromises that could serve as a platform for further constructive dialogue.

Following the July 19, 2006 capture by the Islamic Courts Union (ICU) of the town Burkakaba, near Baidoa, where the Somali Transitional Federal Government (TFG) is based, Ethiopia sent a column of vehicles and troops to Baidoa. The takeover of the town near Baidoa was most likely an ICU probe of the extent of Ethiopia's commitment to the TFG, rather than a planned attack in a Baidoa aborted by the Ethiopians' arrival.[81]

Two weeks after the Khartoum summit, on September 18, 2006, eleven people including six alleged assassins were killed in Baidoa in an unsuccessful attempt to assassinate Somalia's interim president, Abdullahi Yusuf. The president was unhurt in the attack but his brother was among the killed, and 18 people were wounded.[82]

The assassins detonated a car bomb when the president's convoy left the parliament building. A second blast went off shortly after the first one. No one inside the building of the parliament was injured.[83] The blasts came as the president started a key session to approve the new cabinet. It is not clear who carried out the attack.

Despite the Khartoum accord the ICU and the TFG remained deeply divided over several key issues including the proposed deployment of a peacekeeping force. The minister of foreign affairs of the TFG declined to speculate as to who was behind the blasts, but suggested they were probably linked to the proposed peacekeeping mission issue.[84]

A government spokesman, Abidirahman Muhammad Nur, said: "We really do not have the expertise to uncover the whole attack that was well organized by the same groups that are carrying out attacks in Iraq and Afghanistan."[85] The ICU's chairman, Sheikh Sharif Sheikh Ahmad, condemned the attack and blamed Ethiopia, which backs President Yusuf, saying it wanted a pretext to send troops to Somalia.[86]

On October 18, 2006, at a meeting in Nairobi, aimed at salvaging peace talks with the ICU, the TFG's President Yusuf appealed for international support against the ICU. Yusuf for the first time directly accused the ICU of planning to assassinate him and other government officials.[87]

"As a result of the investigation, our security forces have seized recent ICU documents listing a considerable number of TFG leaders condemned as infidels and a target for immediate physical elimination," Yusuf said in a statement obtained by the Reuters news agency.[88] He cited a document that he said approved both his and Prime Minister Ali Muhammad Gedi's assassination.[89]

On November 30, 2006, three car bombs exploded at a government checkpoint outside a TFG base in Baidoa, killing 8 people, including two policemen. According to TFG police reports, one of the three suicide bombers was a veiled woman.[90] No one claimed responsibility for the attack. This was the second suicide attack in Somalia since the ICU came to power in Somalia (June 2006).

Somaliland and Puntland and the ICU's Islamic Revolution

After the victory over the warlords of Mogadishu and the ongoing conflict with the TFG, the next targets of the Islamic movement were the autonomous regions of Puntland and Somaliland.

On October 9, 2006, during a visit of Sheikh Sharif Sheikh Ahmad in Dubai, he said that regarding Puntland and Somaliland, he viewed the two entities differently:[91] "Puntland is an autonomous state and we are negotiating with them to join the ICU. ... However, we understand the grievances of Somaliland and we want to tell them our readiness to address these historical mistakes."

Sheikh Dahir Aweys represented even a more hostile position and accused the Somaliland people of worshiping an idol. "The Somaliland people forgot to worship Allah and instead worship an idol called Peace," he said in a statement to the media.[92]

From the middle of October the tension between the ICU and Puntland and Somaliland escalated and turned into violent conflict.

The ICU and Puntland—November 2006

On November 5, 2006, fighting broke out between the ICU forces in Gilinsor, in the Mudug province in central Somalia, and the militia of Abdi, Qeybdid, who had links to the autonomous government of Puntland.[93] The fighting came as some religious leaders from Puntland had set up an Islamic court in north Galka'ayo. The formation of the court has already intimidated authorities in the region who threatened that they would either kill or deport its founders.

The ICU chief of national security Sheikh Yusuf Indaha'adde explained in a press conference that his fighters were attacked by militia loyal to Abdi Qeybdid and Puntland fighters. The ICU forces fought back forcing the enemy to retreat.[94] He indicated that the ICU has supported the fresh Islamic court recently formed at North Galka'ayo under the administration of Puntland. Puntand's rural affairs minister Ali, Abdul Awarre has denied any involvement of forces from Puntland in the fight.[95]

The ICU and Somaliland—October-November 2006

On October 17,2006, Awdal News Network published an article titled "Suicide bombers heading for Somaliland."[96] According to the article, based on an internal document written in Arabic and dated 6 Ramadan 1427 of the Hijri calendar (28 September 2006), the decision blasts the Somaliland leadership for being apostates who reneged from Islam and opted to work with Jews and Americans at the expense of their nation and religion.[97]

"The Shura Council of the Perseverance Alliance has decided to send 30 young martyrs to carry out explosions and killings of the Jewish and American collaborators in the northern regions," the document said.[98] The list of targeted personalities include Somaliland president Dahir Riyale Kahin, Foreign Minister Abdillahi Muhammad Duale, Finance Minister Hussein Ali Duale, Defense Minister Adan Waqaf, Aviation and Transport

Minister Ali Muhammad Waran Adde, Minister of Information Ahmed Dahir Elmi, and other seven senior officials.[99]

The Council said the decision was made "After the Follow Up Committee of the Perseverance Alliance submitted reports related to the circumstances in which religious scholars live in the northern regions (Somaliland), and after the reports mentioned the personalities that carried out the torture against Islamic clerics and after the Council watched a video footage of the torture of Sheikh Muhammad Ismail."[100] Somali Islamist media have repeatedly shown the alleged torture video of Sheikh Muhammad Ismail, an Islamist cleric jailed in Hargeisa for alleged terrorist acts.

Other, measures recommended by the decision include forming a committee tasked to circulate the alleged torture video footage and stir protest marches and dissent in the Somaliland towns of Buroa, Las Anod, Erigavo, and Buhodle. These are all towns known to shelter a large—so far peaceful—opposition to the Hargeisa government; Buroa being the center of Islamist activity in Somaliland.[101]

The Islamist council also decided to train 3,000 young mujahids hailing from the northern regions, or Somaliland, that are currently living in the southern towns of Mogadishu, Kismayo, and Guri Eel. These would later be dispatched to Somaliland the document reveals.[102]

In an interview with "Awdalnews" early October, Somaliland President Dahir Riyale Kahin said that the footage seemed to be a fabrication, underlining that Somaliland was investigating the case and would present the outcome to the public. "We don't use torture as an investigative method and we don't torture anyone in our prisons. It is against our values and our laws, "President Kahin added, pointing out that the whole episode could be a ruse by some people trying to use the name of Islam for their own agenda. Mr. Kahin confirmed that the man was suspected of being behind the explosives found in Hargeisa during the parliamentary elections in September 2005.[103]

The ICU, however, seems to have made some inroads in Somaliland recently, particularly with the recent departure to Mogadishu of Sheikh Ali Warsame, a former leader of Al Itihad. Mr. Warsame, who until 2006 lived in Buroa, is also the brother-in-law of Mr. Aweys, the main author of the document threatening Somaliland.[104]

Meanwhile, a number of demonstrations against the alleged torture video took place in major Somaliland towns such as Hargeisa, Buroa and Erigavo. A number of Somaliland clerics have also issued statements, calling for the Somaliland government to apply Islamic Sharia without any delay.

On October 13, 2006. A mob led by extremist clerics burned many copies of *Haatuf* newspaper. *Haatuf* is highly critical of Somali Islamist movements, terming them "terrorists" and was the first to report on their Buroa-based Somaliland link.[105]

The ICU view the *Haatuf* newspaper as a powerful independent voice that stands in the way of their ongoing efforts to mobilize support within Somaliland.[106] *Somaliland Times*, the English-language publication of *Haatuf*, said the newspaper burners were led by Mubarak Ahmed Diriye, who has been suspected of having ties to ICU in Mogadishu.[107]

External Involvement in the Conflict between the TFG and ICU

From the early stages of the confrontation between the ICU and the TFG both sides were backed by external forces. The most significant external involvement was that of Ethiopia, which had sent military forces to protect the TFG in Baidoa, and that of Eritrea, which had sent arms and a small number of combatants to support the ICU.

Shortly after the arrival of Ethiopian forces in Baidoa, Sheikh Hassan Dahir Aweys called in a radio broadcast[108] for a Jihad (holy war) against the Ethiopian forces that were deployed in Baidoa to protect the TFG. "I am calling on the Somali people to wage a holy war against Ethiopians in Baidoa. They came to protect a government which they set up to advance their interests. We must defend our sovereignty."

As a response to the arrival of Ethiopian soldiers, the ICU mobilized forces and organized anti-Ethiopian demonstrations in Mogadishu.[109] President Abdullahi Yusuf, the head of the TFG, has repeatedly called for international peacekeeping force to be sent to restore peace and order in Somalia, an initiative that the ICU strongly opposes.

The warning of external involvement of Ethiopia and Eritrea was condemned by the United Nations and the U.S. State Department. UN envoy Francois Fall said that he thinks reports of 4,000-5,000 Ethiopian troops in Somalia are exaggerated, but he said there were indications that there are some Ethiopian troops around Baidoa and near the city of Wajid.[110]

According to the Monitoring Group set up under United Nations Security Council Resolution 1407, the Islamists were shipped, via Eritrea, 200 boxes of Zu-23 anti-aircraft ammunition, 200 boxes of B-10 anti-tank ammunition, 200 boxes of Dshk anti-aircraft ammunition, 200 boxes of Browning M2 heavy machine gun ammunition, ammunition for the ZP-39 anti-aircraft gun, 50 rocket propelled grenade launchers, 50 light anti-armor weapons, 50 M-79 grenade launchers, and communications equipments to be mounted on "technicals," (armed vehicles of the ICU militia). This was followed two days later by a consignment of 1,000 short-version AK-47 automatic rifles, 1,000 pairs of binoculars, 1,000 remote-control bombs, 1,000 anti-personnel mines, and ammunition for 120mm mortars.[111]

On July 2006, Eritrea sent to the ICU military supplies at least twice.[112] A TFG spokesman claimed that on July 26, 2006 an Ilyushin 76 cargo plane landed at Mogadishu International Airport carrying weapons from Eritrea for the ICU.[113] A second large cargo plane delivered tons of equipment to the ICU on July 28, 2006.[114] The Eritrean arms supply came shortly after the reports that Ethiopian troops entered Somalia to protect the TFG in the area of Baidoa.

Eritrea and Ethiopia have a long history of tension and hostility and fought a border war in 1998-2000. Supplying arms to the ICU in Somalia by Eritrea would be in defiance of Ethiopia. There are concerns that Somalia will turn into a battlefield between Ethiopia and Eritrea. The UN envoy to Somalia, Mr. Fall, called on neighboring countries to exercise maximum restraint and "not to interfere at this particular moment in Somalia."[115] The U.S. State Department said that there are external parties involved on all sides and called them to avoid actions that might harm peace talks.[116]

In a rare public acknowledgement of Eritrean support for the ICU, Sheikh Hassan Dahir Aweys said Asmara was providing support in gratitude for past help.[117] "The previous Somali government (of Ziad Barre) helped Eritrea during its struggle for independence from Ethiopia. Eritrea helps the Somali people, they are returning back the favor."[118]

Aweys, who attended a meeting in Mogadishu with the UN envoy to Somalia, Mr. Fall, said that the ICU would not participate in peace talks with the TFG until Ethiopian troops withdrew from Somalia. While Aweys ruled out peace talks, Sheikh Sharif Sheikh Ahmad, the former head of the ICU, said the ICU's "peace committee" still had to consider the UN's call for negotiations, which were scheduled to be held in August 2006 in Khartoum, Sudan.[119] The TFG agreed to attend the peace talks with the ICU in Khartoum on August 31, 2006.

Sheikh Hassan Dahir Aweys, in spite of his previous call for Jihad against the Ethiopian forces protecting the TFG in Baidoa, has agreed to peace talks in Khartoum. Aweys, in an interview, explained: "Legally the government is still the government, but we are the power in Somalia.... In order for the government to fulfill its role, and for us to continue doing what we want to do and to provide leadership to our people, we need to come together."[120]

On September 4, 2006 the ICU and the TFG reached an agreement under Arab League mediation in Khartoum. The ICU and the TFG agreed to form a United National army. The agreement didn't specify when the plan would take effect and talks were expected to resume October 30, 2006. The pact stressed that neither side would accept military interference inside Somalia by neighboring countries.[121]

UN Secretary General Kofi Annan praised the deal and encouraged both sides to "ensure a conducive environment for the next round of talks, which will take up crucial political, power-sharing and security issues."[122] One day later, East African leaders gathered for a summit in Nairobi, Kenya. The Nairobi summit was called by the regional Inter-Government Authority on Development (IGAD) that for years led peace initiatives to solve Somalia's political problems.

The summit pushed forward a long delayed plan to send African peacekeepers to Somalia and to wrest the diplomatic lead on solving Somalia's political crisis from the Arab League.[123] The plan faces two major obstacles:[124] the United Nations must lift an arms embargo on Somalia that has been in place for more than 10 years to allow peacekeepers to enter the country, and the African Union must release funds to back the mission, which is expected to cost $34 million a month.

Sheikh Sharif Sheikh Ahmad called the IGAD meeting "a plot against our country." Fuad Muhammad Kalaf, an education official of the ICU, declared that: "We will fight a holy war (Jihad) against them and we will train our students in military tactics. There is nothing wrong with our plan to train students."[125] As a response to the IGAD plan, the ICU organized demonstrations in Mogadishu against foreign interference, calling for holy war (Jihad) against any foreign force on Somali soil.

On September 24, 2006 the militia of the ICU captured the strategic port town of Kismayo. The ICU claimed that the capture of Kismayo came to prevent the deployment of IGAD's international forces. The takeover of Kismayo was a blow to the TFG and IGAD.[126] In response to the growing tension between the ICU and the TFG, Ethiopia has sent more troops to reinforce the TFG in Baidoa. At this stage both Ethiopia and the TFG have denied the deployment of Ethiopian troops in Baidoa and they denied the last reports as well.

The Fighting between the ICU and TFG and Ethiopian Forces

On October 5, 2006, Sheikh Sharif Sheikh Ahmad claimed that Ethiopia started shelling the town of Beledweyne and had caused unknown number of casualties.[127] "Our forces are on high alert because yesterday

(October 4, 2006) Ethiopian soldiers started shelling with mortars and artillery around our bases near Beledweyne," he told a ceremony to inaugurate a new sharia law court in Mogadishu. "We are telling the world that Ethiopian forces are violating our territory," Sheikh Ahmad told the crowd. "It has been sending thousands to Somalia for the last three days...."[128]

Beledweyne is about 30 km from the Ethiopian border and 300 km north of Mogadishu.[129] As they have done in the past in response to repeated eyewitness reports of uniformed Ethiopian troops in Somalia, officials in Ethiopia denied the claim, dismissing it as "propaganda." "These reports are unfounded and categorically false," Foreign Ministry spokesperson Solomon Abebe told Agence France-Press in Addis Ababa. "This is propaganda, they are always using, we are not attacking Beledweyne or any other town in Somalia."[130]

Ethiopian Prime Minister Meles Zenawi again denied sending troops to Somalia, but hinted Addis Ababa would intervene if the Islamists tried to oust the Somali government based in the town of Baidoa.[131] Meles Zenawi, in an address to parliament in Addis Ababa, said Islamist forces were about 15 km from the border in central Somalia and warned that Ethiopia would defend itself. "The jihadists are planning to attack Ethiopia and they are endangering our national security. The Ethiopian government is ready to defend its territory from Mogadishu Islamists."[132] In this speech Meles for the first time told the parliament that Ethiopia had sent military trainers to help the TFG:[133] "We have sent only trainers, who are soldiers." This was, in the first official acknowledgment that Ethiopian troops have been inside Somalia. "Other than this, the army has not entered into Somalia," said Meles.

The first battle between Ethiopian and ICU forces happened on November 19, 2006. Two Ethiopian trucks were destroyed, six soldiers were dead and as many as twenty injured. The battle happened near Balanballa in Golgadoud province, in central Somalia. The Ethiopian convoy ran into an ambush; two trucks were destroyed by landmines and ICU fighters then opened fire on the convoy. The Ethiopian forces have imposed a curfew on Balanballa and began searching for ICU fighters.

On November 22, 2006, hundreds of Ethiopian troops were seen patrolling a road leading to Somalia's transitional government headquarters after the brief but intense firefight in the area. On December 8, 2006, fierce fighting erupted between the ICU and forces loyal to the TFG and Ethiopian soldiers near Dinsoor, 110 km south of Baidoa. "The Islamists have attacked us and we are defending ourselves," Deputy Defense

Minister Salad Ali Jelle told the media from Baidoa. "They have been calling for attacks against our troops and today they have proven to be the real attackers," he said.

In Mogadishu, Sheikh Sharif Sheikh Ahmad, said "heavy fighting" was under way in the Dinsoor area. He told a large crowd after "Friday prayers" that the battle began when a joint Somali government-Ethiopian force attacked Islamist fighters near Dinsoor, where the two sides have been girding for battle for the past 10 days.[134] "Our forces have been raided by Ethiopian troops, so people get up and fight against the Ethiopian troops and oppose a proposed United Nations-authorized peacekeeping mission." "Stand up and defeat the enemies who have invaded our land," he told several hundred people protesting the UN Security Council's adoption of a resolution authorizing regional peacekeepers for Somalia.[135]

The Fall of the Islamic Courts Union

On December 13, 2006 fighters from the ICU have surrounded the city of Baidoa on three sides, declaring an ultimatum for Ethiopian forces to leave Somalia within seven days.[136] "Starting today, if the Ethiopians don't leave our land within seven days, we will attack them and force them to leave our country," said Sheikh Yusuf Muhammad Zaid Indaha'adde, the ICU militias' defense chief.[137]

Heavy fighting erupted on December 21, 2006, hours after the expiry of the ICU ultimatum. The fighting started early in the morning in the ICU-held Beledweyne and Bandiradley townships.[138] The Ethiopians moved tanks and other reinforcements into the battle zone and launched airstrikes against the ICU forces.[139] Ethiopian Information Minister Berhan Hailu said the operation targeted several fronts including Dinsoor, Beledweyne, Bandiaredly and Buur Hakaba. This was the first time that Ethiopia launched airstrikes against the ICU forces.

Sheikh Hassan Dahir Aweys declared that all Somalis Should join a struggle against Ethiopians. He said that he viewed Ethiopia as the single biggest obstacle to uniting Somalia under an Islamic courts system, which would bring peace and stability to the country.[140]

After three days of fierce fighting the ICU forces have deserted several strategic towns in central and southern parts of Somalia, including Buur Hakabaand Dinsoor. Ethiopian forces, accompanied by government forces occupied all strategic towns: Galkayo, Bardiradley, Adado, Buloburte, and Beledweyne.

At this stage of fighting, several hundred people have been killed, other hundreds injured and thousands of people have fled their homes.

On December 25, 2006 Ethiopian jets bombed Mogadishu's airport.[141] On Ethiopian television, the Defense Ministry claimed that the Ethiopian forces would move towards the city of Jowhar, 55 miles north of Mogadishu.

On December 27, 2006 Ethiopian and TFG troops took control of Jowhar. After the fighting in Jowhar, the Ethiopian forces and the TFG troops had swept quickly across the country retaking territories captured by ICU that left before their arrival. On December 27, 2006 evening the Ethiopian and TFG forces arrived at the outskirts of Mogadishu.

Surprisingly, the ICU decided not to fight over Mogadishu to avoid bloodshed and the Islamist fighters fled the city. In the process of the ICU withdrawal from Mogadishu, the ICU distributed guns and arms to their supporters in the town to create havoc in the wake of their withdrawal. Shortly after the ICU withdrawal from Mogadishu, fighting began between armed groups that tried to loot arms storages and offices left by the ICU.[142] Next morning, December 28, 2006, Ethiopian and TFG forces captured the capital of Somalia—Mogadishu.

Ali Muhammad Gedi, the TFG prime minister, promised thousands of war-weary Somalis peace and stability, as he formally took control of Mogadishu.[143] He declared that: "Today is the beginning of a new life, new stabilization and new future for Somalia."[144] President Abdullahi Yusuf and the Ethiopian forces declared a 24-hour ceasefire to mark the Muslim holiday of Eid al Adha on December 30, 2006, as a sign of goodwill.[145]

President Yusuf said that Ethiopian troops would stay in Somalia for now because "the government is not up to the level of tacking back the entire country overnight."[146] President Yusuf said that his forces will take the fight to Kismayo to defeat the last stronghold of the ICU.

After their withdrawal from Mogadishu the ICU forces moved south 300 km to the area of Kismayo as their last stronghold. Shortly after the arrival of the ICU forces in Kismayo, Sheikh Sharif Sheikh Ahmad urged thousands of residents gathered in Kismayo Stadium to celebrate the Muslim festival of Eid al Adha and to defend their country.[147]

"Our country is under occupation so we have decided to fight. We are gearing up to kick these occupiers out of our country." The ICU had rallied several thousand fighters at Jilib, north of Kismayo, and in Kismayo.

Ethiopian and Transitional Federal Government forces engaged the Islamist militias that were hastily building a network of trenches to defend the town of Jilib, north of the strategic port city of Kismayo. The TFG forces and their Ethiopian allies rained down mortars and rockets on the ICU fighters positions around Jilib and Kismayo.

The battle in Jilib began at 5:00 pm on January 1, 2007, and the Ethiopian Air force pounded the ICU positions. By 2:00 am, just nine hours after the fight began, the Islamic Courts retreated, and also withdrew from Kismayo without a fight. Both sides are said to have taken heavy casualties in the fighting. The remnants of the Islamic Courts and its leadership fled Kismayo for the area of Ras Kamboni and into the forests west of Kismayo, to regroup and to open an insurgency.

On January 2, 2007, Ali Jama, the TFG information minister, declared that: "The government has gained control of southern and central Somalia. We will ensure that we restore law and order in that part of the country."[148] He said the government exerted control of the southern port town of Kismayo, the Islamists' last stronghold that they abandoned on the arrival of government troops backed by Ethiopian forces. "We will pursue them (Islamists) until we ensure that they are out of this country," Jama said.

Kenya has reinforced its border with Somalia and U.S. forces are also said to be in the region, including at sea, to prevent foreign militants aligned with the Islamists from escaping. Ethiopia says it has 4,000 troops in Somalia, though many believe that the number could be far higher (20,000 troops).[149] The TFG has not given troop numbers, but is thought by experts to have several thousand. The ICU, who have been offered an amnesty by the TFG if they surrender, say they are ready to negotiate with the TFG, but that the Ethiopian soldiers backing it must first leave.[150]

The TFG and Ethiopian Victory over the ICU

In a televised address, Ethiopian Prime Minister Zenawi said: "Our patience was considered as weakness and we were forced to go war and the alternative left to us is to speedily bring the war to a successful and victorious end in the shortest time possible."[151] The military intervention of Ethiopia in Somalia in support of the weak TFG was an impressive military success but in the long run a strategic risk for Ethiopia and the stability of the region.

Ethiopia has one of Africa's largest, best-equipped, and most experienced armed forces, with more than 100,000 trained personnel.[152] The Ethiopian forces in Somalia, using tanks, artillery and air forces, have defeated in short time the lightly armed and ill-trained Islamic force. But the war they are facing now in Somalia will be a new type of challenge. The ICU already declared their will to conduct a holy war (Jihad) against the Ethiopian invaders and the TFG.[153]

The eastern parts of Ethiopia, through which its forces must travel, are remote and have few resources. Its supply lines and communications were stretched even before they crossed the Somali border. It is also an area inhabited by Somali speakers. Some of them, Somali and Oromo rebels operating in the area, are sympathetic to the ICU.[154]

Inside Somalia the Ethiopians are likely to find few allies and many Somalis, who are united by nothing else, will be determined to resist Ethiopian forces; with whom they have fought two wars in the past 50 years.[155]

Ethiopia faces two levels of potential threats:

- A long-standing pan-Somali claim to the Ogaden region.
- Radical Islam and the threat that Somalia will turned into area of Jihad with mujahidin from the whole Muslim world.

The Ethiopian prime minister said that the Shura Council, which presides over the ICU leadership, has crumpled, adding that the existence of the ICU is no more. "Currently, there are only remnants of the group moving towards the seacoast." Meles reiterated Ethiopia's object is defending the danger posed against it, saying that upon completion of this mission, the Ethiopian army would withdraw from Somalia.

He said the mission will continue until those responsible are put under control. "We are planning to stay there for a month, hopefully it would be completed in days, if not a few weeks at most, but once we have done that we are out of it." "The Ethiopian mission in Somalia is limited and targeted at defending against the attacks of the extremist force on Ethiopia and Somalia. If this is accomplished, Somalis will solve their internal problem."[156].

Meles said his government would provide support to Somalia's Transitional Federal Government (TFG) in the latter's efforts to stabilize the situation in Mogadishu. He said Ethiopia may provide support to help Somalis solve their problems, but he said that what Somalis demand is beyond the capacity of Ethiopia. "Their demand is a huge humanitarian relief assistance and a peacekeeping force."

The risk is that if Ethiopia can't consolidate its military victory to political achievements stabilizing the situation in Ethiopia, Somalia will plunge back into "chaos." In such a "chaotic" situation, the Ethiopian forces will be forced to participate in an endless Somali civil war. But the bigger challenge for Ethiopia is that its army is now facing hostile forces on two fronts: in Somalia and in Eritrea, with whom it fought a war (1998-2000). Ethiopia has accused Eritrea of sending arms and fighters to support the ICU. Many experts expressed the concern that the tension between Ethiopia and Eritrea will escalate into a regional violent conflict.

The Ethiopian government has to take in consideration as well that a big portion of the Ethiopian population is Muslim, and that a violent conflict in Somalia and the tension with their Muslim neighbor, Eritrea, can affect this population. The radicalization of the Muslim population in Ethiopia can turn into a major threat to the stability of Christian-dominated Ethiopia. Ethiopia has inserted itself into a complex conflict with no real plan or road map how to put an end to the inter-Somali conflict.

It seems that the end state of the Ethiopian intervention is to help the TFG to establish a pro-Ethiopian regime that will restore order and peace in Somalia. But the TFG remained as powerless as it has been before the Ethiopian military intervention. "While the joint Ethiopian and TFG forces regained Somalia from the ICU, the TFG troops were no more than passengers on Ethiopian vehicles.[157] There is a risk that the TFG will be unable to govern and that Somalia will return to "chaos."

The "Rise and Fall" of the ICU[158]

- 1991—Somalia descends into civil war between rival clan warlords.
- 1996—Ethiopian forces defeat Islamist fighters (Al Itihad) in the Somali town of Luuq.
- 2004—Long-time Ethiopian ally and warlord, Abdullahi Yusuf becomes Somalia's interim president making Baidoa his base, (TFG).
- June 2006—The Islamic courts take control of the Somali capital, Mogadishu from rival warlords and go on to gain territory in much of central southern parts of Somalia.
- 20 July 2006—A column of Ethiopian trucks, more than 100-strong and including armored cars, cross into Somalia. Ethiopia only admits to having military trainers in the country helping the interim government.
- 21 July 2006—The Islamic court leadership orders a "holy war" against Ethiopian forces in Somalia.
- September 2006—Somalia's interim president, Abdullahi Yusuf (TFG), survives an assassination attempt.
- 25 October 2006—Ethiopian Prime Minister Meles Zenawi says Ethiopia is "technically at war" with the ICU.
- 27 November 2006—The Islamic courts say Ethiopian forces shelled the northern town of Bandiradley and it ambushed an Ethiopian convoy near Baioda.
- 28 November 2006—Eyewitnesses say Islamist fighters ambushed an Ethiopian convoy near Baioda, blowing up a truck. The ICU claim some 20 Ethiopians died.

- 30 November 2006—Ethiopia's parliament passes a resolution authorizing the government to take all legal and necessary steps against what it terms as any invasion by the ICU.
- 3 December 2006—Talks are held between the two sides in Djibouti in an attempt to avert further conflict.
- 8 December 2006—Islamic courts say they have engaged in battle with Ethiopian troops for the first time, southwest of Baidoa.
- 12 December 2006—Islamic courts give Ethiopian troops a one-week ultimatum to leave Somalia or face a "major attack" (holy war).
- 19 December 2006—Deadline for Ethiopian troops to leave Somalia or face a "major attack" expires.
- 24 December 2006—Ethiopia for the first time admits its forces are fighting in Somalia, saying it has launched a "self-defensive" operation against Islamist militiamen. Fighting spreads across a 400-km front along the border.
- 25 December 2006—Ethiopian aircraft bomb Mogadishu airport.
- 26 December 2006—Forces loyal to the transitional government are reported to have taken control of the town of Burkakaba from the ICU. Other areas of southern and central Somalia are also said to have fallen under heavy assault from Somali and Ethiopian troops. Retreating Islamist militias are attacked by Ethiopian jets for a third day.
- 27 December 2006—Ethiopian and TFG troops take control of Jowhar, a strategic town previously held by the Islamists.
- 28 December 2006—Ethiopian-backed TFG forces capture the capital, Mogadishu, hours after Islamist fighters flee the city.
- 1 January 2007—Somali government troops, supported by Ethiopian troops, seize the southern port of Kismayo. The last remaining stronghold.
- 8 January 2007—Ethiopian and TFG forces captured Ras Kamboni. Abdullahi Yusuf the TFG president arrived to Mogadishu.

Notes

1. Somalia's Islamists, Crisis Group, *Africa Report* No. 100, December 12, 2005.
2. Andre Le Sage, "Prospects for Al Itihad and Islamist Radicalism in Somalia," in *Review of African Political Economy*, Vol. 27 No. 89, September 2001.
3. Somalia's Islamists, Crisis Group, *Africa Report* No. 100, December 12, 2005.
4. Ibid.
5. Ibid.
6. Ibid.
7. Ibid.
8. Ibid.
9. Ibid.
10. Rohan Pearce, Somalia: Washington's warlords lose out, Hiraan. Com, News and information about Somalia, July 3, 2006.
11. Ibid.
12. Somali Warlords 'Flee to U S Boat', Al Jazeera.net, June 17, 2006.
13. Somalia: The Challenge of Change, UN Office for Coordination of Humanitarian Affairs, IRINnews.org August 16, 2006.

14. Ibid.
15. Ibid.
16. Ibid.
17. Ibid.
18. Somalia's Islamic militia gets second plane delivery, A.P. Mogadishu, July 28, 2006.
19. Ibid.
20. Somalia: The Challenge of Change, UN Office for Coordination of Humanitarian Affairs, IRINnews.org, August 16, 2006.
21. Ibid.
22. Somali Islamists Refuse Peace Talks, *The New Zealand Herald*, Mogadishu, July 26, 2006.
23. Somalia: Transitional Government, Islamic Courts Agree to Talks, UN Office for the Coordination of Humanitarian Affairs, August 16, 2006.
24. Guled Muhamed, Islamic rebels' advance threatens Somali government, Scotsman. com, August 10, 2006.
25. Ibid.
26. Ibid.
27. Somali Islamists take control of central township, Middle East Online, Mogadishu, August.
28. Abdel Rahaman Yusuf, Somali Courts seizes strategic city, Islam online, Mogadishu, September 25, 2006.
29. Ibid.
30. Muhammad Sheikh, Demonstrations turn violent in Somalia, A.P Mogadishu, ABC News, September 26, 2006.
31. Dahir Farah, Twenty women arrested at protest in Somalia, A.P. Kisamyo, Somalia, September 26, 2006.
32. Somali Islamists in war warning, BBC News, September 26, 2006.
33. Islamists fire on Somali port protesters, ABC online, September 26, 2006.
34. Ibid.
35. Nasteex Dahir Farah, Somalia's Islamic Radicals repel attacks, A.P., Kismayo Somalia, October 14, 2006.
36. Somalia largest mosque opens, Abdirahman Yusuf, Islam online, August 19, 2006.
37. Ibid.
38. Ibid.
39. UN news service, First UN food Agency ship in Mogadishu in more than a decade, New York, September 5, 2006.
40. Somalia: Former Militia Find New Purpose, Mogadishu, UN Office for the Co-ordination of Humanitarian Affairs, IRINnews.org, October 17, 2006.
41. Ibid.
42. Ibid.
43. Muhammad Sheikh Nor, Italian nun shot dead by Somali gunman, A.P, Mogadishu, Somalia, September 17, 2006.
44. Kingdom not funding Islamic Courts, Sultan says, Shabelle Media Network, Mogadishu, July 7, 2006.
45. Ibid.
46. Sungata West, "Mogadishu's Ports to Provide Significant Funding for Somalia's Islamists," *Terrorism Focus*, Volume 3, Issue 28, July 18, 2006.
47. Shabelle Media Network, July 12, 2006.
48. Http:/www.reliefweb.int.
49. Sungata West, "Mogadishu's Ports to Provide Significant Funding for Somalia's Islamists," *Terrorism Focus*, Volume 3, Issue 28, July 18, 2006.

50. Ibid.
51. Ibid.
52. Entire interview with Somali Islamic Court leader Sheikh Sharif, Awdal News Network, Afrol News, June 9, 2006.
53. Khaled Mahmoud, Interview with Head of Somalia's Islamic Courts Organization Sheikh Sharif Ahmad, Asharq al Awsat, Cairo, May 17, 2006.
54. Ibid.
55. Ibid.
56. Entire interview with Somali Islamic court leader Sheikh Sharif, Awdal News Network, Afrol News, June 9, 2006.
57. Somali Net, September 5, 2006.
58. Terrorism Monitor, February 19, 2006.
59. Elizabeth A. Kennedy, A.P, Nairobi, Kenya, Somali Militia Leader Wants Islamic Government, June 26, 2006.
60. BBC News, Ethiopia says Somalia 'a threat', June 26, 2006.
61. Ibid.
62. Ibid.
63. Sunguta West, "New Islamist Leaders Emerge in Somalia," *Terrorist Focus*, Volume 3, Issue 27, July 11, 2006.
64. Ethiopian Reporter, June 17,2005.
65. Sunguta West, "New Islamist Leaders Emerge in Somalia," *Terrorist Focus*, Volume 3, Issue 27, July 11, 2006.
66. Ibid.
67. Jamestown. Org. terrorism news, June 16, 2006.
68. Peter Pham, Sheikh Aweys won't go away (at least by himself) *World Defence Review*, July 06, 2006.
69. Rod Nordland, Africa is Taliban, *Newsweek International*, July 31, 2006.
70. Ibid.
71. Entire interview with Somali Islamic court leader Sheikh Sharif, Awdal News Network, Afrol News, June 9, 2006.
72. Rod Nordland, Africa Taliban, *Newsweek International*, July 31, 2006.
73. Sunguta West, "New Islamist Leaders Emerge in Somalia," *Terrorist Focus*, Volume 3, Issue 27, July 11, 2006.
74. Shabelle Media Network, June 12, 2006.
75. Mohomed Olad Hassn, Defections from Somalia's western-backed interim government continue, Canadian press, Canada.com, July 27, 2006.
76. Ibid.
77. Somali Leader accuses Iran, Libya and Egypt of supporting Islamic militants, A.P. Baidoa, July 29, 2006.
78. Somali lawmaker fatally shot outside mosque, A.P. Baidoa, BostonHerald.com, July 28, 2006.
79. Ibid.
80. Ethiopia, Somalia: Stalemate at Baidoa, Stratfor, July 20, 2006.
81. Ibid.
82. Somali Leader survives bomb blast, BBC News, September 18, 2006.
83. Ibid.
84. Ibid.
85. Somali president describes attack, BBC News, September 19, 2006.
86. Ibid.
87. U.S., Eritrea arming Somali Islamists, Al Jazeera.net, October 19, 2006.
88. Salad Duhul, Three suicide car bombs kill eight in Somalia, A.P, November 30, 2006.

89. Ibid.
90. Ibid.
91. Awdal News Network, Somali Islamists swear to "Spread Islam worldwide," October 9, 2006.
92. Awdal News Network, Afrol News, Suicide bombers heading for Somaliland, October 17, 2006.
93. Aweys Osman Yusuf, Somalia fierce fighting takes place between Islamists and Puntland forces, Mogadishu, Shabelle Media Network, November 6, 2006.
94. Ibid.
95. Ibid.
96. Awdal News Network, Afrol News, Suicide bombers heading for Somaliland, October 17, 2006.
97. Ibid.
98. *Political Economy*, Volume 27, No. 89, September 2001.
99. Somalia's Islamists, Crisis Group, Africa Report 100, December 12, 2005.
100. Ibid.
101. Ibid.
102. "Somali Islamists refuse peace talks," *The New Zealand Herald*. July 26, 2006.
103. Ibid.
104. Ibid.
105. Awdal News Network/Afrol News, Islamists burn Somaliland newspaper, October 16, 2006.
106. Ibid.
107. Awdal News Network, Afrol News, Suicide bombers heading for Somaliland, October 17, 2006.
108. Somalia Islamic leader orders holy war against Ethiopia, A.P Baidoa, July 21, 2006.
109. Ibid.
110. Ethiopia, Somalia: Stalemate of Baidoa, *Strafor*, July 20, 2006.
111. Muhammad Sheikh Nor, Arms flown in for Islamic militants-Somalia, A.P Mogadishu, July 27, 2006.
112. U.S., Eritrea arming Somali Islamists, Al Jazeera.net, October 19, 2006.
113. Ibid.
114. Ibid.
115. Somalia warning for Horn rival, BBC News, July 27, 2006.
116. Ibid.
117. Ibid.
118. Muhammad Sheikh Nor, Somalia's voice opposition to peacekeeping force, Mogadishu, Guardian online, September 6, 2006.
119. Rob Crilly, I'm prepared to talk peace, says leader of Somalia's Shark Corts, Mogadishu, Times online, September 1, 2006.
120. Ibid.
121. Wangui Kanina, African leaders discuss Somalia military part, Results, Nairobi, September 5, 2006.
122. Ibid.
123. Ibid.
124. Ibid.
125. Salad Duhal, Somalia militia to train students for holy war, A.P in the *Seattle Times*, September 20, 2006.
126. Subdel Rahaman, Yusuf, Somali Courts Seize strategic city, IRIN news, September 25, 2006.

127. Islamist Claim Ethiopia shelling Somali town, Guardian online, Mogadishu, October 5, 2006.
128. Ibid.
129. Ibid.
130. Les Neuhaus, A.P, Addis Ababa, Ethiopia, military trainers sent to Somalia, October 19, 2006.
131. Ibid.
132. Ibid.
133. Ibid.
134. Sahal Abdulle, Islamic militias threaten war on Ethiopia, Mogadishu, Scotsman.com News, December 13, 2006.
135. Ibid.
136. Ibid.
137. Ibid.
138. Al Jazeera, Somalia bracing for war, December 26, 2006.
139. Clashes between Somalia Islamists, government spread new fronts, bandir.com, December 26, 2006.
140. United Nations Issues call for peace during lull in Somalia's fighting, Mogadishu, A.P, December 26, 2006.
141. Salad Duhul, Ethiopia bombs Mogadishu airport, A.P, Mogadishu, December 26, 2006.
142. Les Nevahus, Somalia's PM promises peace, A.P, Mogadishu, December 29, 2006.
143. Ibid.
144. Ibid.
145. Ibid.
146. Somalia: Mogadishu in chaos as Islamic militia leave, IRIN news.com, Nairobi, December 28, 2006.
147. Ethio.com, Ethiopian troops head southwards, December 30, 2006.
148. Somalis claims control of all Islamist-held territories, AFP, Baidoa, in Khaleey Times online, January 2, 2007.
149. Artillery rains down on Somali Islamists, Reuters, in Ethio.com, December 31, 2006.
150. Ibid.
151. Martin Plaut, Ethiopian army forces Somali test, BBC News, December 25, 2006.
152. Ibid.
153. Ethiopian PM denies U.S. involvement in Ethiopia's counterattack, Ethio.com, December 28, 2006.
154. Ibid.
155. Ibid.
156. Ibid.
157. Matt Bryden, International Crisis Group. In Tia Goldberg, Somalia's stability lies in Ethiopia's hands, Africa. Txt, December 28, 2006.
158. BBC News, Timeline: Ethiopia and Somalia, January 10, 2007.

7

Is the Islamic Courts the New Taliban?

Many experts and politicians expressed their concern that Somalia would become the "Afghanistan of Africa" with a Taliban-style Islamic radical regime. Indeed, we can find many similarities between Somalia in 2006 and Afghanistan in 1996, in spite of all the geopolitical and cultural differences between them. In the following part a comparative study will analyze the parallels and the differences between the phenomenon of the Taliban in Afghanistan and the Islamic courts in Somalia.

The Taliban and the Road to Power[1]

The Taliban movement began its political and military activity in the city of Kandahar in southern Afghanistan. There are a number of reasons why Kandahar was selected as the starting point for building up the movement's power and strength: First, Kandahar is the birthplace of Mullah Omar, founder and leader of the movement. Second, Kandahar is a city with religious significance for Muslims (since 1751).

The movement took control of Kandahar via political moves that resulted in some of the local militia commanders joining the movement, and quick military strikes that resulted in the surrender of militia commanders who resisted. From the beginning, the movement learned to employ unusual means, including an extensive publicity campaign warning that harm to the Taliban—who were described as religious figures—was tantamount to harm to Islam. The movement also learned to play the divisions and rivalries between factions in the various Mujahidin movements and military militias in order to recruit some of them to its ranks and create preferential power relations that would make it relatively easy to quash the remaining pockets of resistance.

Kandahar became, therefore, the Taliban's main area of power and influence. From there, the movement spread to other parts of the country.

In a short period of time, the Taliban succeeded in enforcing Islamic law in Kandahar and reinstating order and security for a population that had suffered from a lack of law and order for almost twenty years. The Taliban's success in Kandahar led to many Pashtuns in the south joining its ranks because they saw in the Taliban the hope for a normal way of life and ending the country's civil war and anarchy.

In the first months after its establishment, the Taliban's main efforts focused on securing influence and control over the Pashtun population. For this reason the Taliban first undertook a struggle against Hekmatyar's movement which, until the appearance of the Taliban, had been the major political and military leader among the Pashtun population.

In 1994 Hekmatyar was embroiled in fierce battles against Rabbani's regime (the ruler of Afghanistan) and was also at odds with most of the leaders and commanders of the other Mujahidin movements. The Taliban took advantage of Hekmatyar's weakness and occupation with the struggle against Rabbani's government. Within a few months (October 1994-February 1995), the Taliban conquered most of Hekmatyar's strongholds in the south of the country and around Kabul.

During these months Rabbani's government encouraged the Taliban's activities and saw it as an ally in the confrontation with Hekmatyar and the Shiite Hizb-e-Wahadat. In battles around Kabul in February 1995, the forces of Rabbani's government took advantage of the military pressure the Taliban was putting on Hekmatyar from the south and conquered most of his strongholds around Kabul. But the alliance between the Rabbani government and the Taliban was short-lived. As early as March 1995 the minister of defense, Sheikh Masoud, and President Rabbani understood, perhaps too late, that they themselves had created an incalculable threat against their rule by helping the Taliban gain victory and advance toward Kabul.

On March 9, 1995, after Hekmatyar's forces around Kabul had been defeated, the Taliban reached an agreement with the siite Hizb-e-Wahadat, which resulted in the retreat of the Shiites and transfer of their positions around Kabul to the Taliban. At this stage it was clear to the Rabbani government that the Taliban was threatening Kabul directly. Therefore on March 10, 1995 their forces launched an extensive attack which forced the Taliban to retreat from the Kabul area.

The government forces' attack on the Taliban led to the latter's first defeat on the battlefield since the beginning of its campaign in October 1994, and was a turning point in the Afghan civil war. From March 1995 on, most of the struggle took place between the Taliban and the Rabbani government, with other militias becoming pawns of these two in the struggle for control of Afghanistan.

In the ensuing months (March-September 1995) the Taliban continued to fight government forces, especially around Kabul, while the government was also facing the forces of the Shiite Hizb-e-Wahadat, Dostum's Uzbeki militias and Hekmatyar on other fronts, mainly in the north and west of Afghanistan.

A significant development took place on September 5, 1995, when the Taliban conquered the important provincial city of Herat from Ismail Khan, an ally of the Rabbani government. Conquest of this city, mainly inhabited by Tajikis and Shiites, heightened the ethnic aspect of the struggle between the Pashtun Taliban and the Shiite and Tajiki minorities in Afghanistan.

On September 13, 1995 the Rabbani government initiated mass demonstrations outside Pakistan's embassy in Kabul and publicly blamed Pakistan for involvement in Afghanistan's internal affairs via its protégé, the Taliban. A formal rift was thus created between the Rabbani government and the Pakistan government which, despite its official denial of connections with the Taliban, continued to support the movement through financial and military aid. The success of the Taliban movement led to the end of Pakistan's support for Hekmatyar's movement. His political and military isolation caused him to try to temporarily improve his relations with the Rabbani government and from a coalition with the Hizb-e-Wahadat and Dostum the Uzbeki.

In October 1995, encouraged by their victory in Herat, the Taliban decided for the second time to conquer Kabul. They were forced, however, to conquer a number of strategic areas around the city. Their attempts to penetrate the suburbs of Kabul were rebuffed by the Rabbani government forces. In the months that followed, static fighting around Kabul and in other parts of the country continued with no significant progress made by the Taliban.

During this time the movement cemented its control in the regions it had captured, with Kandahar serving as the movement's center of control and influence. In April 1996, 1000 senior religious leaders from throughout Afghanistan met and elected the leader of the Taliban, Mullah Omar, the Emir of the Believers, and divested Rabbani and his government of their religious authority.

The declaration of Muhammad Omar as Emir of the Believers was an important milestone in consolidation of the Taliban movement and its leader's status as a political religious entity supported by the Sunni religious establishment, which is very influential in Afghan society. The Taliban continued to secure its control in regions that covered close to two-thirds of the territory of Afghanistan while the Rabbani government's dominance was in practice limited to Kabul and part of the northern provinces inhabited by Tajikis.

The Taliban simultaneously continued to build their military strength in preparation for a decisive attack on the forces of the Rabbani government which began in September 1996. On September 11, 1996, the Taliban launched an extensive battle in eastern Afghanistan, conquering two provinces that the government had held, as well as the important city of Jalalabad, thus opening an important logistical artery along the Pakistani border. After the conquest of Jalalabad, the thrust of the Taliban's offensive was transferred to Kabul and Taliban forces began to effect a closure and siege of the city.

On the night of September 26, 1996, the Rabbani government and the forces it commanded (mainly Sheikh Masoud, the Tajiki minister of defense's forces) left Kabul and retreated northward to Tajiki populated areas that were controlled by forces loyal to Sheikh Masoud. On September 27, 1996, the Taliban forces entered Kabul with almost no resistance, took control of the city and seized control of Afghanistan.

The Rabbani government claimed that this was a temporary tactical retreat to prevent unnecessary civilian casualties in Kabul and that it remained the legal government of Afghanistan. In practice, however, the government had lost all its power and command of the country. The Taliban quickly established a governing council which reigned over most of the Afghan territory and population.

The fall of Kabul into the hands of the Taliban did not bring the end of the civil war. A short time after retreating from Kabul, the Tajikis, Rabbani and Masoud, established a coalition with General Dostum, the Uzbeki, and the Shiite Hizb-e-Wahadat and continued the struggle against the Taliban.

The coalition had the support of Iran, Russia, and the Muslim republics on the Afghan border (Turkmenistan, Uzbekistan, and Tajikistan), which viewed the Taliban victory as a threat to their interests and the ethnic groups affiliated with them. The fall of the Rabbani government and the Taliban takeover of Kabul gave the civil war in Afghanistan an overt ethnic and religious flavor, with the Taliban representing the Sunni Pashtun majority against the ethnic Sunni minorities of Tajikis and Uzbeki and the Shiite Hizb-e-Wahadat.

In late 1996 the Taliban tried to take political steps intended to split the opposition and draw in the Uzbeki General Dostum, whose opportunistic approach was apparent throughout the civil war, temporarily to their side. When these attempts failed, the Taliban launched a renewed military attack to conquer the rest of the country from the hands of the opposition.

In January 1997 the Taliban conquered the important airport in Bagram, north of Kabul, but their attempts to progress further north into the Panjshir Valley, the power center of the Tajiki Sheikh Masoud, failed. In May 1997 the Taliban launched an attack to conquer the provincial city of Mazar-e-Sharif, the main stronghold of Uzbeki and Shiite forces in the north. The Taliban took advantage of internal power struggles in the Uzbeki camp between General Dostum and his deputy, General Malik, who along with his forces defected to the Taliban side, forcing General Dostum to flee by air to Turkey. Through this unholy alliance the Taliban conquered Mazar-e-Sharif.

But the alliance was short-lived. When General Malik discovered that the Taliban intended to divest the militias in the city of their arms, he launched a surprise attack on the Taliban, killing thousands and taking many captive. Malik's betrayal cost the Taliban one of their most severe defeats (the bodies of some 3,000 Taliban warriors were found in the Mazar-e-Sharif area and hundreds of commanders and soldiers were taken captive by the Uzbekis) and the thwarting of a move which might have isolated Rabbani and Masoud in the struggle against the Taliban. After the failure at Mazar-e-Sharif, fighting between the Taliban and the opposition continued on the northern fronts, but with neither side able to achieve a decisive outcome.

In October 1997 the Taliban tried a second time to conquer Mazar-e-Sharif, but Uzbeki forces under General Malik managed to hold off the attack. This time it was General Dostum who grabbed the opportunity. While General Malik was busy rebuffing the Taliban, he returned to Afghanistan. Within a day, the forces loyal to him ousted General Malik and reinstated his control over most of the Uzbeki areas in the country. (The political system of the Uzbeki minority will be elaborated upon below.)

Since October 1997 the Taliban and opposition forces have been fighting on various fronts is the north of the country with no military decision in sight, especially because of massive military aid that Iran provided to Shiite and Uzbeki forces. Nevertheless, Mazar-e-Sharif was finally conquered by the Taliban in August 1998.

Opposition elements also waged terror against the Taliban regime. On August 25, 1999, there was an attempted assassination of leader Mullah Mohammed Omar, when his vehicle arrived at Kandahar (the Taliban's center of power) after a visit to Herat. An explosive device exploded near his car, injuring him lightly and killing six of his bodyguards.

At the same time, efforts were made with no success by various parties to reach an agreement that would bring about the end of the civil war in Afghanistan. The Taliban regime came to its end in Operation Enduring Freedom, conducted by the American coalition after the 9/11 attacks.

The Rise of the Islamic Courts in Somalia

Since the fall of General Ziad Barre's regime in 1991, Somalia has been a "chaotic" fragmented state. Carved up by warlords and clan-based militias, it lacks an effective central government. All the attempts to restore statehood through internationally brokered national governments failed to bring order or stem the violence. The Barre regime had suppressed the political movements for over twenty years. In the political vacuum and power struggles after Barre's fall, militant Islamic movements resurfaced with a vengeance, providing an alternative to the government ranging from commerce to the judiciary. Islamic leaders had first earned legitimacy effectively administering court functions in lawless areas. Mogadishu-based courts also kept militias and have since been major players in internecine fighting.[2]

After a successful campaign in 2006 against the pro-U.S. warlords in Mogadishu, the Islamic Courts now have direct control of Mogadishu's sixteen districts and Somalia's heartland. New Islamic courts had been established in areas under the formal control of the internationally backed TFG. Despite inner wrangling for power, the Union of Islamic Courts has talked with one voice to the international community and in negotiations with the TFG.

Unlike the warlords, the Islamic militia seems to enjoy popularity by offering the prospect of peace after relentless bloodshed; the Islamic movement gains much of its legitimacy also from its anti-American stance.[3] Somalia in (2006) was very much like Afghanistan was in 1996. In the wake of years of civil war, chaotic rule by warlords, and the death and displacement of countless Muslims, a ragtag Islamic militia has moved in to take control of much of Somalia.[4]

After running off some prominent warlords from their entrenched stronghold, the Islamic militia has sought to establish and expand its writ and has threatened to dislodge an internationally backed transitional government made up of veteran warlords with limited authority (TFG).

Businessmen, clan leaders, and the general public, having tired of seemingly interminable factional violence and lawlessness, have lent support to the al-Qaida-aligned, fiercely anti-American Islamic militia, which draws legitimacy from its plans to restore peace and order. The militia has purported to do so by enforcing a court system based on an ultra-orthodox version of the Sharia (Islamic law) and tribal social norms.[5]

The parallels between the predicaments of Somalia in 2006 and Afghanistan in 1996 were striking.[6] In the early days of their rule, Somalia's Islamic Courts Union (ICU) started to operate like Afghanistan's Taliban.[7] Like the Taliban, the Islamic Courts came to power ending an extended period of violent uncertainty. Those who had managed to survive years of insecurity, poverty, hunger and fighting between clans and warlords in either country were ready to welcome any group offering an alternative to instability.[8]

This time (2006), however, the fighting was brief, and by Somali standards relatively bloodless (400 died). Afterward, for the first time, the warlords were chased from Mogadishu. Sheikh Ahmad has warned gunmen aligned with warlords that "any groups that tries to fight the Islamic Courts will be destroyed. The Islamic Courts have overcome the infidel stooges." A visitor in Mogadishu was able to spend five days in the capital without hearing a single gunshot or negotiating a militia roadblock (there used to be 10 just on the road to the airport).[9] The Islamic Courts Union (ICU), has collected the militiamen's guns and rounded up their "technicals" (jeeps with machine guns mounted in the back). "In 15 years, no one was able to do what they did in 15 days," says UN official Saverio Bertolino.[10]

Instead of the rule of warlords, Somalis now have what many are calling an African version of the Taliban, bent not only on imposing a harsh, Wahhabi-style Islam on the country, but allegedly also providing a safe haven for international terrorists.[11]

The ICU militias, like those of the Taliban before them, were reinforced by foreign jihadis, and foreign terrorists have found refuge in Somalia. For example, three foreign Al Qaida leaders indicted for the 1998 bombings of the U.S. embassies in Kenya and Tanzania and who are believed to also be involved the 2002 suicide bombing of an Israeli-owned hotel in Mombasa, Kenya—Fazul Abdullah Muhammad of Comoros, who figures on the FBI's "Most Wanted Terrorists" list with $5 million bounty on his head; Saleh Ali Saleh Nabhan of Kenya; and Abu Taha al-Sudani—are being sheltered in Mogadishu by Somali Islamists.[12]

The movement has appointed a majlis al-shura (consultative council) to be its supreme spiritual and policy-setting body and appointed as its leader Sheik Hassan Dahir Aweys, who is on the U.S. terrorist watch list for his connection to Al-Itihad al-Islamiya (AIAI). In an interview with Aweys praised Osama Bin Laden, likening him to Nelson Mandela, and tried to justify Al Qaida's attack on the World Trade Center.[13] "Since Osama was fighting against his enemy, he could use any tactic he had available to him."[14]

Somalia's Islamic Courts, like the Taliban in Afghanistan, claimed that their goals were to restore peace, order, and stability and to establish an Islamic regime in Somalia. The Islamic Courts began introducing Sharia law in areas under their control, including bans on cinemas in many locations, and on broadcasting the World Cup because it carried alcohol advertisements.

On June 2006 Islamists opened fire on a crowd in a cinema watching the Italy-Germany World Cup football match, resulting in two killed and others wounded.[15] The gunmen purportedly were members of the Islamic militia controlled by the Union of Islamic Courts. Their action was seen by some as a worrisome indication that radicalized Islamic elements could try to impose their fundamentalist views on Somali society. (Public floggings of individuals convicted of minor crimes by Islamic courts have reportedly already taken place.[16]) There have been reports of radical Islamists ordering men to grow beards in accordance with their puritanical interpretation of the Koran.

Despite warnings that the Islamic Courts intend to turn Somalia into a hard-line Islamic nation, its ostensible chairman, Sheikh Sharif Sheikh Ahmad, insisted they had no intention of imposing a Taliban-style Islamic state.[17] However, the appointment of Sheikh Aweys reignited fears concerning the potential radicalization of Somalia, especially his demand that "any government we agree on would be based on the holy Quran," a position at variance with the UN-backed transitional president, Abdullahi Yusuf, who previously fought Aweys's Islamic radicals in his Puntland stronghold, (when he was one of the heads of AIAI).

In contrast to the widely detested warlords, the Islamic Courts portray themselves as based on the Quran, with no clan affiliation. (However, most of the 11 courts established in Mogadishu reportedly were connected with the powerful Hawiye clan.) Interestingly, like the Taliban, Somali Islamists originally received backing from local merchants desirous of ending violence in their country. Funds from Saudi Arabia, Yemen, Gulf states and Eritrea sources reportedly were behind their military successes.[18]

The warlords insist the Islamists harbor al-Qaida supporters and would turn the country into a haven for Islamic radicals. While the warlords have lost their main urban power base, paradoxically some of them have joined the TFG. Traditionally, the Somalis and the Afghans have embraced a moderate form of Islam, but decades of civil war and external Islamic influences, made the populace more radical.

On October 9, 2006, Sheikh Sharif Sheikh Ahmad and Colonel Yusuf Muhammad Siyyad, head of the ICU's security apparatus, said that their rapid victory in capturing large parts of Somalia was "a gift from God" and that they aspired to spread their message worldwide once Somalia was secure in their grip.[19] This was the first time that the ICU, had spelled out their agenda to export their revolution to other countries.

After many years of lawlessness and the rule of corrupt warlords, many Afghans and Somalis have found their religion as a shelter and a source of hope. Fundamentalist Islamic beliefs are gaining power in Somalia today, like in Afghanistan. The Islamic courts are an "umbrella organization" of all kinds and trends of believers, including extremists and militants who have previous links to Al Qaida and that are ready to assist international Islamic terrorists.

The Fall of the Islamic Courts Union

ICU rule in Somalia was short. In January 2007, about a half year after their victory over the warlords of Mogadishu, it came to an end. In a short military campaign (two weeks) a coalition of Ethiopian and TFG forces with U.S. tacit approval, defeated the ICU militias. Like in the Afghanistan case, the ICU was blamed for supporting Al Qaida, and their involvement in terrorism justified external military intervention.

In Afghanistan in 2002, a coalition led by the United States, with the local militias of the "Northern Alliance," defeated the Taliban regime, Al Qaida, and other Islamic organizations that found shelter there. In Somalia, it was again a U.S.-backed coalition of Ethiopian forces, with the local TFG forces, that fought successfully and defeated the ICU. At the end of the U.S. campaign in Afghanistan (2002), the Taliban and Al Qaida leaders escaped and their whereabouts are still unknown. The same has happened in Somalia.

The whereabouts of Hassan Dahir Aweys, the leader of the Islamic Courts, are still unknown. Fazul Abdullah Mohammed, Saleh Ali Saleh

The Taliban and the Islamic Courts

Topic	Afghanistan	Somalia
Religion	Islam (Sunni majority, Shia minority)	Islam–Sunni
Society	Fragmented society, by ethnic and tribal background	Fragmented society, by tribal background
Regime	Communist military dictatorship (1978–1992)	Military dictatorship of Ziad Barre (1963–1991)
Civil war	Communist regime against Islamic movement (mujahidin) (1979–1992)	Civil war between rival warlords and tribes since 1991
External involvement — Super Powers	The Soviet Union invaded Afghanistan and supported the communist regime against the mujahidin (1979–1989)	UN forces in Operation Restore Hope, mainly American forces. Clashed with different warlords (1992–1993)
Radical Islam Movements	The phenomenon of the global jihad – volunteers who came to support the Afghan mujahidin	Al Qaida supported local warlords fighting the UN/U.S. forces. (Black Hawk Down).
Neighboring countries	Pakistan and Iran supported the mujahidin	Sudan and Iran supported the warlords against the UN/U.S. forces
The result of the war – who win?	Victory of the mujahidin, the end of the communist regime. The mujahidin regime of Rabbani. The phenomenon of Al Qaida and the "Afghan alumni"	The withdrawal of the UN/U.S. forces from Somalia
The stability of the new regime	Ongoing civil war between rival mujahidin movements, a failing state	Ongoing civil war between rival warlords, a failing state
The fundamentalist alternative	The Taliban movement (1994)	The Islamic courts (2000)
The Islamic school	Deobandi	Wahabbi/Salafi
External Support	Pakistan, Saudi Arabia	Eritrea, Yemen, Saudi Arabia
Main stages in the conflict	Defeating: -Local Warlords -Hekmatyar mujahidin -The Rabbani regime	Defeating: Local Warlords Confrontations with the TFG
The "End State"	Islamic state ruled according to Sharia	Islamic state ruled according to Sharia
The collapse of the regime	Defeated by U.S. led coalition and the forces of the Northern Alliance, 2002.	Defeated by Ethiopian and TFG forces December 2006.

Nabhan and Abu Taha al-Sudani, three known terrorists behind the 1998 bombings of the U.S. embassies in Kenya and Tanzania being sheltered by the Islamic Courts, are still missing. Sheikh Sharif Sheikh Ahmad, Sheikh Hassan Turki, Aden Hashi, Yusuf Indaha'adde, and others involved with al-Qaida, the Islamic Courts, and training foreign fighters are on the run.

In Afghanistan, the Taliban and its allies are conducting an ongoing guerilla war against the Kharzai regime and the coalition forces. In spite of the coalition efforts, the Taliban is gaining power and on the 5th anniversary of the 9/11 attacks, Ayman al Zawaheiri, Bin Laden's deputy, declared in a audio tape that he believes that the coalition forces in Afghanistan and Iraq were already defeated by the Mujahidin.

The Islamic Courts leaders have repeatedly stated that they would start an insurgency. Shortly after the outbreak of the war with the TFG and the Ethiopian forces, the ICU's defense chief, Yusuf Indaha'adde, called on Muslim mujahidin from all over the world to join the jihad (holy war) in Somalia against the Ethiopian forces. The ICU's call for jihad demonstrates the global nature of the conflict in Somalia.

On January 5, 2007 Ayman Zawaheiri, on an audiotape urged Somali Islamists to launch an Iraq-style guerilla campaign of suicide and other forms of attacks against the Ethiopian forces in Somaila.[20] The military victory of Coalition forces, both in Afghanistan and Somalia, is not the end of the state of war in both countries, nor the end of the radical Islamic threat, but the starting point of an endless violent confrontation against the local and foreign Mujahidin that turns Afghanistan and Somalia into theaters of Jihad.

Notes

1. Shaul Shay, *The Endless Jihad*, Mifalot Publishers, Herzliya, Israel, 2002, pp. 76-80.
2. Nayum Myushtaq, "A New Frontier of Jihadi Islam?," *Mother Jones*, July 24, 2006.
3. Ibid.
4. Koert Lindiyer, Somalia, the new Afghanistan, www.radionetherlands.ni, June 6, 2006.
5. Ibid.
6. Ibid.
7. Sean Sinclair-Day, Islamic Courts Resemble Taliban, *African Affairs*, June 30, 2006.
8. Ibid.
9. Rob Nordland, "Africa's Taliban," *Newsweek* International, July 31, 2006.
10. Ibid.
11. Ibid.

12. Peter Pham, "Sheikh Aweys won't go away (at least by himself)," *World Defence Review*, July 06, 2006.
13. Ibid.
14. Ibid.
15. Harry Sterling, "Somalia could be the next Afghanistan," Canada.com, July 14, 2006.
16. Ibid.
17. Ibid.
18. Al Qaida urges Somali Islamists to attack Ethiopia, SABCnews.com, January 5, 2007. See also: Aljazeera.net, Al Qaida issues message on Somalia, January 5, 2007.
19. Ibid.
20. Somali Islamists swear to "spread Islam worldwide" Awdal News Network, Afrol News, October 9, 2006.

8

Intercultural Conflicts, "Failing States," and Al-Qaida—Reciprocal Links [1]

This chapter assesses the joint characteristics that arose from the analysis of the philosophical and conceptual aspects of conflict. The objective of this study is to explore the links and reciprocal relationships between the three phenomena or processes specified below:

1. The intercultural conflict between the state-oriented culture and the nomadic culture;
2. The intercultural conflict between radical Islam and other cultures, particularly the Western culture;
3. The link and connection between the intercultural conflicts and the creation and existence of the phenomena of "failing states" and "ungovernable regions" (UGRs).

At the center of this discussion stands Al-Qaida—which according to the study's claim represents both the nomadic culture and radical Islam—and the reciprocal relationships between radical Islam and "failing states" and UGRs.

"Failing States" and "Ungovernable Regions" [2]

Failing states and ungovernable regions (UGRs) have become current issues on the agendas of politicians, military personnel, and academia in the West, due the crystallization of the understanding that these states and regions have turned into a significant threat to the security and interests of the West. Two central threats have positioned these phenomena at the center of international interest:

- International terror
- International crime

141

Figure 1
Al-Qaida: The Clash among Cultures and the Failed "States"

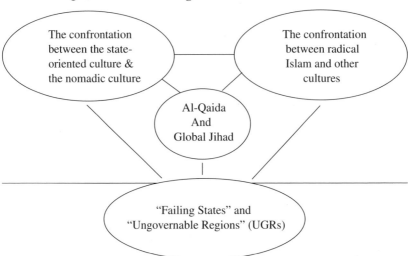

The reality of the twenty-first century has taught us that these two non state-oriented elements—international terror and crime—have turned failing states and UGRs into havens and activity bases from which they can promote their interests regionally and globally.

During the years of the hegemony of the national-countries, states developed political, military, and economic patterns that were relevant and effective for contact between states and state blocs in the international framework. However, the international terror organizations and the criminal organizations posed new challenges to the national-countries and served as a provocation against the main component of the state-oriented entity—the monopoly over the use of force.

International terror and crime act as networks with global dispersion, while the failing states and UGRs constitute the main infrastructure focal points and bases for action. Due to the lack of an effective central government in these places, the organizations' activities are unrestricted and they also receive support and protection from powerbrokers and local interested parties with whom they form alliances and ties.

International terror and criminal organizations do not view territory as an asset of moral significance, but rather as a basis which may be temporary and can be swapped with other territories according to evolving circumstances. To a large extent it is possible to define these organizations as entities with a "nomadic" worldview, which clearly challenge the state-oriented entity and its values.

As stated earlier, the area of the failing state or the UGR serves as a refuge for criminal and terror organizations, however, sometimes it also serves as an arena of confrontation and rivalry vis-à-vis "alien" state-oriented entities acting in the same arena or as a base for attacking neighboring countries.

The provision of solutions by Western countries to these challenges necessitates confrontation on two levels:

1. Confronting the terror or criminal organization;
2. Confronting the regime or powerbrokers that offer refuge to these entities.

The provision of an adequate response necessitates the handling of both levels simultaneously as well as preparation for confronting the regional and global alignment of these organizations, which exceeds the boundaries of the failing state or of the UGR.

Failing States

Failing states stem from the collapse of the governmental and political structure in the country and the loss of the state's ability to enforce law and order. The process is initiated and accompanied by manifestations of anarchy and forms of violence.

The term of "failing state" has different degrees and many definitions. I chose for this study the following one:[3]

A failing state is one in which the government does not have effective control of its territory, is not perceived as legitimate by a significant portion of its population, does not provide domestic security or basic public services to its citizens, and lacks a monopoly on the use of force. A failing state may experience active violence or simply be vulnerable to violence.

Symptoms of state failure can appear in any country in any region of the world, but there are several neighborhoods with concentrations of weak states. Africa produces the largest number of unstable states.[4]

Boutros Boutros-Ghali, the former United Nations secretary-general, described this phenomenon as follows:[5]

A feature of such conflicts is the collapse of state institutions, especially the police and the judiciary, with resulting paralysis of governance, a breakdown of law and order, and general banditry and chaos. Not only are the functions of the government suspended, but its assets are destroyed or looted and experienced officials are killed or flee the country. This is rarely the case in inter state wars. It means that international intervention must extend beyond military and humanitarian tasks and must include the reestablishment of effective government.

The state not only lacks an effective government, but also the situation includes the collapse of the systems that compose the state entity. Therefore, the term "failing states" actually refers to countries that have disintegrated. The term failing state addresses a relatively wide range of situations and serves as the starting point for various interpretations vis-à-vis the phenomenon (legal, political, sociological, etc.). The main political and judicial aspects characteristic of a failing state are:

- The collapse of the government systems, i.e., disintegration of the central government and the other mechanisms that compose the state institutions (the judicial system, law enforcement authorities, the economic system and more), and disintegration processes according to segmentation and cross-sectioning that characterize the society and its political system (interest groups, ethnic and religious groups, etc.), that generate internal conflicts within the country's territorial boundaries;
- The collapse of lawful government, meaning not only disintegration processes, but also disobeying laws and lack of ability to enforce them;
- Loss of the ability to represent the state as a uniform entity within the international system for the purpose of presenting its positions and negotiating with external states and entities.

From the sociological aspect, the failing state is characterized by what the sociologist Max Weber calls "loss of the monopoly over power."[6] In this type of reality, the legal system, the police, and other entities that serve the role of maintaining law and order stop functioning or cease to exist. These entities may join various armed groups or criminal elements that take over the state infrastructures and resources for their own needs and establish a "government" of their own within various regions and populations in the state. This process may be described as a kind of "privatization" of the state, or in certain cases—as criminalization. In this type of situation the state ceases to exist and society reverts to a status of pre-state chaos.

Another central sociological characteristic of a failing state is the brutality and intensity of violence within the society. To quote Arnold Gehlen:

The immediate effect is that the persons concerned become profoundly insecure. The moral and spiritual centers are disoriented because, there too, the certainty of self-evident has foundered. Thus, penetrating to the very core of their being, insecurity forces people to improvise, compelling them to make decisions contre coeur or to plunge blindfolded into the realms of uncertainty, perhaps seeking at any price fundamentals to cling to and give them a sense of purpose. In practice, moreover, insecurity is manifested in the form of fear, defiance or volatility. The effect is to place a heavy burden of control and decision-making on those layers of the personality where life should be lived problem-free amidst the self-evident and the given if people are to be capable of dealing with more demanding situations. In other words, displacement that people suffer due to the shattering of their institutions is expressed as primitivization.[7]

From a legal point of view, it is possible to claim that a failing state is an entity defined as a "state" but in practical terms lacks the ability to function as a state entity. A central component of this phenomenon is the lack of a functionary capable of signing agreements with external factors or of actually implementing them.

The examination of a failing state indicates a similarity in their historical development:

- Colonial occupation that destroyed the traditional social and political structures, but failed to incorporate an effective structural and political alternative according to the Western model.
- The "cold war" inspired the superpowers to support and reinforce corrupt and ineffective regimes due to considerations related to loyalty within the inter-bloc struggle. After the collapse of the Soviet Union and the end of the "cold war," many of these regimes crumbled, leaving political and social chaos in their wake.
- Modernization processes that encouraged geopolitical and social mobility but were not balanced by the building processes of the nation and the nation state.

Although today the number of failing states is relatively low, some of the countries that were granted independence after the collapse of the Soviet Union are gradually joining this category, so there is a fear that this is not simply a marginal phenomenon but rather a "pathological" trend of a changing environment and international system.

Robert Bunker[8] points out a cyclical process in human history of order and chaos that alternate with each other. He claims that the process of institutionalizing nation states and enhancing law and order in Western states began with the Westphalia peace compact (in 1648), while the current era is characterized by a change in direction from order to chaos, an era that challenges the nation state as a regulator of social order.

Historical experience indicates that when the internal violence in a nation state, which can be described as criminal activity or "a private war," grows to a level that threatens the population of the nation state, this entity may collapse if it does not succeed in suppressing the anarchy.[9] The international reality in the current century points to a decline in the status of the nation-state's status as an entity that regulates and organizes social and political systems in parts of Africa, South America, Asia, and areas that were part of the Soviet Union.[10]

Bunker maintains that the threat against the nation state will rise from non-state actors:[11] "The challenge to the legitimacy of the nation state will come from armed non-state actors intent on legitimizing forms of behavior that current societies consider to be criminally or morally corrupt." Based on historical experience, Bunker claims that entities currently defined as criminal and non-legitimate elements according to our normative standards may triumph in the struggle with the state entity and form political entities which in time will constitute a substitute for today's normative systems and ultimately replace them and gain legitimacy.[12]

As the result of the social and political processes described above, the nature of the confrontation also changes. The declared wars between the military forces of the nation state steadily decrease, and we witness the development of new forms of war.

In his article "Privatization of War in the Twenty-First Century," Herfried Muenkler argues that in the fifties and sixties of the twentieth century many new nations joined the international system that did not succeed in obtaining control when managing war and imposing peace, as European states have achieved since the seventeenth century. Thus, internal conflict (civil wars) became a characteristic trait of countries that were established on the ruins of colonial powers, not only in the Third World (like in Somalia), but also in Europe itself (the Balkans).

Thus, it is possible to infer that war is no longer waged between countries and armies, but rather there are more and more conflicts in which sections of the population defined socially, ethnically or religiously fight against each other. In this situation partisans or gangs, warlords as well as groups of international mercenaries, are the main players. The result of this development is the loss of the state's monopoly and a process of "privatization of war." This concept indicates that in the future there will be war between competitive groups on a social and cultural basis, and less on the basis of state interests.[13]

This type of reality currently typifies "failing states," but Bunker points out the inherent threat in the development of violent groups in the United States and the West, such as terror groups or gangs that deal in criminal activity. Based on the assumption that the future threat against the nation state will stem from the generation of alternative organizations that will undermine the state's monopoly on strength, the latter must formulate organizational frames and operation patterns that will enable adequate defense against internal and external rivals.

Ungovernable Regions

The term "ungovernable region" is an amorphous term that generally refers to regions where there is no established government enforcing law and order, or if a government exists, it substantially differs from the governmental and administrative structure customary in the international system (from the "Western point of view"). In contrast to the term "failing state," which relates to a state entity, the UGR may exist within a state where an effective government prevails in most of its territory, with the exception of a region or regions that are uncontrollable.

In recent years "remote" or undeveloped areas with a weak and ineffective central government have become a focal point for the West and the international system. Up to the twentieth century these areas, called UGRs, aroused only minimal interest in the international system, but today the combination of UGRs and the development of the media and modern technologies have turned these regions into major threats against the West and the international system because they have become a haven for international terror and criminal elements and a source that undermines the stability in the vicinity of their own boundaries and overseas.

These regions can be characterized as follows:

- The lack of a central power capable of enforcing law and order throughout the country, or at least in a significant part of its area;
- A backward economic and technological infrastructure;
- Lack of an effective administrative system;
- External powerbrokers acting within the state directly or through internal proxies;[14]
- The internal powerbrokers (proxies) are generally involved in ongoing conflicts;
- There are complex reciprocal links between the exogenous (external) and endogenous (internal) powerbrokers, which decrease the possibility of forming an integrative and stable government;[15]
- The state or the UGR itself is involved in conflict with some of the neighboring countries;

As stated earlier, the UGR constitutes a confrontation arena for internal and external actors. The internal actors can be classified in several main categories:

- Violent powerbrokers fighting each other for control of the territory, the population and the resources;
- Terror organizations exploiting the UGR's area for the construction of an infrastructure and terror activity outside of their territory;

- Terror organizations that make use of the territory and resources mainly for the purpose of activities in external markets;
- Ethnic, political, religious, tribal and other groups struggling for the distribution of the political power and resources in the UGR.

These actors maintain a reciprocal relationship based on the interests of the various sides, while forming coalitions and alliances that struggle against each other. These endogenous actors create external threats against both their immediate and distant environments, in matters related to international crime, drugs and terror.

The terms "failing state" and "ungovernable region" both refer to situations in which the governmental structure ceases to function in the entire state or part of it. The term "failing state" usually refers to a complete deterioration of the state and its institutions, while the term "ungovernable region" refers to a region within the state territory in which the central government has lost control but no new state substitute has been formed and a chaotic state prevails. Thus, it is possible to state that the UGR constitutes part of the disintegration process of the nation state. There are historical examples of UGRs that did not spread and the parallel existence of the nation state functioning in other areas remained feasible, but in most cases the creation of the UGR constitutes an expression of a disintegration process that causes the ultimate deterioration of the country into the chaotic status of a failing state.

This study is focusing on Somalia which, in various stages of its history (after receiving independence), had the status of a failing state. Somalia is the most salient example of a failing state since the ousting of Ziad Barre in 1991.

Somalia as a "Failed State"

Somalia is a perfect example of a failed state. Somalia is regarded as one of the poorest and most backward places worldwide, and possibly is the only state in the world without a government. The origins of the current situation lie in the 1991 collapse of Ziad Barre's regime, which was overthrown by armed rebel movements. The situation soon went out of control after the armed movements fought each other and plunged the country into chaos and humanitarian catastrophe.[16] Somalia's governance vacuum makes the state a comfortable home for terrorist groups seeking refuge or a logistical staging area.

As a result of widespread famine, the United States government and the United Nations sent troops into Somalia in 1992. Their task was to protect relief convoys being sent to the hungry. Although the mission succeeded to save many lives, it failed to convince the armed warlords to stop fighting.[17] The next years saw a humiliating withdrawal of the international forces from Somalia after the 1993 "Black Hawk Down" military debacle, when 18 U.S. troops were killed in Mogadishu.

Since 1991, and mainly after the UN/U.S. withdrawal, Somalia remains a failed state. More than 15 major international peace initiatives have failed. During this period, Somalia disintegrated into several semi-autonomous rival entities:

- The rule of warlords in Mogadishu and other parts of Somalia (1991-2006).
- The semi-independent state of Somaliland (1991-2006).
- The semi-independent state of Puntland (1991-2006).
- The new era of the Islamic courts (2004-2006).

It has also had two transitional governments: the Transitional National Government (TNG) (2000-2004) and the Transitional Federal Government (TFG) (2004-2006). Both governments failed to gain significant popular support and their effectiveness was limited. The "chaotic" period in Somalia (1991-2006) turned this state into a haven for organized crime, piracy, and terror.

In the late 1990s, a new group of warlords dominated Mogadishu. They bought themselves territory and militia loyalty, and made the capital ungovernable until their defeat on June 4, 2006. This group of warlords typically had little professional military or political experience. They financed their fiefdoms by dealing in weapons and drugs, and extortion and illegal licensing. Taking advantage of Somalia's isolation and lack of governance, they directly or indirectly profited from illegal international contracts, including fishing rights, the charcoal trade, and the trafficking of weapons, people, and drugs. Roadblocks in and around Mogadishu were erected for the sole purpose of extortion and intimidation.

Unlike Somalia's traditional warlord class, these faction leaders were not the product of the battle against Barre, but were motivated by competition for resources, greed, and localized power. Their most important channel for political "legitimacy" was the externally supported peace talks, and later, critically, the U.S. regional anti-terrorist strategy, head-quartered in Djibouti.

Organized Crime and Piracy in Somalia

During the period of the civil war and the rule of the warlords, Somalia became haven for all kinds of organized and unorganized crimes. The international community identified three main areas of organized crime activities that threatens the local, regional, and global order and security:

- Arms trade
- Drugs trade
- Piracy

The location of Somalia and the uncontrolled ports of the lawless state turned Somalia into a significant theater and transit area for arms and drugs trade.

- The international community's greatest fear is that arms shipments will flow through the ports. In the past, the smaller port of Marka, less than 100 kilometers from Mogadishu, had been used for arms imports.[18] The ICU had received arms shipments from Eritrea through this port.[19] (In the beginning of March, 2006, for instance, a dhow carrying ammunition for the Islamic movement arrived from Eritrea.) According to a report by a UN panel of experts on Somalia, the arms market in Somalia is supplied by both external and internal sources. Mogadishu's ports are seen as a good point for trans-shipments, especially for arms that are allegedly being received from Yemen and Eritrea. The Islamic courts received arms from Eritrea and from private businessmen in Yemen. A UN report outlined the process by which businessmen in Yemen obtain weapons and ammunition from the general population, which are then shipped to Somalia where the demand and prices are much higher.[20]
- Yet to finance their expansion, the Islamic courts before their fall planned to profit from the various trades that move through the ports, one of which was the lucrative qat (khat) trade. In Mogadishu in 2003, it was estimated that trade in the qat drug plant, whose twigs are chewed as a stimulant, provided significant revenue for the Somali warlords. It was estimated that flights to Mogadishu raised an estimated US$6,000 per day or US$170,000 per month. This revenue has gone to the warlords. Most of the qat sent to Somalia comes from Kenya and Ethiopia. It grows naturally in Kenya and is exported to Somalia from Nairobi's Wilson Airport on a daily basis, landing at small airstrips throughout Somalia. The reason qat flows into Somalia is due to its huge domestic demand. Additionally, once Somalis import the drug, it is often shipped to the Gulf states due to Somalia's cultural and religious linkages with the Middle East, and also due to the convenience of shipping it there. The ICU will now be able to profit from this trade.[21]

Somalia and Piracy

The waters around Somalia are among the most dangerous in the world, with heavily armed gangs prepared to venture far offshore to attack vessels. The pirate raids are part of the anarchy wracking Somalia, which has had no effective government since 1991, when warlords ousted a dictatorship and then turned on each other. On March 15, the UN Security Council encouraged naval forces operating off Somalia to take action against suspected piracy.

Pirate attacks against aid ships have hindered UN efforts to provide relief to the victims of a severe drought in the area. The International Maritime Organization has warned ships to stay away from the Somali coast because of pirate attacks, which surged to more than 40 in 2005-2006 from two attacks in 2004.

There are four examples of the growing threat of the piracy along Somalia's shores:[22]

- First example—three U.S. Navy warships exchanged gunfire with suspected pirates off the coast of Somalia, and one suspect was killed and five others were wounded, the navy said.

  Seven other suspects were taken into custody after the early-morning shootout, said Lt. Cmdr. Charlie Brown, spokesman for the U.S. Navy's 5th Fleet.

  No sailors were wounded in the battle, which occurred at about 5:40 a.m. local time, approximately 25 nautical miles off the Somali coast in international waters.

  The battle started after the USS Cape St. George and USS Gonzales, which were patrolling as part of a Dutch-led task force, spotted a 30-foot fishing boat towing smaller skiffs and prepared to board and inspect the vessels.

  The suspected pirates were holding what appeared to be rocket-propelled grenade launchers, the Navy said. When the suspects began shooting, naval gunners returned fire with mounted machine guns, killing one man and igniting a fire on the vessel.

  Three suspects were seriously wounded and were treated on one of the Navy ships, A Dutch navy medical team was en route, the suspects' nationalities were unknown.

  The navy boarding teams confiscated an RPG launcher and automatic weapons the statement said.

  The Cape St. George, a guided-missile cruiser, and the Gonzales, a guided-missile destroyer, were conducting maritime security operations in the area. They are based in Norfolk.

- Second example—Noel Choong, head of the Piracy Reporting Center of the London-based International Maritime Bureau, told AFP that: "a dozen heavily armed pirates have hijacked a UAE-registered oil tanker along with 19 Filipino crew members off the coast of Somalia.[23]

  "Twelve pirates armed with machine guns, AK-47 rifles and sidearms boarded the tanker off Mogadishu during daylight.

  Choong said the United Arab Emirates oil tanker had earlier discharged its cargo at Mogadishu port and was hit on March 29, 2006 after leaving port.

Maritime officials identified the ship as "Lin 1."

Choong said the pirates are holding the ship off the coast of Somalia and are demanding "a huge sum of money" from the owners for its release.[24]

The international coalition forces consisting of U.S., British and Dutch warships that are helping to police the area have been informed of the hijack, he said.

Choong said the pirates were holding the ship inside Somalia's territorial waters and this could pose a problem should the foreign ships want to intervene.[25]

- Third example—The Korean fishing boat Dongwon-Ho, with 25 crewmembers, was hijacked by pirates in the sea off Somalia on April 5, 2006.

  The fishing boat left Korea in November and was scheduled to return at the end of this year (2006). The vessel was seized along with two other ships belonging to the same fishing company in an area that was part of Somalia's maritime economic zone.[26]

  After the kidnapping incident, the Korean ministry immediately set up an emergency team to liaise with Dongwon Fisheries, and Foreign Minister Ban Ki-Moon sent letters to the foreign ministers of Somalia, Kenya and Ethiopia seeking their cooperation. Korea does not have official diplomatic ties with Somalia.[27]

  After about four months of negotiations the Korean boat and its crew were released, (August 1, 2006).

  The Associated Press in Somalia reported that more than $800,000 was paid for the ransom of the 25 hostages, quoting a Somali militia commander. Abdi Mohamed, the commander, did not say who paid the ransom.[28]

- Fourth example—On February 26, 2006, pirates hijacked an Indian ship the Bhakti Saga, off the Somali coast. Its 25-member crew was only freed on March 29.

Since March 15, 2005, pirates have hit 40 ships off Somalia, but many more attacks have gone unreported. There have been frequent hijackings of boats containing international relief supplies by pirates in the area, but there have not been any casualties reported, and most victims were released in return for money.

Choong urged ship captains to keep their vessels at least 200 kilometers (125 miles) away from Somalia's coast to avoid pirate attacks. "The pirates are armed and they will not hesitate to fire to stop ships," he warned.

In a subsequent incident, pirates fired at a UN food aid ship in an attempt to hijack it. In 2005, the World Food Programme was forced to stop the delivery by sea of relief supplies to nearly a million people who were facing food shortages after pirates repeatedly targeted its vessels.

Since the victory of the ICU over the warlords, the ICU started to implement their control over the Mogadishu port. Later, the ICU has taken control of Haradhere, coast, some 500 km northeast of Mogadishu, which had become a safe haven for pirates.

Sheikh Ahmad, one of the leaders of the ICU said that the warlords had made the Somali coast a no-go area. "The activities of these people [pirates] had made life very difficult for Somalis," he said "Ships were refusing to deliver food to Somalia for fear of being hijacked. We were asked to do something about it and we did.[29] There will be no more hijackings of ships off the coast," he added."[30]

Is Islam the Solution?

The takeover of Mogadishu on June 4, 2006 by the ICU was one of the more important events in the history of Somalia in the last 16 years. The ICU removed a political class of clan-based extortionists and dealers in everything from drugs to people known as "warlords," which had divided and ruled Somalia since the collapse of the Barre regime in 1991.[31]

Warlordism created one of world's most protracted humanitarian crises. In the absence of any significant political, military, or humanitarian intervention, Somalia has suffered chronic impoverishment, exodus, displacement, and international isolation.

However, the military victory by ICU, triggered by a popular revolt against the warlords, achieved what international military intervention and peace talks have failed to accomplish since 1991. Unable to neutralize or control the warlords, the international community ultimately resorted to working with them. Fifteen rounds of internationally sponsored peace talks, held externally, in 2004 resulted in the establishment of the present Transitional Federal Government (TFG), headed by Abdullahi Yusuf Ahmed, a former army colonel.

The ICU has brought order to the streets of the cities of Mogadishu and other places by imposing brutal punishments for criminals. Implementing the Sharia law, they sentence rapists to death by stoning and ordering drug users to be lashed.

Military discipline among the militia was vital but difficult to achieve when a generation of young men depended on extortion and brutality. For many, it became an established means of livelihood. The ICU had previously achieved a reputation for discipline and control by virtue of its intolerance of drugs, including qat; but no Somali government has succeeded in banning qat, an established economic and social habit.

Similarly, the ICU has made clear its intention to "clean up" local video houses, in terms of drugs, alcohol and criminality.

The period of the ICU rule in Somalia was short (months) and the Islamic movement was defeated by the Ethiopian forces and the TFG. During this short period, the ICU restored law and order in the areas under their control and earned the sympathy and support of a big portion of the Somali population. The collapse of the ICU regime left unanswered the question "Is Islam the solution"? for a failed state like Somalia.

The Conflict between Radical Islam and Western Cultures

Samuel Huntington claims that the source of the conflicts in the world at the end of the twentieth century and at the beginning of the twenty-first century is not ideological or economic, but first and foremost cultural. Huntington claims that up until the end of the "Cold War" the modern world was under the dominance of the Western culture, and most of the significant clashes took place in the framework of this culture, or as he terms it "western civil wars."[32]

With the end of the "cold war," the international political system liberated itself from Western dominance, and the center of gravity shifted to reciprocal ties and conflicts between the West and non-Western cultures and between non-Western cultures among themselves. From this stage onward, the peoples and countries associated with Western civilizations ceased to be influenced upshots and victims of Western colonialism. They became active and dominant partners in the propulsion and formation of history. During the "cold war" it was acceptable to categorize the world according to the political systems and the technological/economical development of the countries (developed countries, undeveloped countries, first-world, second-world, third-world, etc.). Huntington believes that today the countries must be classified in terms of civilizations or cultures, while defining civilization as follows:[33] "A civilization is the highest cultural grouping of people and the broadest level of cultural identity people have short of that which distinguishes humans from others."

Civilization is defined via objective components such as language, history, religion, customs and institutions, as well as subjective components such as self-definition or identification of the individual and the group; thus, it is possible to state that the civilization with which the individual identifies is the one that for him constitutes the widest and deepest level of solidarity.

Huntington counts eight central civilizations in the modern world: Western, Slavic, Chinese-Confucian, Japanese, Hindu, Latin American,

Islamic, and **African**. According Huntington's classification Somalia belongs to both the African and Islamic cultures but the Islamic culture is the more relevant and dominant regarding Somalia.

Huntington says that: "most major scholars of civilization except Braudel do not recognize a distinct African civilization." The north of the African continent and its east coast belong to Islamic civilization. Historically, Ethiopia constituted a civilization of its own. Elsewhere European imperialism and settlements brought elements of Western civilization.

In South Africa, Dutch, French, and then English settlers created a multifragmented European culture. Most significantly, European imperialism brought Christianity to most of the continent south of the Sahara. Throughout Africa tribal identities are pervasive and intense, but Africans are also increasingly developing a sense of African identity, and conceivably sub-Saharan Africa could cohere into a distinct civilization, with South Africa possibly being its core state.[34]

Huntington argues that the Islamic civilization is the most militant among the various civilizations in our era, and that it is involved in an inherent conflict with Western culture as well as other cultures. He also points out the conflict's historic roots starting from the period of the crusades, through the Ottoman Empire and Western colonialism, up to the liberation wars of Muslim states.

A quick glance at the map of conflicts worldwide provides convincing support for Huntington's claims, as from Africa to the islands of the Pacific Ocean, Islam is involved in violent conflicts at contact or friction points with other civilizations (known as "fault line wars"). Despite the fact that political reality appears to bear out Huntington's general concept, it is still advisable to criticize and qualify some of his arguments.

Huntington takes a comprehensive and sweeping approach when presenting all of the Muslim states as an Islamic cultural bloc pitting itself against Western and other cultures. But a closer examination of the regimes in the majority of Muslim countries indicates that most of them are secular regimes or administrations with pragmatic and moderate Islamic orientation. These countries are not involved in conflict with the West. On the contrary, they have adopted the "bandwagon" approach and have joined the "modernization convoy" by adopting Western technologies, values and lifestyles.

Huntington does not differentiate between this central trend in the Muslim world and fundamentalist Islamic trends. These movements have admittedly adopted the battle cry of the struggle against Western civilization, but they still constitute a minority in the Muslim world, albeit a militant one.

Consequently, the Muslim world is involved in a profound and harsh internal cultural conflict vis-à-vis the nature and direction of Muslim society; the results of this internal struggle currently dictate and will subsequently dictate the nature of the connections between Islamic culture and Western as well as other cultures. Regimes in many Muslim states have not only adopted the patterns of Western culture, but also rely on military, political and economic aid from the West in order to sustain their existence.

The radical Islamic trends exist and operate in varying degrees of intensity and violence in all Muslim states as well as in some other countries identified with different cultures (China, the Philippines, Balkans, India, and more), in which they act to achieve independence for Muslim minorities. The objective of these entities is to establish religious Islamic states in Muslim countries while replacing secular regimes, and to achieve independence for Muslim communities in countries where they constitute a minority in order to establish new Islamic states.

Thus, radical Islam is involved in struggles against foreign cultures on four levels:

1. The replacement of secular regimes with Islamic regimes in Muslim countries;
2. The struggle of Muslim minorities to achieve independence and establish independent Islamic states;
3. The struggle against ethnic/cultural minorities demanding autonomy or independence from Muslim countries;
4. The struggle against alien foreign cultures, mainly against Western culture, at the fault lines and contact points with Islamic culture.

This reality is consistent with the basic concepts of Islam which regards the world as divided between the area of Islam (Dar al-Islam) and the area of war (Dar al-Harb); the aim of Islam is to bring the true faith to all of human civilization.

Islamic fundamentalism makes use of a range of means and tools in order to achieve its objectives starting from education, propaganda, economic aid and spiritual welfare, through political dissension and culminating in terror and war. An analysis of conflict focal points indicates that their efforts are directed primarily towards a revision of the political reality inside the Muslim world, and to a lesser extent against other cultures.

The new geopolitical reality in the post "cold war" era is perceived by radical Islamic circles as an expression of their success, which places Islam at the front of the confrontation vis-à-vis the Western culture headed by the only superpower, the United States.

One of the prominent phenomena characteristic of the previous millennium and the beginning of the current millennium, which saliently reflect Huntington's concept regarding the cultural conflict, is the trend of the Afghan "alumni" who constitute the vanguard in radical Islam's confrontation with rival cultures. Osama Bin Laden and Al-Qaida constitute the most outstanding expression of the Afghan "alumni" and of the cultural and philosophical concept at the root of this phenomenon.

The Conflict between the Nomadic Culture and the State-Oriented Culture

The end of the twentieth century and the beginning of the twenty-first century are characterized by the "conflict between cultures." As mentioned above, one of the fathers of this concept, Samuel Huntington, argues that after the end of the "cold war" era the source of conflicts in the world is "cultural." As stated earlier, he counts eight main cultures in the modern world and names Islam as the most militant of all.

"The conflict between the cultures" can also be conceptualized and examined from another point of view which divides cultures into two categories; the state-oriented, institutional and territorial culture as opposed to the nomadic culture. Deleuze and Felix Guatteri extensively discussed various aspects of the conflict between the nomadic culture and the state-oriented territorial culture. This chapter will focus on their definitions of the terms "conflict," "war" and the "war machine" in the context of the confrontation between the nomadic and state-oriented cultures.

The roots of the confrontation between the wanderer (nomad) and the farmer lie in the conflict between Cain and Abel as related in the Book of Genesis. The expulsion from the Garden of Eden propelled man from a state of plenty to a reality plagued by scarcity, competitiveness, force, and a battle for survival. The fourth chapter of Genesis recounts the dramatic confrontation between Cain and Abel, which culminates in Abel's death and Cain's decree to become a nomad—"a wanderer you shall be in the land" (Genesis 4:12). This is the first testimony and primary mythological explanation for nomadism and for the inherent conflict between the nomad and the permanent dweller, and between the nomadic culture and the state-oriented, territorial culture.

Jacques Derrida, Deleuze, Guaterri and other philosophers regard nomadism as a philosophical concept that involved in perpetual conflict against the state-oriented, tyrannical philosophy, as they choose to define it. The nomadic society and the nomadic "war machine" are in constant movement from the conceptual point of view, although sometimes this does not involve actual physical movement. The nomadic concept opposes "domination" that the state-oriented perception enforces in all matters related to organization, space and time.

The philosophical, state-oriented discourse always relates to the law, institutions and contracts which jointly embody the concept of the state's sovereignty; it is this aspect that the nomadic concept views as dominating or tyrannical, or to quote Deleuze: Even in the Greek polis (city-state), (which is perceived as the epitome of democracy), the philosophical discourse relates to tyranny and conceptual force, or at the very least it existed in the shadow of this tyranny.[35]

Nietzsche was one of the first to bring up this complex issue for discussion. He argued that philosophical thought and discourse must be nomadic and free of the bureaucratic and procedural discourse. Thus Nietzsche, claims Deleuze, turned thought into a war machine and a battering ram reflecting a counter-philosophy that constantly challenges the state-oriented philosophy.[36]

Deleuze and Guaterri indicate several substantial differences between the state-oriented and nomadic approaches:[37]

- The state-oriented approach, which is founded on the definition of the state's sovereignty, is constructed in the form of a *(graded) vertical hierarchy*. The philosophical and constructive logic are based on this concept of structural and logical dependency arranged layer upon layer. By its very nature, the vertical structure creates a dictatorial pattern, since without the enforcement of conceptual and structural order the vertical structure will collapse. The nomadic approach does not accept the vertical structure and logic. The nomadic system is a *horizontal system*; on the philosophical and structural level there is no clear hierarchy, and the structural links are amorphous and less structured.
- *The territory*—The concept of "territory"—the permanence and the context of place—constitute the basic foundations of the state entity, which defines itself through the delineation of boundaries. Boundaries represent a basis not only for the physical definition of the state entity, but also address the conceptual dimensions of this entity. The nomadic outlook negates the notion of "boundaries" as well as the concept of "state." Nomadism signifies conceptual and physical de-territorization, which expresses itself in constant movement. The state does its best to

settle its components, and to establish and patrol their movement and organization. However, the nomadic concept interprets this attempt in terms of compulsion and tyranny on the part of the state entity, and expresses the essence of its existence by opposing any attempt to settle or regulate it.

Nevertheless, Deleuze and Guaterri point out that there is no "quintessential nomadism," and a paradox exists in the very fact that nomadism defines itself as different than the state entity. Moreover, there is the danger that if the nomadic perception emerges victorious, then it will also turn into a state entity.

- *The concept of time*—The concept of time is perceived differently in the state-oriented entity than in the nomadic culture. In the state-oriented culture, the perception of time is also contingent upon conceptual boundaries of the entity and represents part of the definition of the boundaries. The nomadic culture is in constant flow, in both dimensions of space and time. In the nomadic perception, the concept of time does not serve to delineate boundaries, but rather exists as a point of reference and orientation in the course of history. In the following sentences Deleuze and Guatteri encapsulate the nature of the difference between the state and nomadic entities:[38]

"As a non-disciplinary force, the Nomadic war machine names an anarchic presence on the far horizon of the state's field of order."

Deleuze and Guatteri point out two types of war; the first, "the real war," and the second; the pure idea of war.[39] They perceive the pure idea of war as[40] "a war machine that does not have war as its object and that only entertains a potential or supplementary synthetic relation with war."

The war itself logically contradicts the existence of the state-oriented entity and constitutes a form of antagonism directed against all forms of sovereignty. The nomadic movement is also based on fundamental antagonism that opposes any regulated form or flow related to normalization and order. To illustrate, the two elements can be compared to the quiet and regular flow of water in a river as opposed to the turbulent churning of water in whirlpools, thus creating a swirling disorder.

It is possible to identify historical confrontations between nomadic entities and state-oriented entities in the three countries at the heart of this study. These confrontations occurred not only between powerbrokers within the state-oriented territory, but were also integrated in struggles waged against external powerbrokers, particularly colonial forces, that attempted to implement state-oriented order in spaces characterized by nomadic cultures.

The consequence of these confrontations was the formation of an unstable space whose components are located at different levels of intercultural confrontation. Somalia represents the most salient example of the victory of nomadic forces and the actual dismantling of the state-oriented framework, while Sudan and Yemen are involved at different levels of the conflict, the result being that these regimes are constantly being challenged by the nomadic components that strive to dismantle them.

Areas involved in cultural confrontation constitute a preferred action arena for nomadic power entities; their very presence and activity in the arena contribute to the intensification of the confrontation between the nomadic and state-oriented cultures.

The confrontation between the nomadic culture and the state-oriented culture may lead to the creation of "ungovernable areas" (UGRs) and "failing states," which serve as a hothouse for nomadic entities. The latter pose a threat and cause instability in their immediate vicinity and beyond it, thus creating a "Catch-22" situation. This can be described as a vicious cycle in which nomadic forces confront state-oriented forces and cause the undermining and collapse of the failing state; the next step is the development of a local nomadic entity that also attracts external nomadic entities. This presence prevents the rehabilitation or construction of a new state-oriented identity, and the space becomes a focus from which the nomadic entity threatens to continue spreading towards nearby state-oriented entities as well as more distant ones.

Al-Qaida as an Expression of the Merging of Radical Islam and Nomadic Culture[41]

Osama Bin Laden moved from Saudi Arabia to Pakistan and from there to the Afghan front. In the Pakistani city of Pashwar, Bin Laden established an organization that dealt with the recruitment, absorption and training of Muslim fighters from all over the world who volunteered to participate in the Jihad against the Soviet Union in Afghanistan. Already at the beginning of his career, Osama Bin Laden adopted radical Islamic views that regard Islam as involved in an existential struggle against the more powerful forces of the superpowers as well as against secular and corrupt Arab regimes acting according to the interests of their powerful patrons. According to Bin Laden's tenets, radical Islam is involved in a struggle to banish the corrupt leaders from the Muslim world and found a utopian community of Islamic believers—the "Umma."

Bin Laden claims that Islam has no boundaries and that the Muslim national states are the artificial creations of colonialism and imperialism, whose goal was to cause a fake separation within the Muslim world, thus perpetuating the control and involvement of the Western powers.

Therefore, radical Islam represents a nomadic concept that negates the state-oriented entity and regards it as an expression of the physical and conceptual tyranny of the Western culture, which represents the state-oriented culture.

Bin Laden adopted the slogan, "not east, not west," which is accepted by those faithful to radical Islam: In 1979 he first focused his struggle upon the Soviet Union, and accepted aid from the United States, Saudi Arabia, and other "corrupt" Arab regimes to achieve his objective, but even then he never concealed his opinion that after victory in this struggle, the West's turn would come.

The war in Afghanistan saliently reflects the conflict between the state-oriented concept and "war machine" and the nomadic concept and "war machine." The Soviet Union and the communist regime in Kabul expressed the vertical, graded state-oriented concept, on the philosophical, conceptual and practical level, while the Afghan mujahidin, who were assisted by the "internationale" of volunteers from all over the Muslim world, like Bin Laden, expressed the concept of the nomadic "war machine." This machine was built horizontally and was composed of scores of organizations and groups lacking a regulated or permanent structure and without defined procedures of cooperation, whose only loose link was the joint goal—defeat of the communist regime and banishment of the Soviet Union's forces from Afghanistan.

The nomadic "war machine" of the mujahidin is in perpetual movement on various levels:

- Operating a chaotic campaign without a clear delineation of boundaries outside of Afghanistan, within Afghanistan in the areas outside of Soviet control, inside Afghanistan behind the Soviet lines, and even inside the government centers in Kabul and other cities. The operation of this type of chaotic campaign is meant to undermine the operative, structured and institutionalized rationale of the state-oriented order.
- A perpetual motion and flow of concepts and ideas all designated to jointly undermine the graded and state-oriented ideology and doctrines prevalent in Kabul, while simultaneously creating new subversive concepts (mostly Islamic).

The mujahidin movements were the most characteristic model of the nomadic "war machine": They were in constant motion with the aim of undermining the physical and conceptual boundaries of the Afghan state; they generated ideas and concepts that were free of the state-oriented, tyrannical rationale; they fought a chaotic campaign that neutralized the advantages of the state-oriented superpower and gave the nomadic machine superiority. And indeed, in 1990 the nomadic "war machine" defeated the Soviet Union, which pulled its forces out of Afghanistan, and two years later the communist regime fell in Kabul leaving control in the hands of the mujahidin.

Deleuze and Guatteri foretold the inherent paradox when a nomadic system turns into a state-oriented one. The Afghan case constitutes an interesting example of the opposite phenomenon: Even after their victory over the communist regime and the Soviet Union, the mujahidin movements continued their nomadic modus operandi. Thus, in the years 1992-1996 Afghanistan remained in a chaotic state, and the attempt to found a vertical, graded system that would result in a state-oriented government failed. In actual fact Afghanistan was "controlled" by a nomadic "war machine" that perpetuated itself via a complex system of powerbrokers that fought each other, thus preserving the chaotic and non-institutionalized reality that characterizes the nomadic system as an non state-oriented system.

The rise to power of the Taliban regime in Afghanistan during the years 1996-2001 wrought only slight change within the system's structure, because the internal power struggles in the arena persevered. Moreover, during these years two parallel systems existed which were constantly at loggerheads with each other: One system, a semi state-oriented system of the Taliban regime; and a nomadic system that fought it in the form of the coalition of the "Northern Alliance."

At the end of the war, an even more salient nomadic "war machine" was created in the form of the Afghan "alumni," whose most prominent representative is Osama Bin Laden. The Afghan "alumni" are not identified with any particular state or movement, but rather express a radical religious-cultural trend that believes in the relentless struggle of Islam against heretic Muslim regimes and adverse cultures.

One can indicate four main channels of activity adopted by the Afghan "alumni:"

1. Incorporation in the activities of radical Islamic organizations in their native countries (Egypt, the Maghreb countries, Somalia, and others) and the leadership of these organizations;
2. Establishing new terror organizations, such as Al-Qaida under Bin Laden's leadership;
3. Establishing "independent" terror cells without a defined organizational link or affiliation while sustaining cooperation with other Islamic terror organizations;
4. Joining areas of conflict involving Muslim populations, e.g., the Balkan, Chechnya, Kashmir, Tajikistan, and the Horn of Africa.

As stated earlier, Al-Qaida and its leader, Osama Bin Laden, are the most prominent examples of the nomadic concept both from the aspect of its physical dimension and its conceptual dimension. At the end of the war in Afghanistan, Bin Laden decided to continue the Jihad against the enemies of Islam, and he positioned the United States as a central target of this campaign. During the years 1992-2001, Bin Laden "wandered" between Afghanistan, Saudi Arabia, Sudan and Afghanistan until his "disappearance" following the American offensive in Afghanistan at the end of 2001.

Bin Laden represents the nomadic concept of the wanderer who does not settle down nor does he establish himself within a state-oriented system, but rather he is perpetually on the move. From his point of view, territory expresses only a functional and temporary need; in other words, it is essential to his ability to further his goals, but he does not form a permanent link with any particular territory.

Al-Qaida was designed according to the nomadic concept as an organization without a clear, graded structure. It is composed of cells and groups spread all over the world and sustains conceptual and organizational links with countries that support terror (such as Sudan, Iran, and more), as well as Islamic organizations that hold similar worldviews.

The organization's goal is to fight an uncompromising battle against the United States, the West, and Zionism that can also be defined as entities that reflect the state-oriented concept. The organization openly contests Western cultural concepts in every area; on the ideological-religious level it calls for the destruction of the Western rival and the establishment of an Islamic culture in its stead; on the economic level, it exploits the economic establishment of the Western world for its own purposes and acts through it to demolish this infrastructure, based on the understanding that most of the power of the Western culture is drawn from its economy; on the military level it established a nomadic "war machine" that confronts the superior power of the Western state-oriented "war machine" by posing challenges that render it vulnerable and irrelevant.

The organization functions according to the nomadic concept, at any place and at any time, and creates disarray that undermines the foundations of the state-oriented rationale. The flexibility, agility and independence of the various components of the nomadic "war machine" constitute an acute problem for the state-oriented "war machine" of the West, which functions within the framework of the restrictions and limits that the graded state-oriented order forces upon itself.

A study of Al-Qaida's areas of activity indicates some main characteristics:

- The organization prefers to position its central headquarters and organizational infrastructure inside the territory of a Muslim state governed by a sympathetic radical Islamic regime that supports the organization and its chosen direction, such as the Taliban in Afghanistan and the Sudanese regime headed by Hassan al-Turabi.
- The organization bases its infrastructure in countries that are steeped in internal and external power struggles as well as economic woes, as this enables the development of mutual dependency between the organization and the authorities; the authorities offer the organization refuge and support in establishing the organizational infrastructure, and in exchange the organization offers the government economic and operational aid in its struggles against its adversaries. This was the case in Afghanistan and subsequently in Sudan.
- Due to the nature of its ties with the government in the host state and as a result of its worldview, the organization acts in external arenas of confrontation, sometimes in cooperation with the country where it claims refuge or in its name. This was particularly prominent in Al-Qaida's activity in Sudan, when the organization helped Sudan and its ally Iran in their struggle against the U.S. presence in Somalia; and also in Afghanistan when the organization acted as the emissaries of the Taliban regime and its patrons in Pakistan against Indian forces in the disputed Kashmir region.
- The organization does not perpetrate terror activity within the boundaries of the host country, but generally acts outside of the country, in order to refrain from embarrassing its "hosts" vis-à-vis attack victims.
- Despite the attempt to draw a clear line between the organization's responsibility and its host's, there have been cases where the victim country has pointed an accusatory finger at both the organization and the host country and have taken a toll from both. A salient example of this would be the cruise-missile attack perpetrated by U.S. forces against Al-Qaida targets in Afghanistan and Sudan following the attacks on the American embassies in Kenya and Tanzania.
- The extent of the willingness of host countries to pay the price for their support of the organization varies from country to country, and even changes inside each country when the political and military circumstances fluctuate. Thus, due to heavy American-Egyptian-Saudi pressure, the regime in Sudan preferred to ask Bin Laden to leave the country, while the Taliban regime in Afghanistan remained loyal to the organization and paid the price by losing its government as a result of the U.S. offensive in the war against terror.
- "Failing states" and UGRs constitute areas of activity for Al-Qaida. The organization acts in these regions to reinforce infrastructures and perpetrate attacks against its adversaries, while exploiting the lack of governmental control or the weakness of the central government,

and relying on radical Islamic entities that support the organization. Examples of this phenomenon can be seen in the Al-Qaida attacks in Yemen; the attacks at the end of 1992 perpetrated in connection to the U.S. involvement in Somalia, the attack against the USS Cole in 2002, and more. In Somalia, the organization aided Aidid's forces in their anti-U.S. activities in this country.

Al-Qaida also recruits collaborators and terrorists into its ranks from among the residents of the "failing state" or the UGRs, and they act from within the organization's ranks and represent it in various arenas worldwide.

- The nomadic character of Al-Qaida prevents the creation of total and irreversible dependency between the organization and any specific state-oriented territory, and thus, if the organization should lose its infrastructure in a certain region, it can rehabilitate and rebuild itself in another region.
- From the philosophical point of view, radical Islamic states constitute the preferred location of activity for Al-Qaida because their ideology matches the organization's worldview. Nevertheless, due to the inherent nature of these countries, they embody a contradiction and conflict of interest between the nomadic entity and the state-oriented entity. This is reflected, for example, in the Sudanese decision to give in to the pressures to banish Bin Laden. This example indicates that the state-oriented system placed the governmental, state-oriented interest (the government's survival) at the head of its priorities and sacrificed the conceptual-ideological component in the process.

In contrast to the Sudanese case, which represents a salient state-oriented system (albeit a shaky one), for the most part the Taliban regime maintained its nomadic nature and remained uncompromising from the ideological aspect. Its relentless support for Al-Qaida ultimately led to its destruction in the confrontation with the Western state-oriented "war machine."

The September 11 terror campaign prominently reflects both the confrontation between the nomadic "war machine" and the state-oriented "war machine," as well as the cultural conflict between Islam and Western culture. On September 11, 2001 four passenger planes were hijacked in the United States; two of the planes crashed into the Twin Towers in New York, causing their collapse, and a third hijacked plane crashed into the Pentagon complex in Washington. A fourth airplane crashed in a wooded area in Pennsylvania, but it is believed that its target was the Capitol building.

The targets of the terror campaign, which were chosen carefully, are prominent symbols of Western culture in general, and of the United States, in particular—which leads and represents this culture. The Twin Towers were the symbol of financial power (the World Trade Center), while the Pentagon is the symbol of the military power of the United States and the West.

The terror attack expresses the profound cultural and conceptual asymmetry between the United States, which represents the state-oriented concept, and Bin Laden, who represents the nomadic concept.

The attack was perpetrated by several small groups of terrorists (nomads) who came from various Muslim countries (Saudi Arabia, Egypt, and more). The hijackers took over the planes without firearms and in some cases even without any weapons, and turned the airplanes themselves into attack weapons.

The use of an aeronautical mode of transportation to destroy the symbols of the state-oriented "war machine" is symbolic because it represents the ultimate form of mobility. As stated earlier, the Twin Towers and the Pentagon are both architectural monuments that represent the achievements of the Western state-oriented culture. These two stationary monuments, which constituted the embodiment of the state-oriented "tyranny" in the eyes of the nomadic Islam, were destroyed with instruments that were also created by the modern West but reflect the movement and dynamics that are particularly characteristic of the nomadic culture.

The terror attack of September 2001 exposed the weakness and vulnerability of the state-oriented system despite its absolute power, which significantly exceeds that of the nomadic "war machine." The "war against terror" declared by the United States following that terror campaign also constitutes convincing testimony vis-à-vis the problematic issues inherent to the confrontation between the nomadic and state-oriented systems.

The United States declared Al-Qaida and the Taliban regime in Afghanistan (which had provided refuge to Bin Laden) as the primary goals of its war against terror. The state-oriented "war machine" of the United States defeated the state-oriented "war machine" of the Taliban and the components of Al-Qaida within it, with ease. The infrastructure of Al-Qaida in Afghanistan was destroyed and some of its commanders and fighters were either killed or taken prisoner. However, Bin Laden and most of the organization's leaders have so far evaded the Americans, and what is more to the point, Al-Qaida's "horizontal" and decentralized organizational infrastructure was almost unaffected.

This experience teaches us that the infrastructure of the state-oriented "war machine," like that of the Taliban, can be destroyed through the use of the equipment, technology, and doctrine that are at the disposal of the Western "war machine," but the nomadic infrastructure necessitates completely different handling and confrontation. The nomadic culture's concepts of time and space, as well as its organizational narrative, pose a threat to the state-oriented logic and act to undermine its foundations through their very existence, even before the operational capabilities of the nomadic terror infrastructure have been translated into attacks. Thus, the definition of the confrontation as a "war against terror" addresses only a limited conceptual dimension of a far deeper and wider confrontation between the cultures. The component of terror constitutes only a single symptom, albeit an important one, of a confrontation with far greater implications.

Somali society, history, and tradition are of nomad nature. The lawlessness and the "chaotic" environment are reflections of the nomadic nature of Somalia. Therefore, it is not a historical coincidence that Somalia since 1991 is a "failed state" and a potential haven for other nomad entities such as Al Qaida.

The victory of the ICU opens a window of opportunity to restore order and based on a Taliban-style Islamic system. The victory of the ICU shocked regional capitals, which fear radical Islamic state on their borders, because such a state would export the Islamic revolution to the neighboring Muslim communities in Ethiopia (in Ogaden), Kenya, Djibouti, Tanzania, and even to further destinations.

The United States and other Western governments were concerned by the possibility that Somalia, under a Taliban-style regime, becomes a haven for Islamic terror organizations.

Shortly after the ICU victory, Osama bin Laden in an audio recording broadcast in July 2006, called the mujahidin in Somalia to fight anyone who will intervene against the ICU and the implementation of the Islamic doctrine.

Sheikh Aweys dismissed the American allegations regarding the links between the ICU and Al Qaida. Aweys claimed that "America knows that Al Qaida is not in Somalia and that their fear is simply that they don't like to have an Islamic government here."[42]

In January 2007, Ethiopian forces and the TFG defeated the ICU and gained control over the southern and central parts of Somalia. The ICU and their followers and supporters, including "foreigners" are now on the run and returned to a fundamental nomadic model.

In conclusion, Somalia in the near future will remain a theater of conflict between the local and global nomad war machines and the state oriented system represented by Ethiopia and other TFG backed by the regional states and organizations (AU and IGAD), and the United States.

Notes

1.   This chapter is based on: Shaul Shay, *The Red Sea Terror Triangle*, Transaction Publishers, New Brunswick, U.S.A, 2005.
2.   Ibid.
3.   The Failed States Index, Foreign Policy and the Funds for Peace, May/June, 2006, www.foreignpolicy.com.
4.   Ibid.
5.   See the closing speech delivered by the former UN secretary-general Boutros-Ghali at the U.N. conference dealing with public international law: "Towards the Twenty-first Century: International Law as a Language for International Relations: (13-17 March 1995, New York), Documents, p. 9.
6.   Max Weber, Staatssoziolgie (ed. Johannes Winchelman), Berlin, 1996, p. 27.
7.   Arnold Gehlen, in Heiner Keupp, Last and der Erkenn this: Der Menschals soziales Wesen, Munich/Zurich, 1995, p. 1995, p. 105 (ICRC translation).
8.   Robert S. Bunker, "Epochal Change: Ear over Social and Political Organization," Parameters, Summer 1997, 9.15.
9.   Ibid., p.18.
10. Robert Kaplan, "The Coming Anarchy," *The Atlantic Monthly*, February 1994, pp. 44-766.
11. Robert S. Bunker, "Epochal Change: Ear over Social and Political Organization," *Parameters*, Summer 1997, p. 17.
12. Ibid., p. 19.
13. William S. Lind , "Defending Western Culture," *Foreign Policy*, 84, (Fall 1991), pp. 40-50.
14. Literature refers to two categories of actors: Endogenic actors (internal actors) and exogenic actors (external actors).
15. Ibid.
16. Harun Hassan, Somalia: Exit into history? Open democracy. A.P, February 23, 2004.
17. Sunguta West, Mogadishu's ports to provide significant funding for Somalia's Islamists, Terrorism Focus' Volume 3, Issue 28, July 18, 2006.
18. *Somaliland Times*, May 20, 2006.
19. Somalinet News, June 15, 2006.
20. Sunguta West, Mogadishu's Ports to Provide Significant Funding for Somalia's Islamists, *Terrorist Focus*, Volume 3, Issue 28, July 18, 2006.
21. Ibid.
22. Navy exchanges fire with suspected pirates, *Ashraq Alawsat*, March 19, 2006.
23. Pirates hijack UAE tanker with Filipino crew off Somalia, *Ashraq Alawast*, April 3, 2006.
24. Ibid.
25. Ibid.
26. Ibid.
27. Ibid.
28. Ibid.

29.   Somalia: The challenge of change, UN Office for the Coordination of Humanitarian Affairs, irinnews.org, August 16, 2006.
30.   Ibid.
31.   Somalia: transitional government, Islamic courts agree to talks, U.S. Office for the Coordination of Humanitarian Affairs, August 16, 2006.
32.   Samuel Huntington, *The Clash of Civilizations and the Remaking of World Order*, Simon & Schuster, New York, 1996.
33.   Ibid.
34.   Samuel Huntington, *The Clash of Civilizations and the Remaking of World Order*, Simon & Schuster, New York, 1996., p. 47.
35.   John Lechte, Fifty key Contemporary Thinkers, Routledge, 1994.
36.   Gilles Deleuze, "Nomad Thought," in David B. Allison (ed.), *The New Nietzsche*, MIT Press, Cambridge, 1998, p. 149.
37.   Ibid.
38.   Ibid., p. 148.
39.   Ibid.
40.   Ibid.
41.   This chapter is based on the book by Yoram Schweitzer and Shaul Shay, *The Globalization of Terror*, Transaction Publishers, New Brunswick, NJ 2003, pp. 58-63.
42.   Rod Crilly, I'm prepared to talk peace, says leader of Somalia's Sharia courts, TimesonLine, Mogadishu, September 1, 2006.

9

The Campaign against Global Terror[1]

The Al-Qaida attacks in the United States on September 11, 2001 were like an earthquake that provoked the United States into declaring a relentless war against terror. The threat of Islamic terror against the United States and the West were nothing new, and contending with challenges posed by Al-Qaida and other radical Islamic organizations already began in the early 1990s, but only the September 11 attacks illustrated the full power and graveness of the threat to the United States and the entire world, and necessitated a substantial change in the world's attitude towards the problem of terror.

The war against terror is directed against two central targets:

1.   Terror organizations;
2.   The states involved in terror.

When combined, these two aspects create international terror, which can be defined as follows:[2] The use or threat to use violence for political gain by an individual or group acting for or against an existing regime. The act is aimed at influencing a wider target population than the direct victims of the action, while the victims, the perpetrators or their contacts are unrestricted by geographical boundaries.

The various forms of countries' involvement in terror have been unified under the concepts "terrorist states" or state-sponsored terror." These concepts create a very rough generalization of the various levels of involvement of countries in terror, thus a more focused distinction is required that classifies the involvement of countries in terror according to the following categories:[3]

- *States supporting terrorism*—This category includes states that support terror organizations via financial, ideological, military and operational aid;

- *States operating terrorism*—Countries that initiate, direct and execute terror attacks via patron organizations, while avoiding direct government involvement in the terror;
- *States perpetrating terrorism*—States that perpetrate terror throughout the world via the country's security systems (security and intelligence mechanisms).

A fourth category can be added to these categories, the "failing state," which turns into a "hothouse" for terror organizations as the result of the lack of an effective government.

Paul Wilkinson defined the various types of state terror as "direct or indirect involvement of a government, via formal or informal groups, in the creation of psychological and physical violence against political or physical targets or another country in order to achieve tactical and objective targets that it is interested in."[4]

State-oriented terror is characterized by an ambivalent approach to international law and order. On the one hand, states that utilize terror are willing to deviate from the international norms and from the "rules of the game" in order to inflict damage on the enemy and achieve their own goals (a prominent example of this can be observed in the "students'" occupation of the U.S. Embassy in Iran and the holding of U.S. diplomats as hostages in 1979). On the other hand, a country that utilizes terror endeavors not to reveal its involvement in this activity in order to prevent retaliatory measures against it.

Cooperation between a country and a terror organization is usually sustained on the basis of religious, ideological, or political solidarity, and on the basis of joint interests. The extent of control that the "patron" maintains over the terror organization varies according to the basis for cooperation and the level of the organization's dependence on the "patron."

As mentioned earlier, the country's involvement in terror may be either direct or indirect and exist on different levels of aid and cooperation (political, economic, operational). In most cases, the ties between the "patron" state and the terror organization are of a clandestine nature; by using citizens of other countries the country can shirk responsibility when the activity is exposed and avoid criticism and sanctions by the international community.

Terror may be an additional or alternative tool to activating military force in order to achieve the country's objectives, while the state supports an act of terror against another state with which it is involved in conflict, but this may also apply to a situation in which the countries are not officially involved in hostile confrontation.

Terror may be effective for the achievement of goals when there is doubt whether they are achievable through direct military confrontation, such as undermining the political stability in the target state or incurring damage to that country's diplomatic and economic ties with other countries.

It is possible to indicate three stages in the global campaign against terror declared by the United States:

- *Stage 1*—Destruction of Al-Qaida's infrastructure in Afghanistan and removal of the Taliban regime that sponsored the organization;
- *Stage 2*—The campaign against Iraq and against Al-Qaida affiliated terror cells;
- *Stage 3*—The campaign against additional countries that support terror and the continued struggle against Al-Qaida terror cells and other terror organizations worldwide.

In the first stage of the war against terror, the "coalition against terror," headed by the United States, launched its offensive against Al-Qaida in Afghanistan and the Taliban regime that served as sponsor to Bin-Laden and his organization. The coalition acted in Afghanistan, a country that clearly had all of the characteristics of a "failing state," while utilizing the Taliban regime's enemies, the members of the "Northern Alliance," in order to eradicate the Taliban's regime and destroy Al-Qaida's infrastructure in this country.

The combination of American air superiority, the ongoing activation of special forces and the aid provided to the "Northern Alliance," which carried out the main offensive on land, led to the rapid collapse of the Taliban regime and the Al-Qaida activists. Although Taliban leader Mullah Muhammad Omar and Bin-Laden along with his organization's senior leaders did succeed in fleeing, the Taliban regime collapsed and even more important—the infrastructure of the Al-Qaida organization in Afghanistan was eradicated and hundreds of organization members, including senior activists, fell into the hands of the U.S. coalition. The American message during the first stage of the war against terror was unequivocal:

- The United States would fight a relentless war against Al-Qaida and all other terror organizations, and would act to eradicate them.
- Any regime offering patronage to terror organizations will pay a heavy price for this policy.

The eradication of the Taliban regime in Afghanistan signaled a warning to various countries that in one way or another cooperated with

Al-Qaida and other Islamic terror organizations. The fate of the Taliban regime must have loomed before Muamar Kadafi in Libya and the Sudanese and Yemeni rulers when they rushed to deny any accusations regarding involvement in terror and even declared their willingness to cooperate with the United States in its battle against terror.

When attempting to calculate Al-Qaida's profit/loss reckoning following the 9/11 terror campaign, one might say that it was a tactical victory but a strategic loss. The tactical victory stems from Al-Qaida's success in surprising the United States, killing thousands of its citizens in its government and economic centers, and inflicting huge damage upon its economy. The terror campaign granted Al-Qaida unprecedented media coverage, which helped to nurture the powerful image of the "Islamic front" headed by Bin-Laden, thus presenting them with a significant achievement from the point of view of morale.

On the other hand, Bin-Laden failed to achieve his main goal, which was to provoke the United States into taking massive and aggressive retaliatory steps against the Muslim world, in the hope of inciting a frontal confrontation between Islam and the West. Not only did this type of confrontation never take place, but rather a wide international coalition formed, with the backing of Muslim countries, that granted the United States support in the military campaign fought against the Taliban regime.

This campaign led to the removal of the Taliban regime in Afghanistan and to the inflicting of severe damage upon Al-Qaida's infrastructure in Afghanistan. Its bases and training camps were eradicated, and the thousands of confiscated documents exposed the plans and *modi operandi* of the organization. The organization sustained heavy losses from among its leadership, some of whom were either killed or caught, and thousands of its fighters were killed or taken prisoner. Thus, Al-Qaida lost (at least temporarily) its operational bases in Afghanistan, which constituted an essential component in its global terror infrastructure.

In addition, the organization sustained a heavy blow to its prestige as a result of the successful military campaign which the United States waged against it in Afghanistan, and the "unbeaten" image that the Afghan mujahidin (with Bin-Laden at their head) so carefully nurtured following their victory over the forces of the former Soviet Union was suddenly distorted.

It is important to emphasize that the campaign against Al-Qaida and the Afghan "alumni" (with Bin-Laden as their leader) is still in its initial stages, and its results depend first and foremost upon the West's determination to continue the struggle and upon its capability to provide a suitable and effective response to the threat of global Islamic terror. Failure to deal this response to the threat may enable Bin-Laden and his men to recover and rehabilitate the organization's infrastructure, and cause even graver damage than they have already.

The West must comprehend that the heavy blow sustained by Al-Qaida did not demolish its force, and it particularly did not diminish the strength of the terror cells supported by Al-Qaida, which are linked to it and are currently waiting in many countries worldwide to continue to promote the agenda of the Global Jihad. These cells are made up of trained and determined fighters who mainly thirst for revenge.

The nomadic character of Bin-Laden's terror network, including all of its branches, enables it to not only survive these blows but continue to operate. The survival of its senior commanders, with Bin-Laden at its head, as well as his deputy, Aymam al-Zawaheiri, and several other senior activists, and the escape of hundreds of Al-Qaida members from Afghanistan, via Iran and Pakistan, to countries that allow them to function—with their full knowledge or as a result of the absence of an effective central government—enable the organization to renew its preparations for continued terror activity.

For more than a decade, and with greater intensity since 1996, hundreds of young Muslims arrived in Afghanistan from all over the Muslim world, as well as other countries worldwide—including Western Europe, Eastern Europe, Asia, North America, Australia, and Africa—underwent training in guerilla warfare and terror, and were sent back to their own countries. Thus, a pool of trained terrorists loyal to the concept of Global Jihad was created.

These terrorists were assembled in terror cells, with each cell composed of a small number of activists "programmed" to perpetrate terror attacks against Islamic foes. The exposure of terror cells in Europe (Britain, France, Italy, Spain, and Germany), in Asia (the Philippines, Malaysia, Indonesia, Singapore, and India), in the Middle East (Jordan, Egypt, Lebanon, and Israel), and in North America (United States and Canada)—before and after September 11, 2001—serves as concrete evidence of their *modus operandi*, intentions, targets, and the inherent danger that they pose.

Despite widespread thwarting activity against the organization and its supporters worldwide, since September 11, 2001 Al-Qaida has succeeded in perpetrating a series of grave attacks at various global targets with the assistance of other radical Islamic organizations; the synagogue at Djerba, Tunisia; a nightclub in Bali, Indonesia; the French oil tanker *Limbourg* in Yemen; the Paradise Hotel in Mombasa, Kenya; targets in Riyadh, Saudi Arabia; and in Casablanca, Morocco.

Moreover, a year after the collapse of the Taliban regime, resistance to the government of Hamid Karzai and the presence of United States and coalition forces in Afghanistan is steadily increasing. The Taliban movement, Al-Qaida, and the radical Islamic organization of Hikmatiyar are gradually re-establishing their power and influence in the country, and are conducting guerilla warfare—which they define as Jihad—against Karzai's "puppet government and the American and coalition forces."

Parallel to the continued fighting in Afghanistan and the global struggle against Al-Qaida infrastructures worldwide, the United States extended the front of the war against global terror and toppled Saddam Hussein's regime in Iraq. President George Bush defined three of the countries that support terror as extremely dangerous and called them "the Axis of Evil." These three countries were Iraq, Iran and North Korea. The United States accused these countries of involvement in terror and of attempts to develop and acquire weapons for mass destruction. The combination of an "irresponsible and aggressive" regime, alongside a policy supporting terror and non-conventional weapons is justifiably perceived by the United States as an intolerable threat against peace in the free world.

As stated above, of the three countries that make up the "Axis of Evil," the United States chose to contend first with the Iraqi regime. While the campaign in Afghanistan was conducted with the full backing of the United Nations and the international community, prior to the offensive in Iraq the United States encountered difficulties in recruiting world sup-port, and many countries—including U.S. allies in NATO—expressed reservations vis-à-vis a U.S. offensive in Iraq. Nevertheless, even without international support, the United States initiated a campaign in Iraq at the head of a small coalition, and within less than a month defeated Saddam Hussein's regime and took over Iraq.

The offensive in Iraq made it clear to states that support terror that the United States is determined and unwavering in its war against terror, and that any country that continues to support terror is risking a confrontation with the United states and its fate may be similar to that of Afghanistan and Iraq. The invasion of Afghanistan and Iraq by the U.S.-led coalition has brought about the encirclement of Iran—another of the "Axis of Evil" countries—and the world "leader" in wielding terror for the promotion of its goals.

The United States is currently presenting the Iranians with two demands:

- To cease the use of terror;
- To cease the development of weapons for mass destruction.

If Iran refuses to meet these demands, it might find itself on a collision course with the United States and its allies.

The importance of activating military force has been understood since the dawn of history. The activation of military strength in Afghanistan and in Iraq in the war against terror confirmed the necessity to use force from time to time. Nevertheless, in the framework of the campaign against states that support terror it is also possible to apply a combination of pressures as well as economic and political sanctions, which may well be no less effective than the use of military force.

Confirmation of the latter can be found, for example, in the regime of international sanctions imposed on Libya following the exposure of its involvement in the explosion of the Pan American airplane over Lockerbie at the end of 1988. The effective set of sanctions imposed on Libya by the Security Council (Resolution 748, March 1991) ultimately changed Libya from a country that actively supports terror—among the most brutal attacks in the history of international terror—into a country that supports terror passively and cautiously. In light of this development, it is likely that the United States will first strive to persuade Iran to cooperate and accept the U.S. demands, but if that country does not acquiesce, the United States will activate various types of leverage and will save the military option as a last resort.

The intensity of the terror campaign in the United States and the damages it inflicted caused major upheaval in the consciousness of the public at large and among decision-makers all over the globe. It also caused shifts in international relationships at the bilateral and multilateral levels. However, the American experience vis-à-vis the Iraqi campaign has proven that it cannot expect automatic support for its steps in the war against terror. Countries act according to their own basic interests, which do not necessarily correspond with those of the United States. Thus, in the matter of the offensive in Afghanistan, unprecedented cooperation was formed between the United States and Russia, which enabled U.S. military cooperation with CIS countries (formerly part of the Soviet Union) such as Georgia and Uzbekistan.

These states permitted U.S. military forces to use bases in their territories for the attack of targets in Afghanistan and in exchange the

United States granted them economic aid. The cooperation between the United States and Russia ultimately led to the signing of a historical cooperation agreement between Russia and the NATO countries in the matter of combating terror. However, in the matter of the offensive in Iraq, Russia was one of the primary opponents to the U.S. military campaign, and it still maintains that the United States erred when it set out on the campaign.

The relationship between the United States and China also underwent changes as a result of the September 2001 events. The relationship between these countries is shadowed by the competition between the two powers, which have different and sometimes opposing interests. In addition, the relationship was further strained due to the incident of the American intelligence plane caught in China. Nevertheless, the two achieved cooperation in light of the shared threat posed by Islamic terror. China, which faces the threat of Islamic terror in its Xinjiang region, also supported the international coalition against terror. However, similar to Russia, China was also adamantly opposed to the U.S. military campaign in Iraq, and claimed—on the basis of its own considerations—that the United States should not be granted legitimization to unilaterally demand the replacement of regimes and act forcefully against them.

In an interim summary of the war against terror to date (January 2007) the following results are to be noted:

- The United States has proved twice (in Afghanistan and in Iraq) that terror-supporting regimes pay the highest price—the loss of their power.
- U.S. military and technological superiority enables it to defeat adversaries like the Taliban regime in Afghanistan and Saddam Hussein's regime in Iraq in a fairly short period of time and with a minimal death toll.
- The toppling of regimes that support terror does not ensure the establishment of a stable and democratic alternative administration; in this area the United States has achieved only limited success to date (if at all);
- The experience accumulated in Afghanistan and Iraq indicates that the ousting of a regime that supports terror in itself is insufficient; the long-term presence of forces and the investment of significant financial resources are prerequisites for the foundation of a new and stable administration that will prohibit the growth of terror in the country.
- The handling of the regimes in Afghanistan and Iraq constitutes a warning signal to states that support terror, most of which actually joined the coalition against terror in an attempt to avoid becoming a target of an American offensive in the future.

- The war against states that support terror has encountered political difficulties due to a conflict of interests on the part of countries that are ostensibly members of the counter-terror coalition. This fact is clearly reflected in the lack of support for the U.S. offensive in Iraq, and this trend is expected to recur and even intensify in future campaigns against countries such as Iran.
- The lack of a consensus and cooperation leaves the United States to bear the brunt of the burden of the counter-terror campaign. In the absence of operative cooperation and the investment of input by the international community, even the United States will find it difficult to sustain a large number of campaigns in various confrontation arenas.
- The destruction of the terror infrastructures in Afghanistan and Iraq inflicted damage on Al-Qaida, but it did not significantly impair the organization's operational capabilities and infrastructures worldwide.
- Al-Qaida has a world-encompassing infrastructure (globalization of terror), consisting of autonomous cells capable of perpetrating attacks and expanding the organization's covert infrastructures.
- Al-Qaida has an impressive capacity to renew and rehabilitate itself, so that the apprehension of senior commanders and fighters does not leave a vacuum in the organization, and its ranks replenish themselves.
- The global war against terror, which began with the annihilation of terror infrastructures in Afghanistan and which includes various thwarting measures all over the world (freezing funds, arrests, and more), has somewhat diminished the operational capabilities of the organization's cells, and these are "satisfied" with less spectacular and complex attacks than those of September 11 (although they are painful enough).
- There is effective, world-encompassing cooperation among Islamic terror organizations, which assist each other in the perpetration of attacks and in the ongoing struggle against the U.S.-led coalition.
- In contrast to the effective cooperation among the terror organizations, the free world has encountered difficulties in uniting its ranks and enhancing joint cooperation in the war against terror.
- The United States and the coalition presence in Afghanistan and in Iraq are perceived by large sections of the local populations as an "occupation." Thus, guerilla and terror combat are gradually developing in these arenas against the foreign presence and against the governments regarded as "puppet regimes," which are acting under the sponsorship of the foreign powers. Both Afghanistan and Iraq turned into theaters of Jihad and mujahidin from the Muslim world joined the fighting in these theaters.
- This reality makes it difficult to cope with terror and forms processes that make the ability to defeat and eradicate terror seem remote and far removed from realization.

Rehabilitating "Failing States" as a Component of the War against Global Terror[5]

"Failing states" like Somalia endanger the stability of the international system because national states constitute the foundations of world order. Global security is based on states whose role it is to prevent internal chaos and reduce the spreading of domestic anarchy beyond their borders. The state serves as the intermediary between the internal social, economic, and political systems and the external global system.

The phenomenon of the "failing state" began to develop and spread at the end of World War I, due to the crumbling of the Austro-Hungarian and Ottoman empires. This phenomenon persevered with the collapse of Western colonialism after World War II, and the dismantling of the Soviet Union at the end of the 1990s. In 1914, the number of recognized states in the international system was fifty-five. In 1960 this figure rose to ninety, and with the end of the Cold War and the disintegration of the Soviet Union, their number grew to 192.

The states were not created equal, and they vary in population, resources and governments. A modern state must grapple with far more complex demands and challenges than those faced by countries in the past. Today, the modern state is expected to supply its population with proper government, security, and economic prosperity, as well as education, health, and welfare services. Moreover, it is expected to inspire a feeling of unity and national pride, but primarily the state must provide collective and individual security and public order.

In reality, many of the newly created states are too "weak and fragile" to survive as national states, and they face risks and difficulties that may cause their decline to the status of "failing states." This deterioration from the status of a "standard state" to a "failing state" involves processes which can be identified and provide advance warning as they transpire.

- *The economic aspect*—A rapid decline of the standard of living while the economic elite is comprised of favored sector-related groups (family, tribe, etc.); a severe shortage of foreign currency, which leads to a scarcity of basic food products and gasoline; a sharp decline in the government's ability to provide basic services in the areas of health, education, transportation and more; a corrupt bureaucracy and government that take over the limited resources and transfer funds to private accounts outside of the country.
- *The political aspect*—The government is in the hands of a minority or a single ruler; sections of society feel that they are not represented by the government and are discriminated against in comparison to

the elite that is identified with the administration; The government, which in the past was perceived as an entity acting on behalf of the general good, is currently perceived to represent the interests of certain sectors. Thus polarization is created in society and the government sustains its power through control and subjugation; the freedom of speech and personal security of the individual are impaired; and the state's dwindling resources are invested in the ruler's safety.

When a stop is not put to the political and economic decline, the state reaches a decisive stage of the loss of governmental legitimacy, public order becomes uncontrollable, and the government loses its monopoly of power to halt the process of collapse. In this sort of scenario, a preventive policy must be implemented, crisis management, and handling must be initiated, and sometimes there arises a need for external intervention.

Robert Rotberg claims that the process whereby a state becomes a "failing state" is reversible, i.e., it is possible to put a stop to the deterioration processes in a country, rehabilitate it, and restore its status as a functioning state—even after its systems have collapsed and it has become a "failing state."[6] He claims that it is possible to prevent the decline of a state to a "failing state" mainly through external intervention.

Saving the state from the collapse processes entails two basic conditions:

- The signs attesting to the state's collapse are identified at a relatively early stage.
- The existence of an external entity willing to invest the necessary input for the prevention of state collapse.

External intervention may be reflected in the following ways:

- The involvement of a superpower that undertakes the state's rescue and rehabilitation;
- The intervention of a regional organization willing to undertake this mission;
- UN intervention.

Sometimes there is also the possibility of incorporation and cooperation of several external entities in the rescue and rehabilitation processes preventing state collapse, starting from economic and/or military aid, through the prevention of the establishment of a dictatorial regime, which may induce collapse, and culminating in military intervention aimed at restoring public order and stability. A salient example of the latter is obviously Somalia, where the 1993 attempt by the United States and the United Nations to initiate rehabilitation failed dismally.

It is possible to indicate several central processes in the rehabilitation of a failing state:

- Cessation of violence—bringing the rival parties to a ceasefire and initiating negotiations as well as preservation of the ceasefire through an external, neutral force.
- Humanitarian aid—via state aid and international humanitarian organizations.
- Establishing a temporary government—The temporary government must include representatives of all of the relevant powerbrokers, act to restore a central government capable of ruling and providing all of the population's needs, and lay the foundation for the election of a representative government.
- Establishing security forces—Establishing an army and police force to replace the sectarian powerbrokers, which will be placed at the disposal of the temporary government in order to enforce government control. These security forces will be founded, trained and supervised by external international entities.
- Rehabilitation of the administrative system—Rehabilitation of the administration and renewal of the state's provision of services to its citizens.
- Rehabilitation of the judiciary system—Rehabilitation of the judiciary system, which will function jointly with law enforcement entities to restore personal and public security in the country.
- Rehabilitation of the political system—The creation of a democratic political system (insofar that this is possible) and the establishment of an administration representative of the entire population including all of its components.
- Economic aid—International economic aid to rehabilitate the local economy and develop the state's capability to become incorporated in global economy.

These processes may be implemented either gradually or concurrently, according to the unique circumstances in each country.

The "preventive" steps—those designated to prevent the creation of "failing states"—and the actions to rehabilitate the "failing state" constitute a crucial component in the war against terror, as terror in general and Islamic terror in particular regard "failing states" and "uncontrollable areas" as optimal and fertile activity areas for the establishment of infrastructures and power focal points.

This theory is soon to be tested, in the aftermath of the two campaigns that the United States waged to topple the regimes in Afghanistan and Iraq. In both cases the United States must act to rehabilitate and rebuild these countries after the military offensive. Afghanistan was defined as a "failing state" even before the latest war, after over twenty years of bloodshed that led to the destruction of the state and to the dismantling of its economic and governmental infrastructures. Iraq, on the other hand, was ruled for over twenty years by a dictatorship that terrorized the population and enforced law and order with an iron fist. The ousting of the regime caused a "governmental vacuum" and a state of chaos.

In both cases it would appear that the United States is encountering considerable difficulties in its efforts to establish stable governments that will restore the status of "normal states" and enable the states to function properly within the international system. The instability in both states is already leading to the formation of local opposition powerbrokers, acting via terror and guerilla warfare against the U.S. forces and the U.S.-supported local leadership, which is regarded as an illegitimate governmental entity that must be ousted.

Somalia is the most significant example of a failing state—until 2007 all attempts to restore law and order and to rebuild an effective government ended with failure. The emergence of the Islamic Courts represents the Islamic solution to the "chaotic" situation. But the Islam is not the only solution for a "failing state." Far from the media and the international public interest, we may found a relatively peaceful and democratic alternative to the Somali "chaos" in Somaliland.

Somaliland as an Alternative Model

Somaliland is the northeastern part of Somalia. Somaliland was a British protectorate until June 26, 1960, when it gained its independence. However Somaliland ceased to exist as a sovereign state after the union with Italian Somalia in the south and the partners from the Somali republic.[7]

Somaliland had reclaimed its sovereignty and abandoned the union on May 18, 1991, after the collapse of the Barre regime. Somaliland has followed a very different trajectory from the rest of Somalia, which turned into a "failed state."

Over the last 15 years Somaliland has adopted a process of internally driven political, economic, and social reconstruction. Somaliland developed its unique political and social system combining tradition with Western democracy. Somaliland's democratic transition began in May 2001 with a plebiscite, a new constitution that introduced a multiparty electoral system, and continued in December 2002 with local elections that were widely described as open and transparent.[8]

Somaliland's presidential election of April 14, 2003 was a milestone in the self-declared, unrecognized internationally republic's process of democratization. Nearly half a million voters cast ballots in one of the closest polls ever conducted in the region: when the last votes had been counted and the results announced on April 19, 2003, the incumbent president, Dahir Rayale Kahin, had won by only 80 votes.[9]

As the country celebrates its 15th independence anniversary on 2006, it boasts of having its own national flag, currency, army, and police force, a bicameral parliament, executive bodies of government, a developing educational system (including a number of universities), and an improving health system. It also has a burgeoning private sector, which has booming business.

Somaliland's increasingly credible claims to statehood present the international community with a thorny diplomatic dilemma. Recognition of Somaliland, although under consideration by a growing number of African and Western governments, is still vigorously resisted by many members of both the African Union (AU) and the Arab League on the grounds that the unit and territorial integrity of member states is sacrosanct. Furthermore, the creation of a future Somali government that claims jurisdiction over Somaliland threatens to open a new phase in the Somali conflict.

The victory of the ICU in south and central Somalia, the confrontation between the ICU and TFG and the threat of a radical Islamic state in Somalia turned the Somaliland question into a critical stage. The victory of the TFG and its Ethiopian allies over the ICU, removed the immediate threat of radical Islam to Somaliland, but left open the question of the existence of an independent Somaliland as a part of a future political solution to the Somali crises. The United States and its allies in the Horn of Africa have to recognize Somaliland as an alternative model to the former lawlessness of the warlords era and to the radical Islamic alternative of the ICU.

The United States and Its Confrontation with Islamic Terror in the Red Sea Region

The US declaration of war against terror contains intentions regarding global confrontation of the problem. The general characteristics of the campaign against terror were discussed in the two previous chapters, therefore in this chapter we will focus on the issue of America's method of contending with the problem of Islamic terror in the particular region discussed in this study.

The global and overall aspects vis-à-vis the concept of the campaign against terror have serious impact regarding American policy in this geographical focal point. Following the American declaration of war against terror, the names of Sudan, Somalia, and Yemen arose alongside that of Afghanistan—which was the first target of the war—as countries that maintained ties with Al-Qaida and which might become targets of the campaign to be waged by "the coalition against terror." In light of this threat, the leaders of these countries rushed to declare, each in his own way, that their countries were not linked with Al-Qaida and Islamic terror, and that they were willing to cooperate with the United States in its war against terror.

At the same time as the offensive in Afghanistan, the United States initiated contacts with the governments of Sudan and Yemen and with various powerbrokers in Somalia, in order to actively recruit them in the war against terror. Alongside the contacts and talks, the United States sent boats, marines, and special units to the Red Sea whose mission was to patrol these countries' coasts and prevent the arrival of activists from Al-Qaida and other terror organizations fleeing Afghanistan. The presence of the American and coalition forces was meant to put pressure on the rulers of the countries in the region and enable the United States to take military action in the area if necessary (although the scope of the forces currently deployed there would enable only limited special campaigns).

The policy adopted by the United States vis-à-vis the countries in this region was based on the "stick and carrot" method. The rulers were promised military and economic aid in exchange for their cooperation in the war against terror, alongside the threat that if they refused, they would be risking political, economic, and military action on the part of the U.S.-led coalition against their governments.

As a result of the Sudanese declaration regarding its willingness to join the war against terror, and after apparently proving this intention by taking practical steps, the economic sanctions imposed on the country due to its involvement in terror were lifted, and the United States began intensive mediation efforts in order to achieve a ceasefire and launch peace talks between the regime in Khartoum and the rebels in the south, an act which has met with success to date.

Yemeni President Salah was promised military and economic aid in exchange for joining the war against terror. After improving its cooperation in the investigation of the attack against the USS Cole and following action taken against Al-Qaida activists in its territory, Yemen was granted

U.S. economic and military aid, including the provision of combat means and the training of Yemeni forces in counterterror missions.

It would therefore appear that the concrete threat posed by the United States and the coalition against terror to strike out at the regimes that support terror, based on the same format as the destruction of the Taliban regime in Afghanistan and Saddam Hussein's regime in Iraq, instigated a change in the approach of the governments in Sudan and Yemen. These regimes were forced to choose between their allegiance to their worldview and support of radical Islam, and the real danger to their governments' survival. For the time being, the consideration of survival has prevailed, forcing a compromise (if only a temporary one) on the ideological and cultural levels. However, this policy forces the rulers to contend with heavy domestic pressures from the direction of opposition circles and mainly from the entities identified with radical Islam. In these circumstances, only intensive and ongoing U.S. and international pressure will preserve the policy that these countries have adopted, and any lessening of the pressure may modify the equation and allow these countries to continue supporting radical Islam.

In light of this situation picture, the United States must take cautious and balanced action in order to refrain from causing these regimes to collapse, which could lead to the creation of chaotic situations including loss of central governments and the creation of nomadic entities. The latter are openly hostile to the West, a fact that diminishes the political and military influence wielded by the United States and the West, as has been the case in Somalia during the last decade.

The attack against the French oil tanker *Limbourg* (October 2002) and the attacks against Israeli targets in Mombasa Kenya (November 2002) serve as painful reminders to the United States and the rest of the world that the war against Islamic terror in this region is far from over. Thus, when claiming responsibility for the attacks in Mombasa, Al-Qaida specifically referred to the struggle in the arena of the Horn of Africa.[10]

From the same place that the "Crusader-Jewish alliance" sustained a blow four years ago, i.e., in Nairobi and in Dar al-Salaam, in the U.S. embassies there, here again the warriors of the Jihad from the organization of Al-Qaida have returned in order to strike a painful blow against this treacherous alliance...

... These two actions come and destroy all of the dreams of the "Jewish-Crusader alliance" in this area, and prove the failure of the United States and its allies, which amassed their huge navies in order to surround and lay siege to the Horn of Africa so as to pursue the Jihad fighters in this area and prevent them from penetrating it or dispatching supplies, and to ensure that the attacks that struck them four years ago will not recur.

The Bush administration clearly identifies the risk inherent to the spread of Islamic terror throughout Africa in general, and in eastern Africa in particular. Against this background, President Bush undertook an African tour in the course of which he visited five countries (Senegal, South Africa, Botswana, Uganda, and Nigeria), with the aim of signaling a message to all of the countries on that continent. President Bush emphasized the U.S. commitment to assisting African states in their battle against starvation and AIDS as well as the promotion of democratic values.[11] During his visit, the president also underlined his determination to persevere in the war against terror, including upon the African continent. It is to be noted that even prior to the president's African tour, a plan was prepared by the Pentagon to establish U.S. bases throughout Africa, in order to enable ongoing activity against terror organizations, in the light of indications gathered by U.S. intelligence agencies that the activities of Al-Qaida and other terror organizations were on the rise in this continent.

As of September 2001, a task force of the U.S.-led coalition has been active in the region of the Horn of Africa. The commander of the U.S. force, Major General John Stellar, stated that the force includes some 1,300 soldiers, about 900 of which are members of special units stationed at the Lemonier base in Djibouti. The force is equipped with transport planes and helicopter gunships, which enable immediate action in the entire action arena.[12] General Stellar also operates a sea task force, which patrols the movement of ships in the Bab el-Mandeb Straits along the shores of the Horn of Africa.

This task force has been granted the approval of the states in that region—Djibouti, Yemen, Eritrea, and Ethiopia—to act within their boundaries if the need arises. An example of American operational capabilities in this region is reflected in the termination of several Al-Qaida activists in Yemen (November 5, 2002), via an UAV armed with missiles that hit the car in which they were traveling.

To date, the overall strategy implemented by the United States in the war against global terror has instigated changes in the policies of Yemen and Sudan, ostensibly turning them into U.S. allies in the war against terror. The combination of U.S. military presence in the region as well the offering of economic and political enticements constitute the main leverage preventing states that formerly supported terror from reverting to their erstwhile policies. An expression of the success of U.S. policy can also be seen in the peace accord between the Sudanese government and the rebel forces in the country's southern provinces. Another step that can be attributed to the American policy is the agreement between Sudan, Yemen and Ethiopia to increase cooperation in the war on terror.

Nonetheless, the huge area, teeming with a large and poverty-stricken Muslim population, constitutes an wide field of action for Islamic terror organizations, and therefore in the foreseeable future eastern Africa will continue to constitute an arena with a high potential for terror attacks and the development of terror infrastructures that will pose a threat against the United States and the Free World.

The War against Terror and Somalia

After the losses of 1993 ("Black Hawk Down") the United States left Somalia in a "chaotic" statelessness. The ongoing clashes among the local warlords, the TNG, and later, the TFG and the Islamic courts, made Somalia a potential "safe haven" for Islamic terror organizations. The United States identified Somalia as a potential threat in the global war against terror and has developed a regional strategy to confront the threat.

A Belgian based International Crisis Group (ICG) said that: "Somalia is the largest potential safe haven for Al-Qaida in Africa.[13]

Somalia is an Al-Qaida recruiter's dream—with rampant unemployment, travel restrictions, and no government or foreign investment—and young Somalis will turn to terrorism for money and, occasionally, because of shared ideology. Schools run by Islamic charities are graduating large numbers of students with no prospect of meaningful work. Drug dealers and militias looking to restart conflict over economic interests find easy recruits, further destabilizing the area and sowing the seeds of radicalism.[14]

In Somalia, contact was initiated between American security entities and various powerbrokers in the country. However, due to the lack of a central, effective government the American were forced to initiate separate contacts vis-à-vis each one of these entities, all of which sought to elicit U.S. support in internal power struggles. Thus, each promised to join the U.S. war against terror and accused its domestic opponents of supporting Al-Qaida and Islamic terror entities.

The United States established the Djibouti base in 2003, with smaller bases or points of contact in the region including in Ethiopia, Kenya, and northeastern Somalia. The focus of the U.S. strategy is an anti-terrorist one, although they are also establishing programs to dig wells and assist in humanitarian projects.[15]

Reports in the U.S. media claimed part of the anti-terrorist strategy in the region was to support the warlords in Somalia and encourage them to seize individuals suspected of terrorism or Islamic extremism. This has always been officially denied by the U.S. government. It became an "open secret," with reports of money being dispersed from Nairobi by U.S. intelligence agencies. In Mogadishu, the United States was perceived to be behind the "anti-terrorist" coalition set up by the warlords on 18 February 2006, called the Alliance for Restoration of Peace and Counter Terrorism—ARPCT. Local reports—although unsubstantiated—claim that Qanyare, Dhere and Bashir Rage (a founding member of the alliance) have from time to time kidnapped "suspects" in Mogadishu and handed them over to U.S. agents.[16]

Former CIA Director Porter Goss is alleged to have visited Kenya in February 2006, to coordinate a campaign against Al-Qaida with Somalia warlords (the U.S. embassy in Nairobi simply states that it has "no information" about such a visit).[17] According to the TFG and Kenyan security sources, this visit was followed by a CIA mission to Mogadishu that distributed as much as US$2 million in funding to ARPCT warlords.[18] Assistant Secretary of State for African Affairs Jendayi Frazer stated that she did not know if the ARPCT warlords were receiving U.S. assistance, but made clear that "We will work with those elements that will help us to root out Al-Qaida and to prevent Somalia becoming a safe haven for terrorists, and we are doing it in the interests of protecting America."[19]

The narrow focus of the United States on the capture of some foreign Al Qaida militants, implicated in attacks on the U.S. embassies in Nairobi and Dar al Salaam in 1998 and the Israeli-owned hotel near Mombasa in 2002,[20] backfired and ended up empowering the Islamists (ICU) that it sought to undermine.[21] Ultimately, the perceived role of the United States provided a popular focus for resentment and served to strengthen the Islamic Court's position.

The ARPCT was engaged in heavy fighting with the ICU and after several months of heavy fighting was defeated by the ICU. State Department counterterrorism coordinator Henry Crampton acknowledged that the Bush administration failed to correctly assess the power of the ICU and the popular support they enjoy.[22] The failure of the concept supporting the ARPCT created a new challenge for the U.S. policy in the Horn of Africa. The TFG remained, after the defeat of the ARPCT, the only obstacle on the way of the ICU to gain control over most of the Somali state.

The Ethiopian support to the TFG reflected the common interest of Ethiopia and other states in Horn of Africa and the United States to remove the Islamic threat in the region. Washington backed the warlords in their losing battle against the Islamists in spring 2006, and tacitly approved Ethiopia's military intervention to support the TFG. In December 2006, it has even been passing aerial surveillance reports to Addis Ababa, according to U.S. news reports.[23] Preoccupied with the specter of Islamic terrorism, Washington is thus party to an attempt by Ethiopia to replace a popular de facto government in Somalia, the ICU, with a widely reviled official one, and it is a dangerous gamble.[24]

Ethiopian Prime Minister Meles Zenawi denied U.S. involvement in the country's counterattacks on Somalia's Union of Islamic Courts (ICU).[25] "The U.S. hasn't contributed a single bullet, a single soldier or a single military equipment to this operation," Meles told a press conference in Addis Ababa.

> "We have with the U.S. longstanding arrangements to share intelligence on terrorist activities in the neighborhood and that sharing of activities in the neighborhood and that sharing of intelligence has not been stopped during the conflict. This is the sum total of our close partnership with the U.S. and the so-called involvement of the U.S. in the Somali crisis."[26]

On January 9, 2007, the United States conducted air strikes against suspected Al Qaida targets near Kenya-Somalia border. On January 10, 2007, Pentagon spokesman Bryan Whitman officially acknowledged that U.S. combat aircrafts had struck a suspected terrorist hideout in southern Somalia.[27]

He said the operation involved one or more AC-130 planes and was based on intelligence reports that principal Al Qaida leaders were in the area. "We are going to remain committed to reducing terrorist capabilities when and where we find them and the operation was an example of that."[28]

White House spokesman Tony Snow expressed a similar view at his daily briefing. "We have made it clear that this is a global war on terror, and this is a reiteration of the fact. People who think that they are going to establish safe haven for al-Qaida any place need to realize that we are going to fight them," he said.[29]

In Mogadishu, Somalia's interim president endorsed the air strike. Interim President Abdullah Yusuf told reporters al-Qaida terrorists had been using his country as a safe haven and as a base for their operations for years. Yusuf said the United States had a right to attack the al-Qaida leaders, who he said were involved in the bombings of the U.S. embassies in Kenya and Tanzania in 1998.[30]

The target of the air strikes was Fazul Abdullah Muhammad, a senior Al Qaida commander that the United States accused of perpetrating the terror attacks against the U.S. embassies and against Israel, tourists in the Paradise Hotel, and an Israeli commercial airplane in Mombasa, Kenya, in 2002. Two other most wanted Al Qaida terrorists that U.S. forces are looking for in Somalia are: Abu Talha al-Sudani, a Kenyan, and Saleh Ali Nabhan.

The U.S. air strikes in Somalia failed to kill any of the three Al Qaida suspects they targeted, but killed up to 10 of their Somali allies. This was the first known direct U.S. military intervention in Somalia since the failed peacekeeping mission that ended in 1994.[31]

Meanwhile, Fazul Abdullah Muhammad's wife and the wife of Saleh Ali Saleh Nabhan have been arrested in Kenya after fleeing the coastal Somali town of Ras Kamboni, Kenyan intelligence sources say.[32]

The air strikes in Somalia are a part of the U.S. multidimensional campaign in the Horn of Africa. The United States sees the break-up of the Union of Islamic Courts as an opportunity to try to remove what it regards as a serious threat from al-Qaida in the region.

The U.S. strategy is to hunt the Al Qaida operatives in Somalia and to ensure that the ICU and their supporters do not regroup and post a threat to the TFG. The Americans and their Somali and Ethiopian allies therefore feared a guerrilla war that might threaten efforts to establish the new government. They are determined to stop the Islamic Courts from resuming power.

The U.S. 5th Fleet has been patrolling the Somali coast to prevent any escape of Al Qaida and other radical Islamists by sea. In order to upgrade the U.S. military capabilities in Somalia: the U.S. Navy had moved an aircraft carrier to the Somali coast to beef up the naval cordon.[33] U.S. aircraft have carried out reconnaissance flights over Somalia and it is believed that the United States provided Ethiopian forces with intelligence support during the recent offensive.[34]

According to Somali sources, small U.S. special operations forces are providing military advice to Ethiopian and TFG forces in Somalia. Somalia's deputy prime, Hussein Aidid, said American special forces were needed on the ground to capture remaining extremists. "They know how and they have the right equipment to capture this people."

The United States and other governments are acting to shore up the government of President Abdullahi Yusuf (TFG) by encouraging the formation of an African Union force to act as peacekeepers. The Security Council gave its approval for such a force in Resolution 1725 in December 2006, before the Ethiopian offensive. The resolution was implemented in 2007 and an AU peacekeeping force is operating in Somalia.

The U.S. State Department called for all Somalis to achieve "genuine national reconciliation" and reiterated its support for an African peace-keeping force to be deployed in the country. "The current situation in Somalia provides a historic opportunity for the Somali people to achieve a broadbased, inclusive·government" it was said in a statement on December 29, 2006.[35]

Secretary of State Condoleezza Rice announced that the United States is providing $16.5 million as an initial "robust" response to meet humanitarian needs in Somalia following the re-establishment of control over the country by the Transitional Federal Institutions.[36] In a January 4, 2007 statement, Rice said Somalia has a "historic opportunity to being to move beyond two decades of violence and the international community has to join the United States in supporting humanitarian and reconciliation efforts.[37]

The secretary of state said, the United States is providing $11.5 million for food aid that will be distributed through the World Food Programme. Also, $1.5 million in nonfood assistance is being given through UNICEF, and $3.5 million is being provided through the UN High Commissioner for Refugees and its implementing partners for assistance to Somali refugees.[38] "These resources will help an additional 18,000 people displaced by recent floods and conflict," Rice said. "We intend to seek additional substantial assistance to help Somalia with humanitarian, security, and reconstruction efforts."[39]

Concluding Remarks about the War against Terror and the Somali Crises

A brief interim evaluation of the TFG government since its victory over the ICU does not inspire great hope regarding the TFG's ability to restore order, security and an effective government in Somalia.

A short time after the collapse of the ICU regime, in which local warlords controlled various areas of Somalia and its capital, Mogadishu, incidents of robbery and looting, inter-tribal agitation, and shooting incidents escalated. The activity of pirates, which had ceased during the ICU's regime, resumed and in March 2007 a ship carrying UN humanitarian aid to Somalia was hijacked.

However, aside from the return to "chaotic" characteristics, which typified Somalia during the period prior to the ICU's ascent to power, a new dimension was now added to the violence in that country—the Jihad of Islamic entities against the TFG and foreign forces (the Ethiopians and the African Union peacekeeping force in Mogadishu).

To illustrate the severity of the problem, one need only note that in the first two weeks of March 2007, 16 shooting incidents took place in Mogadishu. These incidents involved mortar fire, a roadside explosive charge and shooting from light arms. Three rebel attacks were perpetrated against the Ethiopian forces, two against the Ugandan unit in the African Union peacekeeping force, and the remaining eleven incidents were carried out against TFG government and military targets, including an attack against the presidential palace.

The rebel forces, the majority of which are associated with the ICU, are supported by Al Qaida and the Global Jihad. These organizations continue to reiterate their commitment to the Jihad in Somalia. However, Muslim countries like Eritrea and Yemen and NGOs within the Muslim world are also assisting Islamic entities to conduct the Jihad in Somalia. Following the victory of the TFG and the Ethiopian forces, Somalia has become an arena for Jihad and the site for a showdown between the anti-terror coalition, led by the United States, and the Global Jihad.

The "Somali Affair" has thus enabled an examination of the confrontation between the coalition of the global war on terror headed by the United States and the Islamic ICU in Somalia. Since the events of 1993 (Black Hawk Down), the United States has regarded Somalia as a potential focal point for the development of Islamic terror. This assumption proved to be true in 1998 when perpetrators sought and were granted refuge in Somalia after attacks in Kenya and Tanzania. The Itihad al Islamiya organization appears on the U.S. State Department's list of terror organizations.

Following the September 11, 2001 attacks and the American campaign against terror that was launched in Afghanistan in October 2001, the United States assumed that Al Qaida entities fleeing from Afghanistan would try to find refuge in the area of the Horn of Africa in general and Somalia in particular.

As part of its efforts to apprehend terrorists affiliated with Al Qaida and the Global Jihad, the United States tightened its ties with Ethiopia, Somalia's historical adversary, which supported the transitional Somali government (TFG). The latter was located at Baidoa and lacked influence in much of Somalia, including the local warlords in Mogadishu who had joined forces in a single organization (ARPCT) with the United States' blessing. By initiating these steps, the United States chose two power brokers that were unpopular among most of the Somali population.

For the most part, the Islamic movement—the Islamic Courts Union (ICU)—developed as a grassroots organization designated to correct the "chaotic" situation in Somalia and restore law and order. Due to the fact that the organization grew at different focal points, it came to contain a wide range of moderate and extremist leaders. In order to broaden its power base and stabilize the central government, the Islamic movement confronted U.S. allies in the Somali arena in two phases—initially the ARPCT and subsequently the TFG.

American assistance and support for the ARPCT, and the American decision to avoid all contact with the ICU, despite appeals from that organization's moderate leaders, such as Sheikh Ahmad, strengthened its militant factors and brought about the election of Sheikh Aweys, who is affiliated with Al Qaida. The American fears regarding the ICU had become a self-fulfilling prophecy.

After the defeat of the ARPCT, and when it appeared that the ICU would also rout the TFG forces, the United States activated its other ally in the arena—Ethiopia. With U.S. blessings, Ethiopia launched a military operation in order to save the TFG. Thanks to Ethiopia's overwhelming military advantage, Ethiopia together with the TFG forces succeeded in defeating the ICU, taking over Mogadishu and paving the way for a TFG-led government within a short period of time.

Already during the fighting stages between the ICU forces and the joint Ethiopian and TFG forces, the United States initiated direct action in Somalia against targets that were suspected of serving as bases for Al Qaida terrorists (who had been wanted by the United States since the 1998 attacks). The American attacks, however, did not achieved the desired effect. Today, the victory of the U.S. allies in the Somali arena appears to be a short-term gain and a long-term loss.

Al Qaida and the Global Jihad attempted to sponsor the ICU during its initial stages in Somalia, but the organization's leaders, including Sheikh Aweys, were careful to avoid any link to Al Qaida in order to win international legitimacy. After the collapse of the ICU regime, the moderate voices were silenced in the Islamic movement and its leaders declared a Jihad in Somalia against the TFG government as well as the Ethiopian and foreign forces that had taken over the country. Al Qaida and the Global Jihad organizations, which regard Somalia as a new arena for confrontation in addition to the existing arenas in Afghanistan and Iraq, echoed this call.

After its inception, the ICU (or at least some of its leaders) aspired to avoid any solidarity or affiliation with Al Qaida, though radical components in its ranks offered refuge to a handful of Al Qaida activists who had been hiding in Somalia since 1998. However, after the collapse of the

ICU, a mutual interest and operation plan developed between the latter and the Global Jihad, and U.S. fears that Somalia would become a Jihad arena were realized. Moreover, the presence of Ethiopian soldiers and the AU peacekeeping force on their soil, and particularly in Mogadishu, is perceived by most Somalis, even those who are not affiliated with the ICU, as a foreign occupation of their land. The TFG is regarded as a group of collaborators with enemy elements and it has failed to win legitimacy among the majority of the Somali population.

During its short existence, the ICU government was able to restore law and order as well as personal and public security in most areas of Somalia under its control, which earned it widespread support. The return to the "chaotic existence" under the TFG and the growing violence only served to reinforce solidarity with the Islamic movement, which demonstrated, albeit for a limited period, that there exists an alternative to the "chaotic" state in this country.

Under the existing circumstances, it appears that Somalia will once again be submerged in anarchy for the foreseeable future in which tribal and other warlords, as well as Jihad fighters, will struggle against the central government (TFG) and the foreign forces—the Ethiopians and AU forces supporting them. This situation plays directly into the hands of Global Jihad elements, which know how to exploit it for the continued development of Jihad infrastructures, similar to the pattern in Afghanistan and Iraq.

If the struggle of the Jihad elements prevails and the foreign elements are forced to leave Somalia, thus enabling radical Islamic elements to take control, the Global Jihad will be able to claim credit for a major triumph against the counterterror coalition. The main question on the agenda is how to prevent this eventuality. In light of the above-mentioned processes, the "Somali Affair" is a particularly hard nut to crack as the only model that has succeeded to date to restore law and order, even for a short period, was that offered by radical Islam.

Thus, the alternative for the "Islamic model" must contend with difficult objective circumstances and power brokers that will do their utmost to undermine this sort of move and prove once again that Islam offers the only viable solution. When approaching the issue of Somalia's future, one must consider that the rehabilitation of this country, which for the past 25 years has been embroiled in a chaotic state of violence without a central government, constitutes an extraordinary challenge both for Somali society and for international elements that must support this sort of program.

Contending with the "Somali Affair" thus necessitates simultaneous and combined activity on several levels:

- The domestic Somali level
    - o **The political system**—The TFG in Somalia must take action to expand its power base and intensify its legitimacy in the eyes of the Somali population. In this framework, the temporary government must initiate a dialogue with the following entities:
        - Leaders of the central tribes
        - Moderate Islamic leaders (some of whom are members of the ICU)
        - Local warlords in Mogadishu and other parts of Somalia
        - Capital holders in Somalia and worldwide

This dialogue must lead to the establishment of a parliament that will represent all of the components of Somali society and a government that will include the current adversaries of the temporary government from among the tribes and mainly the Islamic movement.

The establishment of a joint national unity government and a parliament that will represent the majority of the power brokers in the country will enable the diminishment and isolation of the radical elements in the Islamic movement and the Global Jihad entities that support them.

- **Preparing the country's constitution**—It must be acceptable to most components of the emerging political system. The institutions essential to the country's function will be established on the basis of this constitution:
    - o An effective government and an administrative system that will implement the government's policies.
    - o Law enforcement agencies (police, domestic security service, tax systems, etc.)
    - o A legal system, which can be based on the infrastructure of Islamic courts developed by the ICU. Placing the legal system in the ICU's hands may contribute to its cooperation with the new governmental system.
        - **Building a national Somali army**—Establishing the national Somali army on the basis of the TFG forces with the addition of existing militias, including the ICU militia. The Somali military will be organized, trained, and equipped through international aid, mainly from Western countries. Once the military and defense capabilities of the national Somali army reach an adequate level, it will be possible to remove any foreign military presence in that country (see subsequent discussion).
        - **The country's economic rehabilitation**—A prerequisite for Somalia's stabilization is the dramatic improvement of

the population's economic conditions. Somalia's economic rehabilitation will require significant international aid in the form a "Marshall Plan" which must be implemented by the West in cooperation with affluent Muslim countries. The unity government will need to initiate cooperation with Somaliland and Puntland to regulate the relationship between them (possibly on a federal basis).

On the International Level

The international community led by the United States and the West, in cooperation with moderate Arab countries and the African Union, must act on several levels in order to stabilize the government in Somalia. The main steps are specified below:

- ◆ **Security**—Sealing Somalia's borders at sea, in the air and on land is critical in order to prevent the infiltration of Islamic Jihad entities and to thwart the smuggling of combat means to subversive factors in Somalia. An international military presence is required in Somalia in order to help the government fight its opponents. Military involvement should be evident in several areas:
  - o   Aid in establishing, organizing and training the national Somali army.
  - o   Undertaking the main struggle against the government's opposition until it develops its own effective forces.
  - o   Due to the animosity of the Somalis toward the Ethiopian presence in the country, it is advisable to replace the Ethiopian forces with AU forces that can perhaps be supplemented or replaced by forces from Arab League countries, which would be more acceptable.
  - o   The gradual removal of foreign forces when the government's forces are capable of carrying the defense burden.
- ◆ **Economy**—The international community, particularly Europe, the United States, and Muslim countries (mainly the Persian Gulf states), must develop a "Marshall Plan" for Somalia's economic rehabilitation. The immediate and dramatic improvement of the Somalis' economic conditions constitutes a critical prerequisite for attaining the population's support for the state, the unity government, and the rehabilitation of its institutions. Due to the lack of government mechanisms and the absence of a functional economy, the countries offering aid will have to help to establish relevant institutions in Somalia that will enable the correct utilization of the incoming economic aid.
- ◆ **International policy**—The international community will be obligated to grant the Somali government legitimacy and it must allow its representatives to resume their proper place in various regional and international bodies, and facilitate the rehabilitation of the country's international relations. At the same time, the regional and world community must act against countries and organizations that oppose

Somalia's rehabilitation process, by threatening to impose sanctions and other penalties on countries and organizations that choose to defy this policy. At the same time, the global war on terror must continue on all fronts as well as in Somalia and the Horn of Africa. Although the international community has not taken effective action to facilitate Somalia's rehabilitation in the past two decades, the situation in this country is still reversible despite the tremendous difficulties involved.

Leaving Somalia in its chaotic state as a "failing state" or even worse, letting it fall into radical Islamic hands, constitutes a grave risk to the security and stability of the entire region.

Notes

1.   This chapter is based on the book by Yoram Schweitzer and Shaul Shay, *The Globalization of Terror*, Transaction Publishers, New Brunswick, 2003.
2.   Boaz Ganor, *Defining Terrorism*, The Interdisciplinary Center in Herzlia, Vol. 4, August 1998, pp. 21-22.
3.   Paul Wilkinson, *Terrorism and the Liberal States*, MacMillan Education Ltd, 1977, p. 182.
4.   This chapter is based on: Shaul Shay, *The Red Sea Terror Triangle*, Transaction Publishers, New Brunswick, 2005.
5.   Robert I. Rotberg, "Failed States in a World of Terror," *Foreign Affairs*, July/August 2002, pp. 283, 127-140.
6.   Bashir Goth, Somaliland: where peace and democracy make no headlines, Somalia news and information, txt, May 17, 2006.
7.   Somaliland: Democratization and Its Discontents, International Crisis Group (ICG), *Africa Report* No. 66, July 28, 2006.
8.   Ibid.
9.   Claiming of responsibility by Al-Qaida in the Islamic website Azzaf Alatrach.
10. *Ha'aretz*, Tel Aviv, July 7, 2003.
11. Islamonline, January 10, 2003.
12. John Prendergast, our failure in Somalia, U.S. Counterterrorism Policy in Empowering Islamist Militias, Washingtonpost.com, June 7, 2006.
13. Ibid.
14. Somalia: the challenge of change, UN Office for the Coordination of Humanitarian Affairs, August 16, 2006, IRINnews.org.
15. Ibid.
16. Andrew McGregor, Warlords or Counter-Terrorists: U.S. Intervention in Somalia, Terrorism Focus, Volume 3, Issue 21, May 31, 2006.
17. *Daily Nation*, Nairobi, May 11, 2006.
18. Ibid.
19. Anouar Boukhars, Somalia's regional proxy war and its internal dynamics, *Terrorism Monitor*, Volume 4, Issue 13, June 29, 2006.
20. Ibid.
21. Shabelle Media Network, June 2, 2006.
22. Ethiopian PM denies U.S. involvement in Ethiopian's counterattack, Ethio.com, December 28, 2006.
23. Ibid.

24. Ibid.
25. Ibid.
26. Ethiopian PM denies U.S. involvement in Ethiopia's counterattack, Ethio.com, December 28, 2006.
27. U.S. confirms air strike on Al Qaida leaders in Somalia, Mogadishu, Shabelle Media Network, January 10, 2007.
28. Ibid.
29. Ibid.
30. Shabelle Media Network, January 10, 2007.
31. Ibid.
32. Paul Reynolds, Twin U.S. arms in Somalia, BBC News, January 9, 2007.
33. Ibid.
34. Ibid.
35. Stephen Kaufman, Somalia: Rice announces nearly 17 million dollars in initial U.S. aid to Somalia, allAfrica.com, January 4, 2007.
36. Ibid.
37. Ibid.
38. Ibid.
39. Ibid.

Index